Praise for *The Northern Front*

'Witty and absorbing ... Essential, and humbling, reading for all those pundits and commentators who think they understand what happened in Iraq.'

Malise Ruthven, author of *A History of the Arab Peoples*

'A vivid picture not only of the events leading up to the war and the chaos of the war itself but also of some of the Iraqi emigrés who were hoping to take over the government of Iraq.'

Ian Gilmour

'Should be mandatory reading for all wannabe foreign correspondents.'
Jonathan Randal, author of *After Such Knowledge,*
What Forgiveness? – Encounters with Kurdistan

'In the finest tradition of radical reporting – anti-war, sympathetic, compassionate and enlightening.'

Phillip Knightley, author of *The First Casualty*

'A beautifully written account of the full sweep of the war and of what it was like to report on it. His diary should in future serve as the starting-point for any proper understanding of the whole contentious business of the Iraq war.'

John Simpson

Charles Glass

THE NORTHERN FRONT

A Wartime Diary

Foreword by
P. J. O'Rourke

Photographs by
Don McCullin

SAQI
London   San Francisco

ISBN 10: 0-86356-770-3
ISBN 13: 978-0-86356-770-4

Published in 2006 by Saqi Books

A full CIP record for this book is available from the British Library.
A full CIP record for this book is available from the Library of Congress.

Manufactured in Lebanon

SAQI
26 Westbourne Grove, London W2 5RH
825 Page Street, Suite 203, Berkeley, California 94710
www.saqibooks.com

In memory of Peter Jennings,
and dedicated to his family

Iraq, 2003.

Foreword

by P. J. O'Rourke

Excessive certainty leads to definite actions, many of them dire, from a too-calculated 'I do' to the firebombing of Dresden. I promise you that Charlie Glass's book will leave you wondering, and wonder is a splendid and under-used human capacity. Charlie takes you to war as modern war is actually fought: it entails so little fighting, yet produces such an awful toll of death and destruction.

Charlie covered the Second Gulf War from the 'northern front', a theatre of war that didn't exist. The importance of its non-existence can hardly be overstated. The future of the Kurds, Turkey, NATO and Iraq itself were all affected. Charlie describes the nation of Kurdistan, the well-organized and effective anti-Saddam Iraqi government-in-exile and the successful planning for peaceful postwar occupation of Iraq – three things that never existed in the most spectacular way.

There is so much to discover if we are ever going to achieve a truly encyclopedic incomprehension of the Middle East. Charlie Glass is the right man to aid us in this endeavor. He has lived and worked in the region, read its literature and history, met many of its leaders, is even partly Middle Eastern by blood and speaks more Arabic than he lets on. We need this intellectual equipment with which to empty our minds.

Charlie performs the small good deed of removing the romance from the profession of war correspondent. The real job of a war correspondent is, as you will see, to go where no one wants you and be poorly fed and ill-sheltered and to wait for the moment when the ostracism and discomfort become indescribable pleasures because their alternative is to be dead. Charlie is a real writer, who will go anywhere for the chance to write about humanity, and humanity is never more human than when it's lying its head off. That's all people do in a war, except for taking occasional breaks to kill each other.

Charlie disabuses us of that notion, bred by TV, that a journalist can be everywhere at once, seeing all there is to see. He also rids us forever of the silly conceit that 'journalism is the first draft of history'. I don't know who said this, and Bartlett doesn't dignify the quote with a citation. But surely it was some tired hack trying on the historian's fancier hat. It's an Orwellian thought (though not a thought of Orwell's) that history gets redrafted. History is for those too squeamish to swallow the dog's breakfast that is reality.

Charlie Glass chews the raw mess. His is a tale of human existence without historical inevitabilities, without comforting big trends, without foregone conclusions of progress or decline. You will find herein no great sweep of democracy or Marxism or markets or Arab nationalism or Islamic fundamentalism or of any of the other grand ideas used by the mighty to extend their might. Such winds may blow through the Middle East, but do they fan fires or heap ashes? Will the peoples of the Middle East be blown away? And if so, in the cyclones of brutality or on the luxury of yachts? I don't know. You don't know. Charlie Glass doesn't know.

Charlie and I don't agree about anything politically. But we do agree upon one thing: it is our fondest wish that a lot more people – especially those more important than we are – knew a lot fewer things for certain. If only the heroes and villains (and let's not bother to try telling them apart) would wake up and say, 'I will be a confused ignoramus all day. I'll put off changing the world until tomorrow morning, and then I may sleep in. Meanwhile, I'll pick up my socks from the bedroom floor and remember to leave the toilet seat down. Maybe I'll try to make an honest buck today. And spend it sensibly. And give a little bit away, if only as a tip in a nice restaurant tonight'.

Introduction

Towards the end of 2002, Iraq attempted to pre-empt United Nations approval of a US invasion by agreeing to allow the UN to inspect its weapons of mass destruction (WMD). That agreement was insufficient to prevent the US, without UN support, from launching its war in Iraq. I doubted that Washington's Arabists, once they seized control of the country, would do a better job in Iraq than Britain had done in the early part of the twentieth century. I met Saddam Hussein's Iraqi opponents in London in late 2002. In January 2003, I went with them to northern Iraq to await the American onslaught. Thanks to the Turkish parliament's refusal to allow the US to invade Iraq through Turkish territory, there was no northern front. The northern front was never necessary to defeat an army that barely existed after its defeat in Kuwait in 1991 and twelve years of economic embargo. This book is an account of the war from the front that never was and among the Iraqis whom Washington's imperial planners would later install in Baghdad as the Iraqi face of an American occupation.

Paris, May 2006

Today is an anniversary, as most days are, of a massacre in the Middle East. In 1983, someone drove a truck past the sentries at the US Marine Headquarters in Beirut. A bomb, said later by FBI forensic analysts to have been the largest conventional explosive ever used, killed 241 American servicemen and shot a cloud into Beirut's morning sky like a miniature Hiroshima. The fact that similar bombings had previously destroyed an Israeli military office in southern Lebanon and the US embassy in Beirut made billeting so many American personnel in one undefended concrete block seem careless, negligent and perhaps criminal. The Marines left Lebanon a few months later, although the Pentagon said they were merely 'redeploying' to the ships. It was not long until the ships sailed away.

I covered Lebanon then for ABC News. Ten years later I quit ABC, disgusted as much with myself as with television. After 1993, my children approached and attained maturity. I travelled; I sought a home, whatever that might mean for an itinerant American, in Tuscany, London and Paris. Two novels failed to find publishers. My essays, book reviews and disgruntled commentaries on the American empire made their way into British and American periodicals. I am halfway through writing a travel book (not a guidebook) on the Middle East, and have run out of money. So it is back to TV news, the mistress whose bed I swore never, ever, to share again.

In 1983, television did not tell the story of the American war in Lebanon. We showed the pictures, but we could not explain why the Marines were there. They were there because Israel's 1982 invasion of Lebanon was unpopular at home and horrified the rest of the world. Israel then persuaded Ronald Reagan's administration to send Marines to oversee the forced departure from Lebanon of the Palestine Liberation Organisation. The Marines would later be duty-bound to return to protect the ravaged West Beirut refugee camps of Sabra and Shatila, whose undefended residents were slaughtered on Israel's watch. Secretary of State George Shultz made Lebanon's Israeli-installed president Amin Gemayel sign an agreement with Israel in 1983. Gemayel harassed his rivals and tortured dissidents. Identified with Gemayel's stupid policies and with Israel's occupation, the Marines became an obvious target – obvious, that is, to everyone but Shultz and Reagan.

The US is now preparing to invade Iraq: another American intervention in an Arab state, another regime change. Will we tell the story any better now than we did in 1983? Will we make the connections we did not then? This time Washington has its own agenda. I am talking daily with ABC News in New York about covering the war. Peter Jennings, the incarnation of ABC, is encouraging. Then again, we're friends. He was best man at my wedding, and each of us gave sympathy to the other when our marriages were dissolving in confusion. Today he warns me, 'Don't fuck up.'

I always fuck up. I am negotiating a deal with Paul Friedman, another friend and ABC executive. Friend or not, he plays tough over money. I'm broke, although I don't tell him this, and accept less than what I was earning ten years ago. (Friedman was expected to succeed Roone Arledge, the P. T. Barnum of television news and the most enthusiastic backer of his 'troops' in war zones, as president of the network's news division. He didn't. Walt Disney bought the company, and Friedman is not a Disneyman. Nor, despite childhood trips to Disneyland and a love of *Old Yeller* when I was seven, am I.)

Like our rulers in Washington, I'm turning my attention from the Levant to Mesopotamia and for the same reason: money. I might not covet Iraqi oil, but I need an income. HarperCollins's paltry advance for my book, *The Tribes Triumphant*, ran out months ago. I've been working on it for more than a year, during which I had to re-mortgage my flat in London. I moved to Paris last February to live more cheaply. The book should have been finished by now, but I write slowly, rewrite more slowly and rewrite again. There is one other reason to witness this war: I love Iraq in general and Iraqi Kurdistan in particular. The Kurds have endured more than any other people in the Middle East since the British and French, having promised them a state in the 1920 Treaty of Sèvres, forced them to live as helots within Arab, Turkish and Iranian national states. They are fine people and deserve better.

Thursday, 24 October 2002
London

I take the morning Paris-London train to see the ABC people, interview Edward Said for a BBC documentary, meet old acquaintances and friends from Iraq, do research on Iraq and deliver a lecture on the establishment of modern Iraq by Great Britain. An article I wrote on the subject for *The London Review of Books* brought a letter from the comedians John Bird, John Fortune and Rory Bremner. They are doing a satirical sketch on Iraq and want a reading list.

Friday, 25 October 2002
London

A documentary maker named Ed Harriman takes me to lunch at an Italian restaurant in Soho to pitch an idea. He wants to produce a film covering the period of my *LRB* essay: from Sir Stanley Maude's conquest of Ottoman Baghdad in 1917 to the toppling of Maude's statue during the 1958 Iraqi revolution. He calls it *Teatime in Baghdad*. It's a good idea, and Britain's experience should be instructive to the US. Harriman, an American expatriate about my age, is hopeful that Channel Four or the BBC will sponsor the film. He imagines a US sale after that. I'm more cynical. I hope that Ed, who has produced many award-winning documentaries, is right and I'm wrong. It's timely – and I need the money.

At the London Library, I read books by some of the Britons who fabricated Iraq and killed thousands of Arabs and Kurds to do it: A. O. Wilson, Gertrude Bell, Sir Percy Cox and other empire-builders who published memoirs. I wonder what version of history Iraq's new kingmakers – Donald Rumsfeld, Paul Wolfowitz, Richard Perle, Zalmay Khalilzad, Colin Powell – will leave as testimony. Michael Austin is at another table in the reading room. We go to the stairway to talk. Taller and a little older than I, intelligent and a transatlantic sailor, he is writing a screenplay based on Steven Kinzer's book, *Bitter Fruit*. It's about another US-driven regime change in the cause of freedom: deposing the reformist president of Guatemala, Jacobo Arbenz, in 1954 to install the mass murderers who protected the United Fruit Company and other US businesses in Central America. Bananas then, oil now. Michael says that Andy Karsch, for whom he wrote and directed *Princess Caraboo*, is producing. It's the kind of project Andy loves. An anti-Zionist Jew and anti-imperialist American, he is courageous for a producer. He did, however, make *Town and Country*.

In the evening, my ex-wife Fiona and two of our children, George and Julia, gather for dinner at our favourite Notting Hill Italian restaurant, Osteria Basilico. Looking at all three of them, I damn myself for every trip I took to faraway lands without them. Fiona and George have already advised me not to worry Julia, who is seventeen, by telling her I am going to Iraq. Instead, we talk about ... I don't remember. It must have been awful for a wife and small children to worry about a man who went to war zones for no better reason than that he did not know how to do anything else. When I leave for Iraq, I'll tell Julia. The last time I left for Iraq, in January 1993, she had just turned eight. It was dawn in London, and she was sleeping. I kissed her without waking her, as I did the other children, sensing on that last morning in our house that my wife would not want me to return. I was right.

That was when George Bush the Elder's bombs crashed into the al-Rasheed Hotel, where the press corps stayed in Baghdad, and killed two civilians. A week or so later, I turned forty-two in Iraq without celebrating. A few days afterwards, Fiona told me on the telephone not to come home. I was shocked, but not surprised, and have not known a home since. Mamas, don't let your babies grow up to be war reporters.

Saturday, 26 October 2002
London

My older stepdaughter, Beatrix, had a boy a few days ago. Julia, Fiona and I go to her new house to see Felix, active at the breast the whole time we are there. Beatrix, now twenty-nine, had just turned four when I married her mother. Her sister Hester was two. Hester has a baby, Orlando, whom I've seen only once in his first year-and-a-half of life. I love Beatrix and Hester, but ex-stepfathers are easily superseded by new stepfathers.

When they met me, I was on crutches from artillery shrapnel that had caught my foot in Beirut in 1976. I tried living full-time with them in London for years – as a domestic news reporter at *The Observer*; as a researcher at London Weekend Television; editing a business magazine; writing for *Newsweek*. When Israel invaded Lebanon in June 1982, I was desperate to go. I got drunk one night and called *Newsweek*'s editor, Rick Smith, to demand he send me. (He sent Tony Clifton, the London bureau chief, who wrote the book *God Cried*, condemning Israel's crimes in Lebanon. Clifton did a better job for *Newsweek* than I would have.) A few months later, I quit. If I hadn't, Rick would probably have fired me.

I went to Lebanon in October 1982, during the early days of Israel's occupation, to write a magazine feature that was never published. I had been ABC's radio stringer there in the early 1970s. In April 1983, the network appointed me Chief Middle East Correspondent, an easy title to obtain when I was its *only* Middle East correspondent. I moved back to Lebanon and found a top-floor flat near the Commodore Hotel. By then Fiona and I had four children, her two girls and our two boys. I left them all and our huge house in Notting Hill to live alone in a small flat 2,000 miles away, writing and calling home every day and visiting every six weeks. It is the stupidest thing I have ever done.

At 6 PM I am at the Albery Theatre in St Martin's Lane. Bremner, Bird and Fortune have finished their matinee performance and are on a two-hour break before the evening show. They have dinner at a little restaurant behind the theatre. Satire may be the only way to expose those who, from their safe havens in Washington and Westminster, propose to send young men and women to kill and die in the oil lands of the East. Bird is reading some of the histories and recommends books to me. They all have questions. What is the source of this quote, that story, some allegation, especially about the Royal Air Force and of the use of poison gas on the Kurds? Their attention to accuracy and authenticity would shame most journalists. Bird says, 'We want to get it right.'

Their revue at the Albery apparently includes a sketch on British desert manoeuvres. Bird says the shortcomings, like tanks that run for no more than an hour in the sand, come straight from Defence Ministry reports. They invite me to see the show any night before it closes, that is, any night this week.

I go to dinner with Kate Reardon, a fashion journalist, friend and former girlfriend (however briefly). She has invited a huge crowd to Cambio de Tercio, a Spanish restaurant in Old Brompton Road. A banker friend of hers from New York knows nothing about me, my work or the war in Iraq. He is, however, a fan of P. J. O'Rourke and remembers my name from P. J.'s *Holidays in Hell*. He quotes passages about a trip P. J. and I made in Lebanon. (P. J.'s Lebanon piece shares, along with an article I did on suicide, the distinction of having been spiked without explanation by Tina Brown – his at *Vanity Fair*, mine at *The New Yorker*. It remains one of his best.) I suspect that when the war starts, P. J. will be in Iraq too.

Tuesday, 29 October 2002
London

Rachel Johnson and I take in Bremner, Bird and Fortune's revue at the Albery. Bremner triumphs as George Bush, Tony Blair, Bill Clinton, Robin Cook and the rest of Anglo-America's bellicose phallocracy. Bird and Fortune's skit on Britain's war preparations pits Fortune as an interviewer against Bird's laconic bureaucrat. Bird's conclusion: Britain, with its equipment designed for Northern Europe, can defeat Iraq – provided Saddam agrees to fight in Northern Europe. A full house jumps to its feet to applaud them for ten minutes.

After the performance, Rachel and I have drinks with Bremner while he eats dinner. Rachel is a columnist at *The Daily Telegraph*, an excellent writer and mother of three. Her husband, my friend Ivo Dawnay, was Foreign Editor at *The Sunday Telegraph* and is now an independent political lobbyist. Her brother, Boris Johnson, edits *The Spectator* and represents Henley-upon-Thames as a Conservative Member of Parliament. I am surprised, given her brother's Conservative connections, that she is as doubtful about the war as Bremner is. She is beautiful, blonde, well-endowed in body and mind: I would ask her to marry me if I did not know she loved her husband. But she seems to be falling in love with Bremner, who is as happily married as she is.

My son Edward calls my cellphone from St Andrew's in Scotland, where he is in his last year doing philosophy and English. He and his girlfriend have just come back from an anti-war demonstration in Glasgow. (I've taken the children to demos from the time they were in their prams – to denounce racism, to legalise cannabis, to stop the ban on hunting, to protect prisoners and stop torture, to preserve the right to trial by jury and to contain the American empire.) I hand the telephone to Bremner who, in his Tony Blair voice, scolds Edward for opposing his and George W.'s war. I expect more scolding from the real Blair before it's over.

Rachel and I go for dinner at San Lorenzo. There we meet Taki Theodoracopoulos – columnist, heir to a Greek shipping fortune, an extreme right-winger with whom I disagree on almost every political issue and one of my best friends. Like Rachel, he opposes war in Iraq. When I disappear to the men's room, I later learn, he makes a pass at her.

Wednesday, 30 October 2002
London

Back to San Lorenzo at lunchtime to celebrate the birthday of my friend Flora Fraser with her husband Peter Soros, her three children, her mother Antonia Fraser and stepfather Harold Pinter. Harold is enraged by the war. He's written about it, given speeches about it and argued about it – despite the fact that he is recovering from a cancer operation. Taki and Harold Pinter, the old right and old left, are lost to George W. and Tony. And the centre? Will it hold?

My older son George and I go to a father-son, black-tie dinner and later meet Julia and one of her school friends for drinks at the Groucho Club in Soho. The two girls have just seen the Bremner-Bird-Fortune show at the Albery and met Rory afterwards. Like Rachel, they more or less fell in love with him. They say most of the Sherborne School for Girls, not exactly a cauldron of radical sentiment, are against the war. Taki, Harold, Rory and company, the Sherborne girls ... where does Blair hear the trumpets, fifes and drums calling the nation to battle?

Thursday, 31 October (Halloween) 2002
London

At the London Library, I read more documents and memoirs from the time of Britain's conquest of Mesopotamia. It is all there, written at the time in arrogance, brought to light now in shame: the bombing of villages, the imposition of unwanted leaders, the rigged referendum, Britain's kidnapping of a popular political leader, the massacres, the contempt for the natives who were forced to live in a state they did not ask for. Saddam inherited and expanded a system that Britain created in 1917: ruling without consent, shooting those who resist. What will the US create when it 'imposes democracy', Washington's latest oxymoron? I read the letters and diaries of Iraq's British guardians, because I am writing a lecture. If I deliver an impromptu speech, I remember later all the things I forgot to say. If I write it in advance to read aloud, I lose touch with the audience. This time, I am trying a compromise: I make little notes on index cards as *aides-mémoires* for an off-the-cuff talk. Like most other compromises, it will be a catastrophe.

The venue is an upstairs room at Orsino's restaurant in Portland Road, Holland Park. My hosts from the Lebanese Centre at St Anthony's College, Oxford, are waiting downstairs, where we have drinks. They are well-dressed Lebanese bourgeois, polite, interested, apparently hoping to hear me deliver the goods. Well ... The plan is for me to give a talk upstairs before dinner and answer questions between courses. Forty-five people attend. I give a short preamble, and amble

I do. I rummage through my index cards looking for an appropriate quote, statistic, fact. I cannot find the ones I need when I need them. I fear embarrassing my son George, who is twenty-five and has a degree in Middle East history from the University of London's School of Oriental and African Studies (SOAS).

A few friends who have no Middle East connections – Rupert Fairfax, Lucy Clive, Willie Stirling and Tracy Worcester – must assume that this stammering, inarticulate buffoon dropping index cards knows nothing. Standing before forty-five puzzled faces impatient for dinner, I abandon the cards. I swallow some *vino rosso* and apologise, 'I'll start again.' I ramble, but the rambling follows the course of Britain's 1917–18 march from Basra to Baghdad; the turf dispute between the India Office and the Arab Bureau; the further conquests; the discovery of oil; the creation of the monarchy, the rebellions and revolts; the lies and deceits and abominations of imperial order in Mesopotamia; Britain's air bridge from Egypt via Iraq to India; Iraq's pseudo-independence; the 1941 anti-British coup; the second British invasion; the Baghdad Pact; and the revolution of 1958.

My conclusion: The US's invasion of Iraq is unlikely to have more felicitous consequences than Britain's did. Then we eat decent Italian food and drink more wine. George looks like he watched me fall from the edge, catch my coat on a branch and slowly climb up before the branch broke.

While we eat, the questions go on and on. Dahlia Salam, whose family I know from Beirut, is with a pro-war Iraqi friend, who says he wants an American invasion. I cannot blame him. Most Iraqis would let the devil himself liberate them from Saddam Hussein. I repeat what Lawrence wrote in *The Seven Pillars of Wisdom*, 'I often told Feisal, "Freedom is taken – not given."' The Arabs' original sin was allowing the British and French empires to expel and replace the Ottomans. Their leaders have pursued foreign sponsors ever since, and sponsors – whether American or Soviet – have their own interests. If the Arabs do not free themselves, they will not govern themselves.

Afterwards, some of us walk back to the house where I'm staying. There my hostess, Amabel Lindsay, is holding a dinner party with, among others, Don McCullin. McCullin and I covered the Kurdish uprising together in 1991. At the time, the Iraqis were taking their freedom. Town after town, garrison after garrison, prison after prison, the north and the south fell to the rebels, who were massing towards Baghdad. The Kurds and Shiites seized fourteen of Iraq's eighteen provinces. Within weeks, the capital itself would have been in their hands. Saddam would have died like Hitler or been hanged in public like Mussolini. But it was not to be. The US, whose president had encouraged the uprising, denied anti-Saddam army rebels access to their arms caches in southern Iraq. At the same time, it withdrew its air protection and allowed Iraq's air force to fly again. Within hours, Don was taking photographs of the victims of Saddam's aerial bombardment.

The Kurds, who had suffered the chemical attack at Halabja in 1988, feared another blast of poison gases. They showed fear. No, what they showed was terror, and they fled to the nearest border. In the south, Saddam returned and massacred the freedom fighters and anyone else in his way. Then, the US did not let the Iraqis take their freedom. Now, it deigns to give it to them. Unspoken then was the apprehension of the US's main Arab clients, Hosni Mubarak of Egypt and the Saudi royal family, that a popular revolution in another important Arab country would set an unfortunate precedent for them. The encouragement to US policy this time comes from Israel.

McCullin, who is sixty-seven and is about to become a father (again) with his new bride, retired from war photography twice. He returned from a seven-year hiatus to come with me to Iraq in 1991, when we did a long piece for *The Independent*'s Saturday magazine. Afterwards, Don gave up war all over again. He and Philip Jones Griffiths are probably Britain's best war photographers, and Don is the least gung-ho journalist I know. His photographs in India and of England's brooding landscapes have been exhibited throughout the world and turned into expensive books. Don does not photograph models, movie stars, minor royalty or game show hosts, but he agrees to cover one more war. His wife, Catherine Fairweather, is due to give birth to a boy in December. That is when the Pentagon says it may invade Iraq. She seems stoic about her new man's departure for the land of strife, 'It's what he does.'

They ask me to be godfather.

Monday, 11 November 2002
London

For the first time in ten years, I visit an ABC News office. The London bureau has moved from Carburton Street in the West End to the Disney building next to the Hammersmith flyover – one of the many architectural eyesores that London's visitors endure on their way in from Heathrow Airport. Inside the cold stone-and-glass reception, surrounded by life-size effigies of Disney cartoon characters, I apply for a security badge. At the old bureau, there were no badges and the only security was an English night watchman who never managed anything more daring than catching an ABC News executive *in flagrante* with his secretary. Now, a team of South African uniformed guards from a private security firm patrol the building. They are polite and young. One of them leads me to the elevator, where music from *Beauty and the Beast* fills the smokeless air.

On the third floor, he swipes a plastic card to open the double doors and leaves me in the newsroom. It is, to my surprise, beautiful. The old newsroom was cramped and never quite worked as a set for a visiting anchor. The space was too narrow, the ceilings too low. It looked like it was built for crooked accountants. The new place is vast: glass-fronted offices on either side of the news desk; windows and daylight in each office; anchor space with a studio camera at one end; and the console and monitors of Master Control behind sealed glass at the other. It is a smaller version of the New York newsroom and looks like a pleasant place to work. It should be, but everyone who works there is a survivor of the latest round of Disney firings. The bureau chief, Rex Granum, is gone. A nice man who had twenty years' experience, Rex received notice a few weeks ago. The last time I saw him was at a memorial service for the intrepid Carlos Mavroleon, who died while on assignment for CBS in Pakistan. His office is occupied by his replacement, Marcus Wilford. Marcus, an English local hire whom I knew when he started at ABC in the 1980s, must share with everyone else in the office the fear that he may be next. ABC has also fired Roupen Vosguimourikian, an award-winning cameraman who began his network career with Peter Jennings in Beirut in 1972, and Bruno Sylvestre, an excellent and long-time producer, in Paris. There are rumours of an ABC-CNN merger, which would see all of ABC's overseas bureaus closed. When I started stringing for ABC in 1973, it had bureaus everywhere – Cairo, Nairobi, Johannesburg, Paris, Rome, Tel Aviv, Moscow, Tokyo, Hong Kong ... It is now down to Jerusalem, Moscow and London, with a few mini-bureaus and stringers dotted around. The more American business expands across the earth, the more the American media retreat.

The place seems sad, but everyone is welcoming. Robin Wiener, a senior producer with whom I worked in the 1980s, gives me a tour. I bump into Gordon Ring, who has run ABC's overseas logistics since he was a kid. He loans me an empty office. There are far more good people than bad here. I'm enjoying the comradeship, drinking coffee with the editors, camera crews and engineers, catching up, hearing the gripes and the gossip. It's a change from the seclusion of writing.

I work the phones, calling every Iraqi I can think of for briefings on the impending war and for help to get to the north of the country. One of my oldest friends in the Kurdish Democratic Party (KDP), Hoshyar Zebari, proposes we meet at a hotel in Kensington in an hour. I am there on time; he is late. This is what I remember about covering the Middle East: garish hotels, coffee in empty bars and a source who is late.

Hoshyar enters the hotel lobby like a salesman making a call, briefcase at his side, tie loose at the neck, grey suit jacket unbuttoned. He is not fat, but is an easy twenty pounds heavier than he was in Kurdistan twelve years ago. Then, when his people were losing again to the monster in Baghdad, he was a trim tribal warrior in the more comfortable baggy trousers of a Kurdish mountaineer. Beside him in 1991 was his contemporary, the then-young Massoud Barzani, who led and still leads his late father's KDP and its armed forces. The Zebaris and Barzanis have a long history in Kurdistan, and it was a Zebari who took the British shilling to turn on the Barzanis in the 1920s. Hoshyar, however, worked for old Mullah Mustafa Barzani, the leading Kurdish nationalist leader of the twentieth century. It was easier for Hoshyar than for others of his tribe to work with their ancient feudal rival. Hoshyar's older sister had married Mullah Mustafa – Mullah Mustafa's son and successor, Massoud, is therefore Hoshyar's nephew.

Hoshyar embraces me with the kind of hug the Russians must have given old Mullah Mustafa, when Stalin took in his band of Kurdish rebels in 1946. (The US had just helped the Shah of Iran to crush the world's first nominally independent Kurdish state, the Mahabad Republic.) Hoshyar had taken me across the Tigris in 1991 at the start of the rebellion, and we survived the war together. The people of Zakho, the first village we entered, welcomed us the way the French did the US Army in June of '44. They hoisted us, a dozen American and British journalists, onto their shoulders. Shots were fired in the air. Speeches were made in our honour. 'Haji Boosh' was thanked through us for leaving the skies clear for them to rescue the country from Saddam's assassins. We were not entitled to credit for Bush's conquest of Kuwait and his call to arms. Nor were we to blame a few weeks later for Bush's betrayal, when he allowed Saddam's forces to rampage and exact revenge.

In the Kensington hotel's empty bar, Hoshyar says Turkey is creating problems for the Kurds. The Turkish government, which has displaced and killed almost as many Kurds in Turkey as Saddam has in Iraq, is setting terms for Iraqi Kurdish participation in the US invasion. Hoshyar has been to Turkey, where officials told him they would resist any Kurdish advance on either Kirkuk or Mosul. The new Islamist Turkish government, not unlike its predecessors, does not recognise a Kurdish stake in either city – both of which are perched above large pools of oil. What would happen, I ask him, if the Kurds go into Kirkuk as they did in 1991? 'The Turkish army would invade,' he said. And then? 'Then, Charlie,' he smiled, 'then Iran has said it will invade to keep the Turks away.' This could be an interesting war.

My goal is to get into Iraqi Kurdistan. It is the only place where journalists will be free of Saddam's and the Pentagon's control. Since 1991, when Hoshyar took us in from Syria, hundreds of journalists have used the route over the Tigris. It was almost romantic to ferry across the rapids on a raft and meet the Kurds on the other side. 'Not anymore,' Hoshyar says. 'Not since CNN.' The Syrian government's only condition for providing the border facility was that no one publicise it and thus upset Saddam. CNN, he says, violated the understanding. When a CNN correspondent broadcast his river crossing, Syria closed the border to the rest of the press. Hoshyar says the Turks do not permit journalists to enter Iraq from their territory. Iran, he says, is being difficult. There is no fourth border for Iraq's Kurds, apart from the smuggling route from the Arab south of Iraq.

I have to find a way in, and that means calling and meeting scores of Iraqis, Iranians, Syrians and Turks. I am applying for Syrian and Iranian visas.

Monday, 11 November 2002
Cambridge

Don Guttenplan, an American writer living in Hampstead, somehow persuaded the BBC to let him produce a profile of Edward Said. Although the BBC is too cowardly to spend more than a pittance and will broadcast it on something called BBC 4 (for which viewers require special digital equipment and therefore has a potential audience of eleven), it is worthwhile. There are few scholars as accomplished, original and polymath as Edward. Don wants to record a long interview for an archive and possibly a book more than he does for the thirty minutes the BBC will broadcast.

Edward Said is in Cambridge with Mariam, his wife, to deliver a series of lectures and to see old friends. He's always been an Anglophile who buys his shirts and ties in Jermyn Street, despite what the British Empire did to Palestine.

Don, his wife Maria and I meet at King's Cross early in the morning for the Cambridge train. We are all affected by the knowledge that this man we admire and love is dying. His leukaemia has been killing him for eleven years already, and his doctors did not anticipate his survival to now. Mariam has told us that he is not well at the moment and has asked us not to tire him. When we reach King's College, we walk up many, many stairs to a sitting room where the director, Mike Dibb, has set up his cameras and microphones. Dibb has read most of Edward's books and is doing the project for love rather than money. There is a blue screen behind the sofa where Edward is to sit, allowing Mike the possibility of superimposing old photographs or other illustrations related to whatever Edward might speak about. Jo Dutton, a charming and multilingual young assistant producer, offers to bring us coffee. A BBC employee, she's overqualified for her job.

Edward comes up the stairs in pain and with difficulty, holding Mariam's arm. Why didn't we use a ground-floor room? He settles in on the sofa. I take a chair. Don, Maria, Mariam and Jo sit on another sofa behind Mike. We begin. Slowly, the tiredness leaves Edward's face. Conversation is a drug, as are writing and playing the piano, which revives him, restores him and despatches the leukaemia.

I have known this man since 1972. We met at a lecture he gave on Michel Foucault in Beirut at the American University. Mariam was with him. We saw one another at dinners and lectures; I was a graduate student in philosophy, he a professor of comparative literature (and so much else) at Columbia, then formulating ideas that would coalesce in his masterpiece, or one of his masterpieces, *Orientalism*.

This past summer, everyone who knew Edward thought he was going to die. He stayed in intensive care, and some friends said goodbye. Then he rallied, somehow. I like to think that this is his time to fight. He is needed to expose Washington's hypocrisy in promising freedom to Iraq while paying to deny it to Palestinians.

Our interview is scheduled to run over two days – four to six hours of tape a day, depending on how tired Edward becomes. I cannot absorb the enormity of his illness, that it is indeed killing this vital, indomitable character, until he answers my first question. I ask about his personal and intellectual preoccupations as a way to create a platform for him to expound on literature, art, music, politics and culture. The answer is one he would not have given a year ago.

'The past several months have been dominated by my illness,' he says, stretching his left arm across the back of the sofa. 'I thought I'd mastered it intellectually. After a summer of infections, I thought I'd get better, but it has taken its toll emotionally. I don't feel that I have a centre that isn't tied up with the disease. I spend a lot of time on it. My doctor is out on Long Island, so I have to go there for tests, and it eats up days. And, of course, there are the effects of the treatment. It's very hard to do anything else. I've even lost the ability to listen to music, and I've stopped playing the piano completely. My energy is drained. Most days, by 4 PM, I don't have any energy left. Sometimes, I can get myself revved up if I give a lecture, but that's it. It's very depressing.'

It does not take him long to revive, to forget his frailty and to enjoy the stimulus of indignation. I ask about his two worlds, the West and the Middle East. 'These two worlds I've lived in all my life seem to be confused,' he says. 'I've had friends who have turned out, surprisingly, to be US imperialists, mouthpieces for the status quo. And that's been a blow to me ... even when I'm at my worst, there is this flash across my mind – an image of Sharon – and I get up straight away.'

By lunchtime Edward has his energy. When we return for the afternoon session before the cameras, he bounds up the stairs. By evening, I am the one who needs rest. On Iraq, he says, 'What Bush and Sharon want is a redrawn map with naked domination of oil.' He laments the fact that the mass media perpetuate the demonisation of Islam, of the Arabs, of the Other, in line with the orthodoxy of power. Here, he feels himself powerless. He has tried, more than most, to penetrate the ramparts that protect a well-fed public from seditious thought.

Tuesday, 12 November 2002
London

Tonight, the proposition for debate at the Royal Geographic Society is 'Bush's cure for Iraq is worse than the disease'. The lecture hall is full, with about 800 people. Women at the door ask those coming in whether they are for or against the motion. To be for it is to oppose the war and vice versa. Public debate is ordinarily a healthy phenomenon, but two aspects of this one are worrying. The leaders who have determined upon war, as Messrs Bush and Blair have done, stand aloof from public debates and ignore public opinion. The other is that we, in the comfort of our Western empires, are deliberating the fate, the lives and deaths, of those who are less powerful than ourselves. Is the decision to wage war a fit subject for debate, when the debaters themselves are neither under attack nor threatened with war?

For the resolution, and thus against war, are Mai Yamani, fellow of the Royal Institute for International Affairs (RIIA), lecturer at SOAS, daughter of Saudi Arabia's former oil minister and a harsh critic of the Saudi royal family; Bruce Kent, a former priest who used to head the Campaign for Nuclear Disarmament; and Michael Quinlan, a think tank researcher formerly at the Ministry of Defence. The war party comprises William Shawcross, author of the book *Sideshow* about Henry Kissinger's destruction of Cambodia, and now a conservative journalist; Charles Powell, once Margaret Thatcher's foreign affairs advisor, now serving on corporate boards; and Richard Perle, the US's own Prince of Darkness, a rightist ideologue, military advisor to the Bush administration, former Likud Party advisor and now on the Pentagon's Defense Review Board. The chair, Rosemary Hollis of the RIIA, explains the form: ten minutes per speaker, alternating between sides; questions from the floor; two minutes for each speaker to sum up; and a vote on the resolution. Lucky us, who get to vote on war against a country most of us have never been to.

The speakers present their cases in turn. The anti-war faction does not defend Saddam, but does question the US's legal and moral right to invade Iraq, and warns of the regional consequences. The pro-war advocates, apart from Perle, do not call outright for war. They say the consequence of war, if it comes, could be the liberation of Iraq and the rest of the Middle East from tyranny. Shawcross makes the softest case for Bush's cure, 'I don't think anyone on this side wants a war.' (He cannot have checked with Perle.) He then lists each *casus belli*: the cooperation that he believes may have taken place between al-Qa'ida and Saddam Hussein; the threat of Saddam's WMD; and the danger of appeasing Saddam. 'Let's hope that he realises this is a last chance to disarm,' Shawcross says. 'Or he could be replaced in a *coup d'état*!'

He seems to believe that Bush's war threat may itself be the 'cure' to force Saddam to disarm or compel senior Iraqi officers to replace him. Charles Powell is more robust. Saddam is 'unmatched for murder, torture', and so on. Powell must have been privy to the reports during his tenure at Downing Street in the 1980s that Saddam deployed illegal chemical weapons on Iranians and then Kurds. Mrs Thatcher, like her alter ego Ronald Reagan, supported Saddam, his war machine and his internal security apparatus. Saddam was 'unmatched' at the time, and Powell should have known it then. That was when Mrs Thatcher berated the *Financial Times* journalist Edward Mortimer for exposing and criticising Saddam's crimes because, she said, his reports hurt British business. She denied that in 1988 Saddam had massacred Kurdish villagers in Halabja with nerve gas, until Gwynne Roberts, a courageous and committed documentary film-maker, brought back soil samples to prove what Saddam had done.

'Saddam has a long track record of arming terrorists,' Powell says, in what must refer to his sponsorship of the Palestinian assassin Abu Nidal. 'He has a track record of using weapons of mass destruction. Also, he has a long track record of defying the will of the United Nations.' This is true, and it happened on Powell's watch and the watches of Thatcher, Reagan, John Major and Bush the Elder. If they had wanted to stop Saddam's crimes, they did not need to invade Iraq. They could have cut his weapons supply. Powell says regime change is not a goal in itself. Like Shawcross – and Bush the Elder in 1991 – he sees deliverance in the *deus ex machina* of a military takeover. He concludes by praising young Bush and Blair for being 'patient rather than rash'.

It is Perle, however, who emerges from the dark to shine his torch on Washington's goals. More portly than courtly, he ascends the podium and chants the real song of power. Like Powell, he recalls Saddam's crimes against humanity and, like Powell, neglects to add where he was when Saddam committed them. The cause is just. The necessity for action is obvious. And the invasion cannot fail. 'How risky is military action? As Saddam is weaker, we are stronger. We will minimise civilian casualties. They will be fewer than if Saddam is left in power.' His great fear is a resurrected Saddam with an atomic bomb. A Scud rocket, he says, could deliver a nuclear payload to the Kurdish north, the Shiite south or, God forbid, Israel. One of Saddam's suicide commandos – Perle does not cite any instance of Saddam's use of suicide bombers – could smuggle an A-bomb in his luggage into New York, Washington, or Harlingen, Texas, and blow it to Hiroshima-dust. These may be the arguments Perle uses at the Pentagon and at the White House, where their mesmeric force sways policy in his direction. At the Royal Geographic Society, the applause is polite rather than enthusiastic when he concludes, 'The alternative to not acting is to leave him to commit the crimes of which we know he is capable.'

Mai Yamani looks like one tough chick, one of the reasons Saudi men keep their women down. Unleashed and behind the wheels of their own cars, they would be more ferocious than any New York feminists. A voluptuous woman whose long black hair has a defiant streak of white, she stands at the lectern with more self-assurance than imperial delegate Perle. 'The air is filled with misinformation,' she says. She points out the lack of evidence of coordination between al-Qaʻida and Iraq. The question for her is, 'Will the US invasion solve the problem or make it worse?' Perle, Shawcross and Powell see a US-sponsored change of regime opening possibilities for democracy in Iran, Saudi Arabia, Egypt, Syria and other lesser principalities of the Muslim East. Yamani believes the opposite. 'Popular reaction [to an American invasion] will force these regimes to become more repressive.' She discourteously mentions that 'the US has never been friendly to democracy in the region', and asks, 'If Bush has a cure, what is the disease? Islamism? Baathism? Secularism? Arab nationalism?' After an invasion, she says, 'the sense of collective humiliation will be intensified'. Far from defeating Osama bin Laden, 'his spirit will invigorate the oppressed'.

Bruce Kent's is a familiar face in Britain. When he was still Monsignor Kent, he led hundreds of demonstrations for nuclear disarmament, gave thousands of speeches and published millions of words. On the Left, he is an old and venerated reminder of a purer, pre-Blairite past. To the Right, he is a sandal-wearing crank. Of the six speakers tonight, he is the most composed, the most elegant, the most practised – as if only slightly varying some Shakespearean soliloquy he has declaimed a thousand times.

'We speak of cures for a patient,' he says. 'What is the illness? That he defied Security Council resolutions? Ninety-one such resolutions have been violated since 1968. The principal violators are ... Israel and Turkey.' Kent is the first to mention Israel, the only state on Earth that is more dedicated to an Iraqi invasion than are Perle, Paul Wolfowitz, Donald Rumsfeld and Dick Cheney. As for Turkey, its treatment of Kurds compares to Saddam's in quality, if not quantity. 'Is it nuclear weapons? If so, he would be only the ninth state to have them, after India and Pakistan. Is it weapons of mass destruction? He used them on the Iranians, but he was our friend.' Kent takes the sermon through the plains of Afghanistan and the requirements of Western oil companies, pausing at the recent UN Security Council Resolution 1441.

'Resolution 1441,' he says, 'gives the United States no right to administer unilaterally the cure of invasion. Articles 41 and 42 of the UN Charter require other options first. There is a legal option: indict Saddam Hussein for war crimes.' The US has resisted indicting Saddam, citing legal obstacles. Organisations that have amassed evidence against Saddam blame politics – that is, Washington's reluctance to expose the role of American politicians and corporations in sustaining Saddam's criminality. 'The Bush doctrine of pre-emptive military action is not a cure,' Kent says, 'but a recipe for anarchy.'

Audience questions – mostly statements from people committed on both sides – consume about an hour before the vote. Young women collect the ballots. Rosemary Hollis announces the result of the poll taken *before* the debate:

178 for the motion that Bush's cure was worse than the disease
126 against
204 with no opinion.

Now comes the real vote. I hand in my ballot. I hope I will not regret my choice, like those who supported the Oxford Union resolution in 1933 not to fight for King and Country. Under international law, individual states, including the US, are prohibited from invading countries that have not attacked them. The UN could have called for an invasion of Iraq under the Genocide Convention in the 1980s when Saddam was conducting the genocide of the Kurds (he called the campaign 'al-Anfal', after a Qur'anic *sura* referring to the 'spoils of war'). It did not. The Reagan and Bush administrations – along with most of Europe and the Arab world – abetted his crimes and supplied him with the tools to commit them.

What is the *casus belli* now? Bush, Jr claims it is Saddam's mere possession of chemical and biological weapons, his record of having deployed chemical agents and his attempt to acquire or manufacture an atom bomb, with a sleight of hand to depict Saddam Hussein as Osama bin Laden. Yet Saddam today has never possessed fewer chemicals and germs, never had fewer missiles with which to deploy them and never had less reason to do so. When he did use them on the Iranian army and on Kurdish civilians, the US – despite Saddam's clear violations of international laws – did not demand disarmament and regime change. When the Iraqi people themselves fought to change the regime in 1991, the American reaction was to lift the ban on Saddam's helicopter gunships, which he then deployed to save himself. The first Bush administration's message, like Bush the Younger's now, was that Iraqis must not liberate Iraq. The US, however, may. This is imperialism. As a citizen of what is meant to be a republic, I vote yes. Yes, I am against war.

After the debate, the vote is:

255 for
198 against
30 don't knows.

Victory for peace. We are not, however, the British Parliament, the US Congress or the UN Security Council. The Pentagon, meanwhile, is predicting a December war. No serious military analyst believes it, because the US has yet to deploy sufficient force near Iraq. John Keegan writes in *The Daily Telegraph* that the US needs months to prepare. I may need that much time to get a visa.

Wednesday, 13 November 2002
London

The mood at the ABC News bureau seems glum. The sackings hurt morale, as do rumours of more sackings and of a CNN merger. Still, the staff soldiers on, waiting for the generals' next blunder: lions, as the Germans said of the British in 1917, led by donkeys. If and when war starts, they will all work overtime. When it is over and ABC counts the money spent, many may be unemployed.

Thursday, 14 November 2002
London

To Cambridge, again to see Edward Said. He is lecturing at Lady Mitchell Hall on 'Humanism and Knowledge: Erich Auerbach's *Mimesis*'. There are no empty seats, and undergraduates are queuing outside. Someone is saving places for Ruth Rogers, Don and Maria Guttenplan and me near the front. Mike Dibb is filming it for his profile and for the archives. Edward is at his best at gatherings like these, where an intellect, to demonstrate its dexterity, manifests itself to other intellects. This talk does not concern Palestine, Iraq or the American empire. Edward does not mention them. Yet, the conclusions can be drawn: think, connect, enquire, challenge.

Edward is drawn to thinkers like Auerbach, a philologist who, like him, dwelled in two worlds or more, thought and read in many languages. He speaks of Auerbach's theory of 'historical coherence', namely that 'each historical period produced similar products'. In 1935, when the Nazis forced him out of Marburg, Auerbach accepted a post in neutral Istanbul. Of *Mimesis*, Auerbach's *magnum opus*, Edward says, 'It is an exile's work.' Auerbach wrote in 1921, 'I am a Prussian and an adherent of the Jewish faith.' I cannot help but see in Edward, a Palestinian out of place in America and an American estranged when in Palestine, a version of what he calls Auerbach, 'a Prussian Jew in exile in Muslim Turkey'. Through Auerbach, Edward guides us on a Dante-esque, purposeful voyage through Heaven, literature, faith and history: the Old and New Testaments, classical and demotic forms of language, St Peter, the Guelphs and Ghibellines, Goethe, Stendhal, Flaubert, French realism and theories of time. He ends his talk, ninety minutes on, by saying that Auerbach was never at ease in Istanbul. Rather than interpret the world in which he found himself, 'he interpreted himself and his culture to his students'.

At a big dinner in a Chinese restaurant afterwards, we talk about the war we know is coming. Edward opposes this war with the moral strength that remains to him – a formidable intellectual arsenal untouched by illness of blood and body. On the way back to London, Ruth Rogers worries aloud that we are losing him. I cannot accept it. It's like the war: it may be inevitable, but it is not acceptable.

Friday, 15 November 2002
London

Salem Chalabi meets me for lunch in Notting Hill. He is the nephew of Ahmad Chalabi, the head of the Iraqi National Congress (INC). He is almost a clone of his uncle, with the same bulbous nose and barrel chest. We call him 'Sam', although for some reason an old girlfriend of mine calls him 'Shmoo'. He's a good guy, who studied law at the University of Chicago and works for a firm of international lawyers in London. In the past few months, he has become more involved in Iraqi politics, working with his uncle and travelling to Washington.

Listening to him, I understand how far behind I've fallen in Iraqi affairs. There are new people in Washington, feuding among themselves on Olympus, each fashioning an outcome for the mortals of Iraq. Sam has become a messenger and a petitioner to these deities. His dreams, like those of millions more in the Iraqi diaspora, is of freedom, of righting wrongs in the homeland. They seek, like the Achaeans, the fall of Troy in order to restore beautiful Helen to Menelaus and set the world right. Washington's Olympians see a drama larger than Iraq's in which all mortals must play their roles. I remember that Robert Graves wrote, and the quote might be inexact, that whatever else it was, the Trojan war was a trade war.

'The Department of Defense,' Sam says, 'wants to train between

5–10,000 Iraqis, but not the existing party militias.' His uncle's INC has no militia. The Kurds have two, one in each half of Iraqi Kurdistan, under Massoud Barzani's KDP and Jalal Talabani's Patriotic Union of Kurdistan (PUK). The Arabs' only opposition militia of any size is the Badr Brigade, armed wing of the Shiite Supreme Council for the Islamic Revolution in Iraq (SCIRI). The US doesn't much care for its Iranian backers or for Shiites, but it lets SCIRI representatives attend Iraqi opposition meetings with the CIA.

Sam says the US is calling for a pan-Iraqi local force. 'We're swamped with applications. We started recruiting in Iraq, but the US didn't want them [the recruits] for security reasons.' Sam believes the security reasons, but I'm more cynical. The US doesn't trust Iraqis. This will be an American show, I tell Sam. Anyone from the British to the Eritreans is welcome to tag along. Anyone apart from Iraqis.

'The US wants a demilitarised Iraq,' he says. 'That means no private armies or *Peshmerga*.' (The Kurds call their fighters *Peshmerga*, meaning 'those who face death'. When they ran away from Saddam's army in 1991, Jonathan Randal – my friend in Paris, who wrote the best book in English on modern Kurdistan, with the worst title [*After Such Knowledge, What Forgiveness?*] – called them the '*Pêche Melba*'.)

A demilitarised Iraq? Not a bad idea, but only the military – which the British created in advance of the state – has ever held Iraq together. Uncoerced, the three parts of Iraq – the Ottoman provinces of Mosul, Baghdad and Basra – would have gone their separate ways. Or the Arab parts might have united with Syria, and the Kurds with their fellows in Turkey or Iran.

Sam fears that Barzani wants two states to emerge from the war: an Arab south and a Kurdish north with its capital in Kirkuk. The INC, he says, proposes 'a more refined federalism'. That means, in his words, 'no private armies', i.e., the Kurds give up their two militias and join the Iraqi national army as individual soldiers. That is not what the Kurds, who will not abandon their self-defence to an Arab-controlled army, foresee.

Anything can happen in this war. In that, we are living again the demise of the Ottoman Empire through the implantation of the

American. Two states, one state, three states, federalism, unity, armies, borders, chaos ... Iraq is up for grabs.

'The CIA is trying to carve Northern Iraq out for itself,' Sam says. 'It has two sub-stations, in Salahuddin and Suleimaniya. In April 2002, the CIA brought Talabani and Barzani to the Farm.' The Farm? Apparently, it's someplace in Virginia where the CIA holds secret meetings. In August, the Bush administration invited various Iraqi opposition leaders – there must be at least twenty – to Washington for meetings with Colin Powell and Donald Rumsfeld. Dick Cheney, true to his Wizard of Oz image, took part by video link. Sam won't say what, if anything, came out of the sessions. Probably nothing.

His uncle, he says, has good relations with Iran – despite his better relationship with Washington's neo-conservative cabal. Because the *mullahs* in Tehran want an end to Saddam at least as much as Rumsfeld and company do – Ayatollah Khomeini called for regime change in Baghdad twenty years ago, about the time Rumsfeld was shaking Saddam's hand – the Iranians 'will not stand in America's way. They will allow the Iraqi opposition to operate across their borders, so long as Iraq is not used as a base for subversion [against Iran].' Why would the US want bases in Iraq, apart from subverting Iran and Syria and dominating Middle East oil?

Tuesday, 19 November 2002
London

Hoshyar Zebari calls, and I go to see him. He says the Iraqi opposition conference details are now set. It is scheduled to take place in London from 10–15 December. The US asked the KDP, PUK and INC to increase the number of delegates from 260 to 300. David Pierce of the State Department and a woman from the National Security Council said the extra forty participants would be independent and liberal representatives. When this was agreed, the Americans returned to Washington. As much as Hoshyar protests that the Iraqi oppositionists are setting their own course, it looks to an outsider that the puppetmasters' strings stretch to Washington.

Thursday, 21 November 2002
London

Two days of Media Chemical-Biological-Radiological Awareness at the ABC bureau in Hammersmith. The instructor is a jocular veteran of the British army named Dave Butler, from the security firm Bruhn NewTech. Sixteen of us – fourteen men, two women – take plastic chairs at a U-shaped table. No one wears suits anymore. Mostly, it's jeans and T-shirts with collars. I recognise most of the people – Fabrice Moussus, Doug Vogt, Abed Itani, Behzad Taidi and Gary Shore are all people I've worked with before. A few are new to me, younger cameramen, editors and sound engineers. This is a tough audience, and I suspect most of them have seen more combat than Dave did in his thirty-two years with Her Majesty's forces.

'My name's Dave,' he begins. 'Welcome on this "sunny" morning to this chemical, biological and radiological course.' The first hour of our first morning is a commercial for Bruhn NewTech, owned by a man named Lars Bruhn – Dave calls him 'our benefactor' – in Denmark. Its headquarters are on Salisbury Plain, near Dave's previous benefactors in the army, and it maintains an office in Baltimore, Maryland, to service its many US Defense Department contracts. Bruhn NewTech does well out of post-11 September fear.

Dave distributes training manuals and forms for us to sign that say we have received CBR kits of full-body chemical suits, gas masks, respirators, boots, gloves and plastic water bottles. 'I think it was Erwin Rommel,' Dave says, 'who said the British had the best training manuals in the world. Luckily, they didn't read them.'

·Dave's teaching method seems to be alternating jokes with warnings – like a boxer following a feint to the head with a blow to the gut. 'I've been in all these hazards for real,' he says.

He operates a slide show from a laptop. After the Bruhn NewTech logo, there is a list on correct behaviour in class, 'Security ... meals ... no smoking ...' Dave adds, 'I'd appreciate it if no one smokes in here.' Smoking isn't allowed anyway in any Disney office. The list flashes on, 'Mobile phones and pagers off ... Toilets ... Health and safety ...'

'There is no story that's worth your life,' Dave says. 'As one famous journalist said to me, "You don't get famous in this business, Dave, without taking a few risks."' Almost everyone here has taken risks. Fabrice, who's risked his life more than most, says, 'The rule used to be, if one person quit on a story, we all quit. But there is pressure from colleagues and New York to take risks.'

Dave holds up a booklet. 'This is the ABC News Safety Policy,' he says. 'Quote: "The personal health and safety of employees is the highest priority. No one should expose himself or herself unnecessarily to danger. No story is worth such risk. Personal judgement should be used in heading away from rather than into a hazardous situation."'

I cannot tell where the ABC quote ends and the thoughts of Dave begin. Fabrice looks sceptical. Dave tries again, 'There is no compulsion to continue a story if the situation becomes too dangerous.' He takes off his watch and turns to a new slide. It says 'Joseph Mannetta', with an email address and telephone number. 'He wrote the policy.' Dave tries another joke, 'Any truth to the rumour you're merging with CNN? I asked Joe, and he told me, "No comment."'

This group misses the joke. All of them believe two things: that they are more professional than most of CNN (which has some talented and experienced individuals, despite the company's weaknesses); and that most of them would be unemployed when the new company – ABCNN or whatever – rationalised its overseas operations.

Another slide tells us Dave won't face unemployment soon. 'Current clients,' it declares in boldface print. 'US Armed Forces, UK Armed Forces, 18 other NATO and non-NATO countries, Media Journalists and Camera Crews, Police, Emergency services and EOD [Explosive Ordnance Disposal] crews.' The company's security clearance goes all the way to 'SECRET' with the UK's Ministry of Defence and the US Department of Defense. The slides click from one to another in quick succession. All of Bruhn's services are mentioned, though we are unlikely candidates for bomb-disposal training. An aerial photograph, which looks like the Luftwaffe took it on a reconnaissance run in 1940, shows Bruhn's complex of offices beside a military base half a mile from the Defence Ministry's chemical warfare labs at Porton Down.

Some of the guys rest their elbows on the table and pretend to be awake. Dave flicks on the lights. 'Anyone want to go to toilet?' he asks. 'Don't worry about asking questions. The real question is: is there a threat?' Good question. Washington and Downing Street have already answered it.

'Some people seem to think we are going to war in the new year,' Dave says, adding, 'I've tagged a little Iraqi threat at the end.'

Not a bad idea, given that ABC is sending us on this course because we are bound for Iraq. A fresh slide names four hostile environments, 'War, Industrial, Accidental and Terrorism'.

'As for war,' Dave explains, 'we know Saddam Hussein has chemical weapons. We know he has biological weapons. Or some kind of dirty bomb. It's more likely he has some radiological device than a nuclear bomb. But put the right equipment on, and you're laughing.'

Friday, 22 November 2002
London

On our second day, we are laughing at one another in ABC's underground car park. We look like spacemen in our protective suits and gas masks. I just hope we won't need them. If we do, we are lost. None of us passes the drills in the time it takes to survive, immediate action drill, immediate decontamination drill, modified decontamination drill, cannister (gas mask filter) changing drill, drinking (through gas mask) drill, urination (in chemical suit) drill, defecation drill and unmasking drill. As bad as the drills are, they cannot compete with Dave's asides:

'There is an AIDS lecture at ten o'clock. Enter by the back passage.'

Putting on the protective gloves, 'I quite like the smell of rubber.'

'I hate this women's-lib stuff. You have to treat them like men.'

'Remember: death can be fatal.'

Dave is, however, trying to teach us something that might save our lives. He shows us a BBC *Newsnight* report from the Iran-Iraq war in 1985. At the time, Iraq was deploying chemical weapons against Iran. The Iranians took a BBC crew to a contaminated area where chemical warheads lay on the ground. It was a good story that told the public what Washington and London did not want it to hear: that Saddam was using illegal WMD to asphyxiate thousands of Iranians. But the *Newsnight* team was itself affected by the poison. The cameraman, Bernard Hesketh, died of cancer that Dave says came from exposure to these chemicals. Another clip, from the documentary Gwynne Roberts made in 1988, shows the dead in Halabja: adults covering their children with their own bodies, some fallen where they tried to run away, some hiding in their houses. It is a modern Pompeii, the effects of a human Vesuvius with brimstone and lava supplied by his friends in Europe and the US. Gwynne wore a protective suit when he dug up contaminated earth and carried it to England for the tests which proved Saddam, Reagan and Thatcher did not tell the truth about Halabja.

At lunch, Fabrice says the world has changed for him since his daughter was born. He's covered more wars than I have. As a cameraman, he gets closer to death than writers have to. When Anwar Sadat was assassinated on 6 October 1981, everyone – including Egypt's senior officers and bodyguards – hit the ground. One person remained on his feet, when armed soldiers broke away from the military parade to shoot their president. That person was Fabrice. If ever you see footage of the assassination, know that he shot it. If he had been a photographer rather than a network cameraman, he would have made millions from sales of his work. But network cameramen do not own their copyright: the corporations, which themselves champion intellectual property as a sacred right, own every frame their crews shoot.

Fabrice says he won't take those risks anymore. He'll go to war, but he intends to return to his daughter in Paris. He is no longer convinced that ABC, under its new owners, will go to the lengths it did in 1991 to help us get out of Kurdistan. (Then, it chartered a 707 to fly us out of southeastern Turkey.) ABC is allowing me, more or less, to assemble the crew that covered the 1991 rebellion – Fabrice on camera and Qassem Dergham, now a freelance cameraman in Lebanon, as sound recordist. But the network will choose the producer. We did not have one in 1991.

Fabrice says he trusts me, something I take as an undeserved tribute. And he trusts Qassem. So, Fabrice will come. I don't tell him, although I do not know why I don't, that he is about the only working cameraman I trust for what may or may not come our way in Iraq. It's not because he's brave. He's honest.

Sunday, 24 November 2002
London

The train from Victoria station this evening smells of drunks and urine. One man in a long woollen coat has passed out on a grimy row of seats. A short woman, drunk and wearing heavy boots, kicks the floor. She speaks to the young man beside her and kicks the floor whenever he, also drunk, seems to lose interest. The train passes the dreary suburban stations south of the Thames: Clapham Junction, East Croydon, Purley, Redhill. The stink of piss on old upholstery is unbearable. At my stop in Surrey, I rush to the door. A woman blocking the aisle asks, 'Are you trying to pass?' *Pass?* I'm escaping. An ancient black cab is parked under the single light outside the station. The driver, an old man, says he knows the way to the address I hand him. The door handle is broken, and the driver leans around to open it from inside. Slowly, he guides the taxi over a series of speed bumps that leads to a main road. There, however, a barrier blocks the way.

'The road's closed,' the driver says. 'We'll take the back way.' How much more back can we get? Dying chestnut trees hover over our route, shielding us from the faint light of the old moon. Shabby apartment blocks stand on either side, dark but perhaps not empty. We come to what looks like a country lane, cottages on either side, and cross over a motorway to a similar lane on the other side.

I ask myself why a Kurd, born in the most beautiful mountains and among the hardiest people on earth, would live in suburban Surrey. Tonight, the Kurds are meeting to talk politics. I am on my way to Latif Rashid's house, huge and rambling and warm, where his brother-in-law Jalal Talabani is staying. Latif and Jalal married Shahnaz and Hiro, the daughters of one of the legendary leaders of Kurdish nationalism, Ahmed Ibrahim. Ibrahim worked for a time beside Mullah Mustafa Barzani and supported his tribal, feudal and near-suicidal policies. His sons-in-law are now, respectively, leader and London representative of the PUK. The PUK governs the southeastern half of Iraqi Kurdistan from its capital, Suleimaniya. Massoud Barzani's KDP administers the other half from Erbil.

The tribes as well as the politicians and businessmen and opportunists of Iraqi exile are gathering to plot the change they know is coming and cannot quite believe. To imagine an Iraq without the tyrant who has ruled it and imprinted his image upon the land and the minds of two generations is beyond many of them. Their grandfathers did not see, in 1917, that the Turks who had ruled their provinces for almost seven centuries would abandon them to European invaders in a few months. They had lost opportunities then – for Arab unity and independence, for Kurdish statehood – and the descendants seek to avoid similar errors. Saddam is going. The US is coming.

All evening, people are coming and going in the sitting room. Talabani and most of the other men are in suits. All of them speak Kurdish and Arabic, and a few speak Turkish. Because I'm there, the conversation is in English. That war is coming is not in question. How to gain from it is. Talabani talks about the new Islamist government in Turkey. 'Those are open-minded people,' he says. 'They will not look on it as the old people did.' And the Turkish army? 'They are trying for two pretexts for intervention: the PKK and the Turcomen.' The PKK is the Kurdish Workers' Party of Turkey, which has waged an insurgency in Kurdish-speaking southeastern Turkey for a generation. Some of them are hiding in Iraqi Kurdistan. The Turcomen are a small Turkish-speaking minority in Iraq. Turkey could invade either to destroy the first or rescue the second. Talabani seems optimistic when he predicts that Turkey would accept an autonomous Kurdish state in an Iraqi federation.

Sitting next to Talabani is Dr Mahmoud Osman, a physician and veteran of many Kurdish wars. His integrity is unquestioned among Kurds I know. Jonathan Randal admires him more than any other Kurdish politician. Dr Osman started his political life with the old

Barzani, worked with Talabani and is now independent and critical of both Kurdish parties.

In all, seven Kurdish men and two Kurdish women sit around a long coffee table laden with Arab sweets. Talabani says he's going to Paris for a meeting of French Kurdish specialists on Friday and asks me for Randal's number. Favouring the US invasion, he wants the Kurds to take part. Their *Peshmerga* fighters must be in Mosul and Kirkuk, he believes, and they must go to Baghdad.

'If there is an American war,' Dr Osman says, 'American protection will go.' Dr Osman is one among many Kurds who believe a war will jeopardise everything they have built – the parliaments, the schools, the civil society, the hospitals, roads, businesses and what may be the freest society in the Middle East – out of the desolation they inherited from Saddam in 1991. The Kurdish zone – an illegal protectorate in which Iraq's Kurds have thrived, despite a KDP-PUK civil war – survives under an American air umbrella. Take it away, and the Kurds fear absorption into a unitary Iraq and loss of their self-government to Baghdad. 'The Kurds have been betrayed three times,' Dr Osman reminds Talabani. 'Not a fourth.'

The three betrayals he refers to were all by US presidents. First, in 1975, having armed and trained Iraq's Kurds with the enthusiastic assistance of Israel's Mossad and Iran's SAVAK, Gerald Ford and his secretary of state Henry Kissinger pulled the plug on them. The Kurds then realised they had been used to pressure Saddam Hussein to sign a border agreement that favoured Iran's claims along the Shatt al-Arab waterway. When Saddam signed the accord in Algiers, his hands were free to punish the Kurds. The punishment was as swift as it was brutal. Deprived of American, Israeli and Iranian support, Iraq's Kurds saw their towns and villages bombed and Iraq's Arab armies reclaiming the land. The surviving Kurds escaped to the highest, coldest mountains and stayed in caves. Others ended up in Iran, Turkey or Syria. I knew some who made their way to Beirut, where I was living then. They joined the region's other mass refugee population, the Palestinians, in questioning both the world order that had been so unjust to them and their own leaders, who seemed to do them no good at all.

The second betrayal, by Ronald Reagan in 1988, was not in fact a betrayal so much as the fruit of his administration's public and clandestine encouragement of Saddam Hussein's wars against Iran and most of Iraq's people. That Reagan's envoy Donald Rumsfeld opened the door in Baghdad in 1983 to renewed diplomatic relations, American largesse, the sale of Bell helicopters and the ingredients for manufacturing chemical weapons is uncontested. The US was aware of Saddam's criminal treatment of Iraq's Shiite Arab majority and his genocide of the Kurds at the time an American fleet cruised the Persian Gulf to protect Iraq's oil exports and weapons imports. Thus, when Saddam sprayed poison on Iraqi Kurds at Halabja in 1988, the US and its British accomplices denied in the first instance that the event had taken place at all and then blamed Iran. It was no betrayal; it was consistent with their support for Saddam. Yet all Kurds refer to this official cover-up of a crime against humanity as a betrayal.

The third American betrayal of Iraq's Kurds – it is too early to say it's also the last – was perhaps the most harmful, unexpected and treacherous of all. The first George Bush prompted the Kurds, as he did Iraq's Shiites and many Sunni dissidents, to risk all they had to stage a revolution and topple the tyrant of whom even the US had wearied when he exceeded instructions by invading Kuwait in August 1990. Bush, after US armed forces secured Kuwait for the American consumer in March 1991, delivered a speech at the arms-manufacturing Raytheon Company – as much a beneficiary of the war as any oil company – in which he called upon the Iraqi people and the Iraqi military to commit regicide.

I was in Iraqi Kurdistan at the time. 'Haji Boosh', the liberator of Kuwait, joined the pantheon of Kurdish epic heroes that included Qazi Muhammad, who led them to one defeat, and Mullah Mustafa, who did the same thirty years later. Bush was about to surpass them. The US had just conquered Kuwait. The skies of Iraq were clear; Saddam could not drop chemicals on rebel Kurds and Shiites from his aircraft. His army was in disarray after its humiliation in Kuwait, and whole divisions were in revolt. Iraqi Shiites had smuggled weapons from Iran; the Kurds brought theirs from Turkey, Iran and Syria. All they needed was the call to arms that Bush issued before the weapons manufacturers at Raytheon.

I am not certain the Kurds were listening carefully. Bush challenged the people and the army to rise. The people did rise, but most of the army, and certainly the senior officers (all of them Baathist loyalists vetted by Saddam and implicated in his crimes), did nothing. Two Arab states – Egypt, the most populous, and Saudi Arabia, the richest – implied they could effect a *coup d'état* among Iraqi officers that would leave the army and state institutions intact. They failed. The Kurds, like the Shiites of the south, heard only the word 'people' and rose accordingly. Within three weeks, the entire south and all of Iraqi Kurdistan were in rebel hands.

Iraq has eighteen provinces – many Iraqis would say nineteen, counting Kuwait – and the rebels had made Baath-free zones of fourteen of them. The convergence on Baghdad was near. But it was not to be. The victorious US generously granted licence to Iraq's armed forces to fly again in what had been a no-fly zone. The permission came from Washington, but the courier who delivered it, General Norman Schwarzkopf, later said the Iraqis had 'suckered' him into allowing them to use the helicopters Rumsfeld had helped them buy. The implication was that Schwarzkopf could not have guessed Iraq's army would deploy its helicopters against insurgents intent on annihilating the regime. He could not have foreseen that the helicopters would conduct aerial reconnaissance of rebel concentrations, drop bombs, fire rockets and deliver troops to the fronts. Could the military genius who had just defeated the Iraqi army, and seen the havoc it had wrought on Kuwait, have assumed that Iraqi helicopters would be used for humanitarian purposes or to save Iraq's General Staff the inconvenience of long drives between Baghdad and their winter homes? When we in the north saw the first helicopters, as still in the sky as the moon, dropping explosives on villages and roads, we knew the rebellion was over.

The Kurdish fighters left the battlefield to be with their families, who feared Saddam's helicopters would deliver poison gas as in 1988. The lucky ones made it to Iran. Those who climbed the mountains to seek refuge among other Kurds in Turkey met the fortified ramparts of the Turkish army and border police, who let them freeze, starve and suffer on barren slopes rather than grant them shelter. The US, having raised and then dashed their hope of liberty, completed its treachery by acquiescing in Turkey's determination to refuse the Kurds a haven. The television pictures of fleeing, weeping, freezing and dying Kurds embarrassed a Bush administration that saw the public relations gain of the Kuwait triumph melting into the rivers of southeast Turkey. While condemning Iran, which turned away no refugees from Kurdistan or the Shiite Arab south, the US arranged a rescue – for Turkey. It saved Turkey the inconvenience of sheltering Iraqi Kurds by proclaiming part of Northern Iraq a 'safe-haven' and reinstating – at least north of Erbil – the no-fly zone that Schwarzkopf had abolished a few weeks before. Slowly, the Kurds returned, rebuilt and warred amongst themselves. Out of the US's gift to Turkey came what was, in fact if not in law, a self-governing Kurdish state.

The fourth betrayal that Dr Osman foresees, speaking for many of his countrymen, is the loss of that state. 'The Americans,' he says (his point is directed at Talabani), 'have promised nothing concrete.' Another man says Washington refuses to use the word 'federal' when speaking of post-Saddam Iraq. Another man complains that the US is sending gas masks to Israel, which has never suffered a chemical attack by Saddam, and none to the Kurds, who have.

'Colin Powell wrote to the Kurdish parliament,' Dr Osman tells Talabani. 'He said, "You are partners." Partners in what? You should be in it [the war], but they may not let you in it. Turkey's condition is that the Kurds stay out. You should be in, but with guarantees for your future.'

I get the impression that, while Dr Osman opposes the war, he believes any military assault on Saddam must include Kurdish fighters to guarantee the Kurds a voice in postwar Iraq. 'America and Turkey,' he says to Talabani, 'when they meet, God knows what will happen to the absent one.' Dr Osman's criticisms are irritating Talabani. They go next door to the dining room and continue their discussion in Kurdish. They could have stayed; I don't understand any Kurdish, apart from the pleasantries, and they are not being pleasant this evening.

Someone mentions that the Iraqi military may yet depose Saddam to avoid war. Latif Rashid responds, 'Iraq is coup-proof.'

An older man in a blue blazer says he knew a Republican Guard

officer under Saddam's predecessor and mentor, President Ahmad
Hassan al-Bakr. 'Another officer approached him about organising a
coup. The officer informed al-Bakr. And al-Bakr told him he knew he
had refused the offer. How did he know? Al-Bakr said, "It is we who
sent this guy to you."'

Latif says, 'The fear is so great they wouldn't risk it.' He makes a
prediction, 'The army will collapse. Saddam will rely on his *fedayeen*.'

Next month, most of Iraq's exile opposition organisations are
meeting in London. Latif says no one should be excluded. All are
invited: Chalabi's INC, the Kurds, the Iraqi National Accord of Iyad
Allawi, SCIRI, parties of Turcomen and of Assyrian and Chaldean
Christians, smaller groups of leftists and Islamists and former Baathists,
the royal pretender, Sherif Ali, and independents. Even al-Dawa?
I ask Latif. Al-Dawa ('The Call') is one of the older Shiite Muslim
clandestine groups that resisted Saddam. Both al-Dawa and the Iraqi
Communist Party, Latif says, have received invitations. Neither has
accepted – or rejected.

'Dave Pierce [an American diplomat] went to see the Dawa,' he
says. 'The Dawa probably don't want to be seen working under a US
programme. There are differences within the Islamic groups. They
believe that if they attend the conference with the US, they would
alienate some of their supporters. Their relationship is not smooth
with al-Hakim.' Muhammad Bakr al-Hakim is an Iraqi Shiite
ayatollah, heads the SCIRI and lives in Iran. 'Iran is supportive of the
conference,' Latif says. 'In the last Iraqi delegation to Washington,
Abdel-Aziz al-Hakim was a member.' (Abdel-Aziz is Muhammad
Bakr's younger brother and deputy.) If Iran had not approved, al-
Hakim would never have gone to Washington. Al-Dawa is another
matter.

Al-Dawa members were abused, detained, tortured and murdered.
Iran, in the midst of its war with Iraq, gave technical and financial
support to al-Dawa, as it did to other Iraqi Shiites who shared
Ayatollah Khomeini's goal of regime change in Baghdad. Iran also used
al-Dawa's cadres for its own ends. In 1983, al-Dawa operatives blew up
the US embassy in Kuwait. That was the year in which Hizbullah, then
a secret Shiite group in Lebanon which took inspiration and money

from the Islamic Republic, sent suicide bombers to blow up the US embassy and US Marine Headquarters in Beirut. The Beirut bombers were never caught – not surprising in the anarchy of the Lebanese war; the Kuwait bombers were. A Kuwaiti court sentenced most of them to prison and a few to death, although none was executed.

The conviction of the al-Dawa bombers was one of the Reagan administration's rare, albeit tactical, victories in its war on terrorism. But it was followed by a series of events that left Iran with strategic victories: the US's expulsion from Lebanon and Iran's acquisition – despite an international arms embargo – of vital American weapons, mainly anti-tank missiles which gave Iran an advantage in the war with Iraq. Briefly put, Hizbullah kidnapped American citizens in Lebanon and issued public demands to exchange its captives for al-Dawa prisoners in Kuwait. Meanwhile, Iran pressed its secret agenda: a shopping list of American arms. The Reagan administration took the bait: Oliver North, Bud McFarlane, John Singlaub, William Poindexter and other Reaganites – many of whom served their own terms in prison for perjury – will forever be associated with what became the Iran-Contra Affair. The Iranians received weapons, Hizbullah released a hostage. Hizbullah would kidnap another hostage, and Reagan would ship more missiles to Iran. By the time the conspiracy was exposed in a Beirut magazine in 1985, there were nearly twice as many Americans held hostage in Lebanon as there had been before. Meanwhile, Reagan used the money the Iranians had paid for the arms to finance the war against Nicaragua that the US Congress – reacting to popular revulsion – refused to subsidise. The end came in August 1990, when Saddam invaded Kuwait and opened its prisons. The al-Dawa prisoners escaped with all the others.

It seems odd to me that the US should now send David Pierce (whom I knew in Beirut in the early 1980s, when he worked as a correspondent of UPI), to talk to people who had destroyed a US embassy and killed American diplomats. It seems odd, as well, that Iran would not oppose the invasion of its Muslim neighbour by the Great Satan.

'Iran,' Latif says, 'cares only that the [new Iraq] regime should not be anti-Iranian.' Chalabi, the Kurds and most of the others who are cooperating with the US are not anti-Iranian. Washington, however, is. Paul Wolfowitz, Richard Perle and the other neo-conservatives responsible for the coming war say Iran's and Syria's regimes are next on the hit list.

We have more drinks, and someone puts hot food on the table. Latif predicts the London conference will attract between thirty and forty exile groups. Four million Iraqis, he says, live outside Iraq. About 20 percent of the population, they left to escape war, Saddam's repression and the poverty caused by UN sanctions. Latif likes to think that democracy in countries where many settled, as he did in England, has had a positive effect on their political outlook.

Dr Osman and Talabani, having concluded their dispute, return to eat and rejoin our conversation. How many Kurds are there in Iraq, I ask Talabani. The usual figure given is 6 million. 'I personally think,' he says between bites, 'we are seven to seven and a half million. There are many Failli Kurds, the Shiites, outside Iraq. Half of them were deported to Iran and Europe in the early Seventies. Saddam accused all the Shiites of being Iranian. They were killed. They were looted. For example, he was one of the Kurdish millionaires.' Talabani indicates one of the other guests. 'They took everything from them. Five thousand intellectuals, university graduates, disappeared. None were released in the last amnesty.'

When Hitler and Stalin occupied Poland, they massacred Polish intellectuals, professionals, aristocrats and officers. Saddam tried the same with the Kurds. Whether the Kurds number 6 million or 7 million, more than 1 million of them live south of the Kurdish areas in Baghdad and other Arab cities. Iraqi Kurdistan is divided into two administrative areas, Barzani's and Talabani's. Won't a war, with the possibilities of Turkish involvement and a new regime in Baghdad that has no commitment to federalism, deprive the Kurds of their autonomy?

A Kurdish businessman named Aza says, 'The two administrations represent 99.9 percent of the Kurds.'

Talabani puts down his food and laughs. 'Let's say 90 percent. We don't want to be like an Arab referendum. Ninety is enough. Me and Massoud Barzani, we got 1 million votes each. All the other parties got seventy-six thousand. I think every Kurd is ready to defend this administration.'

Latif asks when I was last in Kurdistan, and I tell him 1992. It was freezing. I slept on the floor of a friend's house. There was no electricity. Students were asking me to help them obtain European or American visas. People were beginning to return from Iran and to come down from the mountains near Turkey. The villages Saddam levelled had not been rebuilt. All that had changed, Latif said. Then he listed the achievements of the Kurds' non-state, 'Communications. Internet. Mobile telephones. Internet cafés and faxes without censorship. Hospitals. Satellite television. The first thing you notice in Iraqi Kurdistan is the satellite dish on everyone's roof. In Suleimaniya, we have eleven television stations. Radio channels. Newspapers. One hundred and thirty publishers. Books. No censorship. No restrictions on freedom of movement.'

South of the line where Kurdish rule ended and Saddam's began, none of those things – apart from hospitals – was conceivable. Talabani laughs again. 'There are two democracies in the Middle East. Kurdistan and the other place' (Israel).

Latif says, 'We lost our villages.' Talabani, now handed a cup of tea, adds, 'Not one single village survived. All were destroyed.' He puts down his tea and touches a finger for each village he names. If he gives the whole list, we'll be here all night. 'Now, almost all the villages have been redeveloped,' Latif says. 'They have water, mosques, telephones, livestock.'

'For seventy years,' Talabani says, 'the Iraqi regime provided 504 schools. Now, we have 2,076 schools. Now, we have a university with 7,500 students, and 45 percent are girls.'

The two of them begin to sound like delegates of the Kurdish Tourist Board. Latif, 'Roads, sanitation rebuilt. Institutions for youth, women. Now, ten hotels, at least six of which are four-star. One is five-star. There are restaurants and social clubs.'

Talabani, 'Christmas is like in any European country. There is singing and dancing. There is full equality among women and men. Polygamy is prevented. Honour killing has stopped. It's down from hundreds to perhaps seven, nine or, most, ten a year. For the first time in the Middle East, there are four women judges. There is a special shelter for girls who refuse arranged marriages. The old military garrison in Suleimaniya is now Freedom Park.'

Latif, 'There is social security for the elderly.'

Talabani, 'Every student receives 150 *dinars* a month at university, and the university is free.'

The brothers-in-law are speaking not only of the PUK half of Kurdistan, but of the KDP area as well. Where the KDP differs is in official indifference to women's equality and social welfare. In both regions, the gains in the ten years since 1992 are impressive. I remember the desolation, the hopelessness, the terrible psychological burden borne by much of the population whose families had been murdered or tortured, the thousands of acres of land in which the army had sown more than 6 million mines, and the thousands of stone rubbish heaps that had once been villages. On my last visit to Iraqi Kurdistan, it was losing about ten farmers a week to land mines – and dozens more, especially children, were having their legs sawn away by little metal bomblets that German, Italian, French, Russian and American arms dealers had sold to Saddam. The Kurds of Iraq had turned all that around. They had help – Oxfam, the Red Cross, etc, and a few Kurdish exile philanthropists. But they had done most of it themselves against hostility on all their frontiers and despite the UN. The UN enforces sanctions in Iraqi Kurdistan just as it does in Saddam's zone.

Latif, 'Under Resolution 986, Kurdistan is dealt with through the central government.'

Talabani, 'It's because [then-UN Secretary-General] Boutros-Ghali was an Arab. I'll give you two examples.' He describes two factories Kurds wanted to build in his area. One was for cooking oil, the other for cement. Both required foreign engineers in the early stages. The Iraqi foreign minister, Tariq Aziz, would not grant visas to the German and Spanish engineers. Thus, the UN would not help.

Latif condemns the 'low calibre' UN bureaucrats, Palestinian and Sudanese, in Baghdad. 'All they want is to extend their contracts and please the regime.'

Aza the Kurdish businessman offers an example, 'Under the Oil for Food programme, Iraq can buy as much medicine as it wants. A proportion should go to Iraqi Kurdistan, but Iraq puts everything the wrong way. Suleimaniya Hospital does not receive its medicine.'

Talabani returns to the list of accomplishments of his part of Kurdistan, almost as if he were running for office, 'In seventy years of the regime, we had seven hospitals. Now, we have twenty-seven hospitals and 293 health centres. We had 199 doctors, and now we have 900 doctors. We have a medical school now, recognised by Britain, with international examinations each year.'

One of the men who had stayed out of the conversation speaks up. He seems modest, wearing a wool cardigan under his suit jacket. A bushy moustache gives him an avuncular presence, and he smokes between cups of tea. His name is Abdel Razzaq Mirza, the PUK's Minister of Cooperation and Relations. Oil for Food, they all agree, is a disaster.

'The problem,' Mirza says, 'is the UN system and the Memorandum of Understanding.'

Talabani concurs, 'Buying wheat and rice is cheaper from local farmers. It's half the price, and it's better quality. But they [the UN] buy from outside. They are applying the boycott.'

The UN boycott resolution, written by the US, forbids the purchase by the UN of any Iraqi product other than oil. Thus the wheat and rice are purchased from American or other western agribusiness corporations and shipped, at added cost, to Iraq. Mirza believes the programme is killing local agriculture. 'We produce 600,000 tons of wheat locally,' he says. 'Now we get wheat from Australia. Our farmers cannot sell.'

The Australian wheat, bought with the Iraqi oil revenues that the UN administers, is then provided free to Iraqis, including the Kurds.

Latif, 'Resolution 986 and the Memorandum of Understanding were based on humanitarian help for the Kurdish people. We've passed that stage. They cannot spend on development. UN aid is usually sponsored by a country, as in the West Bank. In our case, it's our money. Usually these programmes are short of cash. In our case, we have a $16–17 billion excess.'

'This is our share of the Iraqi [oil] money,' Mirza adds. 'We have the right to have full control in our areas, but we have to observe the state. We should have partnership on allocation and decisions and implementation.'

When the US invades, both the sanctions and the Oil for Food programme will be redundant – legacies of the 'containment' of Saddam. But, I wonder, what will happen to the $16–17 billion surplus in the Kurds' account? In the meantime, shouldn't these Kurdish politicians think of preserving the autonomy that permitted them to accomplish all that they have been describing to me this evening? What guarantee do they have that the new Iraq will be a federal state?

'The first time we mentioned the word "federalism"', Latif explains, 'everyone was hesitant. Then, the [Kurdish] parliament had the formula: a democratic, united, federal Iraq. The Iraqi National Congress in Salahuddin adopted the programme of a federal system in Iraq. But, as for the details, now is not the time to create too many problems. Ideally, we would like a two-state federal system – Arab and Kurd. The Kurdish state would include the Turcomen and Assyrians. Ideally, we would like the region of Kurdistan to be geographically defined. The Arab part, if they want it to be, could be one, two or three states. But that is up to the future Iraqi national assembly.'

It's one-thirty in the morning when I leave, filled with coffee and whiskey and Arab pastries and thoughts about Iraq. I have known some of these men for almost twenty years and was with them during their worst defeat. Is it possible they will win at last? Or is there an inevitable 'fourth betrayal' lurking in US-occupied Iraq?

Monday, 25 November 2002
London

Latif works out of a Knightsbridge building leased by the INC and paid, I assume, from the funds allocated by the US Congress under the Iraq Liberation Act. The PUK, like the KDP, is technically part of the INC. In practice, the Kurds organise their political parties and militias independently of the INC. Coming back to Iraqi politics, I see that the PUK is in fact closer to the INC than the KDP is. Hoshyar Zebari, for example, does not operate out of the Knightsbridge office. He does not need to – he has been here longer than any of them and has more friends in Parliament and the press than either the PUK or INC do. He is also, like his nephew Massoud Barzani, more a Kurdish than Iraqi nationalist. Latif is among his own with the INC Arabs, Sunni and Shiite. Then, again, I may be wrong. It was Hoshyar's party that turned to Saddam's Arabs for help during the Kurdish civil war in 1996.

Anyway, I clear the security screening on the ground floor and walk upstairs to see Latif and Mirza. It's all relaxed in Latif's corner office, people coming and going, cups of coffee, me slouching on a sofa taking notes. These are probably the last days of exile politics. If the US wins the war, these people will have to do the things they have been talking about for twenty years. Even the Kurds, self-governing for the last eleven years, are going to come out of their hermetically sealed isolation and face being a part of Iraq. The word 'democracy' finds its way into almost every sentence. Perhaps if they say it enough, it will materialise.

'There was a time,' Latif, remembers, sitting behind his desk, 'when you couldn't express democracy and rights directly, because this was seen as Western. Now you can. Even the Islamist groups can. That took time for people to appreciate.' Even ex-Baathists and former murderers, who abandoned Saddam extremely late, are speaking about human rights. 'There was a time when people thought Iraq must have a strong single-party government.' Iraq was not alone. Dictators in the rest of the Middle East, as well as in Africa, justified their one-party rule on the grounds that multiple parties destroyed national unity. Any excuse would have done.

'Even before Saddam Hussein,' Latif says, 'there was a dictatorship under the monarchy. The army had a very strong power. I remember pre-1958' – before General Abdel Karim Qassem's military coup that he called The Revolution – 'my father was in charge of the election results in Suleimaniya. There were two candidates, one from the KDP and one from the Iraqi Communist Party [ICP]. They had a coalition.'

When? 'About 1956. I know for sure what happened. My father came back. The KDP candidate was Ibrahim Ahmad' – later, Latif's father-in-law – 'and the Communist was Marouf Barzinji. I know for sure that the results were that the KDP-ICP coalition won overwhelmingly. But the government's candidates were elected.'

Iraq never had a fair election, except possibly for the Ottoman parliament after the Young Turk Revolution of 1906. The British held the country's first referendum – on whether to make the country a monarchy under Emir Feisal of the Hejaz – in 1920. Britain's High Commissioner, Sir Percy Cox, proudly set and achieved a 98.3 percent majority for the new king.

'Iraq is a peculiar country,' Latif says, an understatement of heroic proportions. 'We don't have a date for the formation of Iraq. We have dates for the creation of the army and for the monarchy and so on. It's a peculiar setup for Iraq.'

Wednesday, 27 November 2002
London

Since moving away from London in the summer of 2001, I have noticed on my return visits that nothing works here. The trains of the Underground, compared to those of the Paris Métro, are decrepit and ill-maintained. New Labour's Third Way means No Way for commuters. The Paris trains are cleaner and newer, and the French do not regard public transport as an asset to strip from the public and sell off to the rich friends of politicians. What's more, the French trains stop only in the stations. The London Tube trains prefer to dawdle in tunnels. The Labour apparatchiks swallowed whole the late-Tory view that the public does not exist. There are no patients in hospitals, no passengers on public transport, no clients, no students: everyone is a customer; all services and professions are businesses. The Harvard Business School worldview has infected the US's British colony as thoroughly as the old state socialist model of the London School of Economics did the post-colonial empire that Britain ingeniously named the 'Commonwealth'. Anyway, this is what I think as I sit in a train on the Metropolitan Line that has been stalled for twenty minutes between stations in an unlit tunnel. The people who run this crumbling system are the ones who promise to assist the US in bringing the light of democracy to the Middle East.

Mahmoud Osman lives in Ruislip, a North London suburb reached from central London via three separate Tube lines. More than an hour after I leave Notting Hill, I exit the Ruislip station. Before me stretches a world of suburban stucco for miles in every direction. If Dr Osman were an average exile politician, he would be in Knightsbridge or Belgravia among other exiles who were sensible enough to send their (often stolen) wealth ahead when their government expelled them. He is not a normal exile politician, and he is worth coming all this way to see. He has worked for forty years in Iraqi politics. His Kurdish and anti-Saddam credentials are impeccable, but he does not belong to either the KDP or PUK. The house is modest and lived-in, suitable to an underpaid physician on London's fringe. It is not a grand meeting place with a lavish and gilded reception room, where servants ferry *demitasses* of Turkish coffee to visiting dignitaries and court flunkeys. His is a face that has seen life and death, on the shoulders of a man who, despite his short stature, looks like he has never learned to bow.

He puts me in a soft chair in his sitting room and tells me what he sees happening. The PUK and KDP have not resolved the differences that led to their civil war, he says. That ended, officially, with an agreement signed in Washington in 1988. 'It's called the Washington Agreement, but there was no real agreement,' he says. 'It's a sort of *détente*. This September, they managed to unite the parliaments when Talabani went to Salahuddin.' Salahuddin is Massoud Barzani's mountain lair, above Iraqi Kurdistan's capital in Erbil. 'But there is no single budget. There may be one parliament now, but there are two prime ministers, two governments and two armies.'

Dr Osman does not regard this state of affairs as irrelevant. Survival is at stake. 'They have to make decisions very quickly. There is no time.' The first decision, he believes, must be to form one Kurdish government and to unite the two armies.

If not, what does he think will happen?

'Another defeat.'

He has witnessed too many already. Born in Suleimaniya under the Iraqi monarchy in 1938, he joined the illegal KDP in 1954. The party's leader, Mustafa Barzani, was an exile in the Soviet Union. Party members in Iraq were subject to arrest, torture and execution. Deliverance appeared to come with the army's overthrow of the monarchy in July of 1958. The coup leader, General Qassem, was an Arab nationalist, but he promised the Kurds equality within a new Iraq. 'Qassem brought Barzani back from the Soviet Union,' the doctor recalls. 'He legalised the KDP. The 1958 constitution said the Arabs were partners.' That was how it began in the new Iraq, but none of its peoples escaped or transcended the legacy the British had left them in creating a state that none of them wanted.

'There were mistakes on both sides,' Dr Osman says, an admission I have heard from no other Kurdish leader. Kurdish propaganda tends to present the Kurds as nothing other than victims of rapacious Arabs, Turks and Persians. But their leaders have led them into some obvious traps, which the followers within their tribal society refused to avoid. Declaring the Mahabad Republic, in reality a Soviet puppet-state, at the end of the Second World War was one such mistake. Iran's Kurds, who should have known Stalin would desert them as Henry Kissinger would Iraq's Kurds in 1975, suffered the consequences when the Shah's army returned, determined on vengeance. Another trap was to press the Iraqi state in 1960 for concessions it was too weak to grant. 'The fighting began in 1961,' Dr Osman says. It went on and on, with truces and other interruptions, and has not stopped yet.

Dr Osman was senior commander in the KDP when Mullah Mustafa led his people to tragedy in 1975. The old man was taking assistance from the enemy – the Shah of Iran, who had hanged his Mahabad Republic's prime minister and from whom he fled to save his own life in 1946. Mullah Mustafa compounded his crime, in Arab eyes, by allowing Israeli intelligence agents and military advisors into Iraq to assist his rebellion in the early 1970s. And he trusted the US, although it was obvious to everyone that the Nixon administration was using Iraq's Kurds to put pressure on Baghdad to settle its border dispute with Iran in the Shah's favour.

At that time, I went with Peter Jennings, then ABC News Mideast correspondent, and cameraman Vince Gaito to Iran in a failed attempt to cross the border at the village of Haj Omran, cover the rebellion and interview Mullah Mustafa. The Iranian security forces would not let us into Iraq. They said Saddam Hussein was bombing the road, but we now know the Iranians and Americans were already preparing the betrayal they hoped the world would not notice. (Peter Sturken, another ABC cameraman, stole across the border a few months later to make a documentary film. He nearly died of shrapnel wounds, when Saddam began his systematic annihilation of the Kurds, and had to be evacuated through the mountains on muleback by Kurds who risked their own lives to save his.) The Kurds escaped, as they always did, to the high mountains with their families. Mullah Mustafa, who had lived in Soviet exile for twelve years, spent the last four years of his life as a refugee in Washington.

In 1976, the year after the disaster in which thousands of Kurds died, Dr Osman left the KDP and formed the Kurdistan Socialist Party. He sought help for Iraq's Kurds in Syria, moving to England the year after the 1991 betrayal.

'Since 1992,' he says, 'we have been completely polarised.' In 1995, he says, the US betrayed the Kurds a fourth time; here he adds a betrayal that was not listed at Latif Rashid's house, that of 1995. That would make the 'next one' the fifth – and most Kurds seem to fear another.

'In '95,' he says, 'the Americans, the CIA, promised the Kurds and the INC a *coup d'état* [in Baghdad] on 5 March. The KDP prepared its forces for a month to go to Mosul. The PUK got ready to take Kirkuk. Forty-eight hours before it was scheduled, the CIA went to Talabani and Barzani and said there would be no *coup*. Barzani withdrew his forces, but the PUK and [Ahmad] Chalabi made some attacks. This led to tension between the KDP and Chalabi.' It also led, a year later, to Chalabi's and the PUK's flight from Erbil, when Saddam's forces invaded the city and killed the US allies and agents who had not escaped or gone into hiding.

The divisions within the Iraqi exile opposition, Dr Osman believes, reflect divisions in Washington. He says, as Ahmad Chalabi himself does, that the CIA and the State Department hate Chalabi.

The INC leader's friends are to be found in the Pentagon and among extreme right-wingers in Congress. (He says Richard Perle was just here to see Chalabi.) Dr Osman clearly does not like the way the CIA manipulates its Iraqi puppets, the way the State Department plays favourites, or the way the Pentagon uses others, and so on. They are manoeuvring for policy dominance in Washington, not Iraq.

'I think about America,' he says, 'and I wonder, what will they do in Iraq? The people in Iraq, to begin with, don't have faith in the US. They remember the '91 uprising. People are afraid of that, that the Americans may stop halfway. American policy is not very clear. Most probably, there will be an attack.'

He repeats that the Kurds were 'sold out four times' by the US: 1975, 1988, 1991 and 1995. 'The Kurds are afraid. That is why they are hesitant. When you look at it carefully, the data do not fit. We have been having problems with America. For thirty years, we have been telling them about Saddam. In 1988 and '89, I was in Washington. I couldn't see anyone. Even the human-rights people at the State Department would not see me. They said it would jeopardise relations with Saddam.' A few American journalists – notably Jonathan Randal and Jim Hoagland of *The Washington Post* – tried to persuade administration officials to listen to the Kurds, in vain. Even after the Kuwait war, the US resisted all international efforts to indict Saddam for war crimes.

Now, Dr Osman says, the US is demanding that the Iraqi opposition unite. But he believes the opposition is merely 'a card' for the US to play. 'An American delegation came here to unify the opposition,' he says, 'but this weakens the opposition. In the eyes of the others, they are seen as puppets.'

The Kurds are part of this opposition, but Kurdish leaders are not seen by their own people as American stooges. They administer their areas, and they have an electoral as well as tribal, political and military mandate. More than anyone else in the coming war, the Kurds have something to lose. 'When America has a regime in Baghdad,' Dr Osman says, 'they will lose the American protection. That depends on American and Turkish policy. What I think is that they don't want the Kurds to talk about federation or Kirkuk.' He complains that the

US, although preparing a war that will have an impact on the Kurds, has not given the Kurds 'anti-tank rockets or anti-chemical defences. I think this should be sorted out.'

Last month, the two Kurdish parliaments met together as one for the first time since their civil war. Dr Osman says that a letter was read out from Colin Powell, in which Powell wrote, 'I'm glad to say you are our partners.' Dr Osman asks me, 'What does he mean? Does the Pentagon say the same thing? Does Rumsfeld? They [Barzani and Talabani] should see Bush. Four times, they had a problem with America. They can't have it a fifth time. Nobody will listen to you then.'

The Tube ride back to central London takes another hour.

At four in the afternoon, I'm on time at Ahmad Chalabi's flat in Mayfair for *iftar* ('breakfast'), when Muslims end their sunlit Ramadan fasting for the night. A maid lets me in, and Ahmad's wife Lela hands me a Ramadan drink of fresh apricot juice. Lela is the daughter of Adil Bey Osseiran, who until his death a few years ago was a respected politician and one of South Lebanon's largest Shiite Muslim landowners. She leaves me and goes to put on her shoes and see to dinner in the kitchen.

The flat is luxurious and well-decorated – Chinese porcelain lamps, Persian carpets, silver flower bowls and a vase of yellow tulips. The 1950s oil portraits on the walls are mostly of women, decorous and modest. One portrait is of a vibrant man in military uniform, a sash and medals on his chest, with his hair combed back and his moustache trimmed like a 1920s RAF pilot's. There are books on Islamic architecture and mosaics. An Art Deco chandelier lights a table set for the *iftar*.

Ahmad arrives with his surprise guest, Lela's brother. Ali Osseiran is visiting from Lebanon, where he lives with his wife Sarah and their children. Forced into politics as his father's son, he is foremost a farmer and has come to London for the annual Smithfield agricultural show. Ali and I have been friends for twenty years, but our bond goes a little deeper: in June 1987, while driving to Beirut from his family's house in South Lebanon, we were kidnapped together by Hizbullah operatives. I have not seen him since my last visit to Lebanon, in 1997.

Lela serves a vast Lebanese feast of roast lamb with rice, rolled grape leaves, chicken, yoghurt, stews and vegetables. Ahmad does not eat much, because he never does. Nor do I, because I have a dinner date later. Ali, who has gained a good twenty pounds since our kidnapping, digs in. Most of our talk is personal. I ask about Sarah, who is also Ahmad's niece, and their children. I tell him about mine, whom he knew when he was living in London just after the kidnapping.

We turn to politics. I ask Ahmad about the attacks he and the PUK made in 1995, when the CIA called off its coup. (Dr Osman had spoken of it this morning.) Ahmad says he was with the CIA man, Bob Baer, who wrote about it in his book. 'Bob Baer stood beside me,' he says. 'We beat back two Iraqi divisions. We captured heavy artillery – seven guns. But Massoud Barzani didn't like it. He said, "These guns can be used against me."' How, I wonder, will this Iraqi opposition unite? The only binding they have is their hatred of Saddam. If the US takes him away, what will they have in common?

I speak to Ali about Hizbullah, our former captors. It is now a legitimate political party which enjoys the prestige of having expelled the Americans and Israelis from Lebanon. Won't other Hizbullahs emerge to fight the US occupation of Iraq?

'What you have to understand,' Ali says, 'is that the Islamic Revolution is over, and there is nothing to replace it.'

In the morning, I interview Noam Chomsky at a hotel in Mayfair on camera for our television profile of Edward Said. Chomsky and Said are two of the most prominent opponents in the US of the Iraq invasion – Gore Vidal, Norman Mailer, Lewis Lapham and Howard Zinn are among the others. Chomsky and Said, in their writings and through their friendship for thirty years, have influenced my philosophy and politics more than any other two men I know.

Another crew from the BBC is already interviewing Noam for another programme when we arrive. They are scheduled to stop at ten, but they try to keep going. Mike Dibb and I wait outside the suite, and I hear Carol Chomsky, Noam's wife, ordering the crew to stop. Their time is up. If not for her, I am sure there would have been no time for our interview. The other crew packs up; Mike sets up his camera, lights and microphones. We settle in, and I ask Noam about Edward. He makes some general comments about Edward's integrity and intellect; Edward would say the same of him.

When I ask about Edward's contribution to scholarship, he answers, 'His main scholarly contribution has been to reverse very substantially the way in which we comprehend Western high culture over centuries, its self-image with regard to the rest of the world. I mean, he wasn't alone in this, of course, but he was a leading voice in really reshaping the interpretation and understanding of centuries of cultural tradition going right up to the present. That's a major contribution.'

He says Edward is also 'the major voice for Palestinian rights and the more general question of oppressed people throughout the world. He's done that with eloquence and courage, particularly in the light of both the threats against him and his own personal situation. It's pretty remarkable.' (Death threats from Zionist extremists became so virulent a few years ago that the police had to give Edward protection.)

By 'his personal situation', Noam means Edward's leukaemia.

Noam places Edward in a tradition of resistance, a 'fringe of intellectuals' who have not joined what he has called elsewhere the 'secular priesthood'. Edward challenged the leaders of both his countries, Palestine and the US. 'I think he's in that tradition,' Noam says. 'I mean, what we call a "prophet" is just a bad translation of an obscure Hebrew term that roughly means what we call "intellectual" ... I mean, they were imprisoned and driven into the desert. Hundreds of years later, they were honoured. But the people who were honoured at the time are the ones we call false prophets and flatterers of the court. That goes right through history to the present.' Edward, though, is 'not alone', Noam says. 'There are many who do it. He's unique in his eloquence, visibility, impact and originality of what he's done ... It's not easy to be a dissident, never has been. That's why in the First World War the dissidents ended up in jail.'

When we finish, I walk with Carol down to the London Library in St James's Square. She says Noam is, as ever, exhausting himself with public speaking – now mainly against the invasion of Iraq. She tries to make him turn down some of the requests to lecture. He continues teaching at MIT, writing articles and books and rallying the masses. She has retired from Harvard, where she was a professor of psychology. Her life now seems to involve making Noam rest a little and keeping an eye on her grandchildren. She has also taken up the accordion. He is lucky to have her.

In the evening, the plaza outside St Paul's Cathedral is impassable for the crowds waiting to enter. I arrive early enough to find a pub before the lecture begins. Ruth Rogers is meeting me, and I call to divert her to the pub where I'm drinking Jameson's Irish whiskey. We make our way back to the cathedral in time to hear Kerim Yeldiz, the executive director of the Kurdish Human Rights Project, introduce Harold Pinter. Yeldiz is a Kurd from Turkey, whose abuses of the Kurdish people the US ignores now as it did Saddam's in the 1980s. This evening marks the tenth anniversary of the Project's birth, when it was 'dedicated to the protection and maintenance of human rights within the Kurdish regions of Turkey, Iraq, Syria, Iran and the Caucasus'. Yeldiz is a brave man, who has tried to protect Turkish

Kurds in particular from extra-judicial executions and torture.

Harold Pinter takes the pulpit. Dressed in black, glowering at the thousands of people in this secular congregation, he excoriates the American empire the way Anglican divines once condemned Catholics and Dissenters. He damns the war and 'the criminal regime in Washington'. Then, he says a few words – as in his plays, his rhetorical style is not verbose – about Noam Chomsky. A long pause. He explains why the warmongers hate Chomsky, 'He tells the truth!'

Chomsky's lecture comes to us in a calm, soft voice. He is the antithesis of the demagogue, speaking to intellects, reasoning with people. I've never heard him speak down to anyone. Tonight he presents not so much the case against war, but the prosecution case to convict the guardians of empire.

'No one can predict the outcome of war,' he says. He cites the disquiet within the US foreign policy establishment to emphasise the fact that old lefties and Jeremiahs like himself are not alone in fearing the designs of Cheney, Rumsfeld, Wolfowitz and Perle. The dean of the Kennedy School of Government at Harvard and the military analyst Anthony Cordesman, he says, 'are warning the administration not to heed Israeli fantasies.' For this mostly British audience, he says of Cordesman, 'For those of you who don't know him, he's as hardline as you can be within the realm of sanity.' In contrast to a sane hardliner like Cordesman, there are the hawks in Washington and Israel, 'They think the Arab world is a world of retards, who "understand only the rule of force", in the words of one Israeli analyst.' He goes on to say that war threatens the Kurds, including those in Iraq.

'If the worst can be averted, there are signs of hope,' he says. 'Popular forces can have influence. The Kurdish Human Rights Project has a stellar record in making change. In the coming years, its tasks are likely to be greater.' Later in his talk, after a history of US policy in the Middle East, he returns to the theme that normal people can make a difference, that popular will can restrain power, 'Look at the protests against the coming war. There is no precedent in the United States. The comparison to the Vietnam anti-war movement is misleading. This is the fortieth anniversary of the Kennedy administration's announcement of the bombing of South Vietnam. Protest was non-existent. There were no meaningful levels until the aggression extended to the rest of Indochina. Today, in dramatic contrast, there is large-scale, principled opposition to the war. There is a steady increase in the unwillingness of people to tolerate aggression and atrocities.'

He may be right about public intolerance of military adventures, but the leaders don't care. It is one thing for there to be popular protest – and an anti-war movement in advance of war is an achievement – but it is another for the protests to prevent war. When I see the apostles of invasion – jaws set like stones on tombs – I know nothing will stop them.

Chomsky's theme of American military aid's effects moves from Turkey and the Middle East to the Western Hemisphere, 'Turkey relinquished to Colombia its place as the main recipient of US arms.' Colombia has become a 'typical US terror state', its officer corps a product of the notorious School of the Americas, its peasants and trade unionists ripe for culling. 'America now takes pride that the US Army helped to defeat liberation theology in Latin America. The advocates of the "preferential option for the poor" were punished accordingly. Reagan's war on terror in 1981 opened with the murder of an archbishop and closed with the killing of six Jesuits [in El Salvador], killing tens of thousands in between ... Eighty percent of Colombian atrocities are committed by government paramilitaries and the military, as atrocity is privatised.' He mentions Dyncorps, former US military officers under Pentagon contracts, who are helping to drive Colombians from their land. 'Atrocities are likely to increase with the increase in military aid. They are opening up the land by driving out the peasants, planting mono-crops and taking the minerals.' (It sounds like what the US did to Native Americans a century earlier.)

When he finishes, he reminds us, 'We are primarily responsible for the anticipated consequences of our actions.' Everyone applauds, then stands and claps some more. Chomsky has been doing this – persuading, reasoning, exposing, analysing – for over forty years. His integrity and scholarship have helped many people to denounce war and empire. For a moment in the early 1970s, the movements in which he played a leading part helped to stop the American aggression in Indochina and to start making government accountable to its citizens. Then the corporate state took back the ground it had lost when democracy went too far. Now the public has less space and is losing rights that its activist ancestors in the trade unions, academia and even the press fought to assert. Chomsky and Pinter are in their seventies. Howard Zinn is in his eighties. Edward Said is sixty-six and dying. Are there young radicals to succeed them and urge us to stand together to challenge state power over our lives and the lives of people thousands of miles from Wall Street and the Pentagon?

Saturday, 14 December 2002
London

The taxi stops in early morning traffic on the Edgware Road. On my way to the Hilton Metropole Hotel near the Marylebone flyover, I notice *The Times* headline in front of a newsagent's shop, 'TROOPS START COUNTDOWN TO WAR.' A little further north, banners proclaim, 'BUSH AND BLAIR WILL MURDER THOUSANDS FOR OIL' and 'WE DEMAND AN END TO WESTERN INTERFERENCE IN THE ISLAMIC WORLD'. A few hundred young people, mostly men and boys, stand behind portable steel barriers to display their slogans in bold black letters on orange cloth. Inside the Metropole, one of those garish, impersonal structures that would look familiar to residents of modern Riyadh and Baghdad, another sign welcomes guests, 'IRAQI OPPOSITION CONFERENCE, LONDON, 14–16 DECEMBER 2002. FOR DEMOCRACY AND SALVATION OF IRAQ.'

The conference opens upstairs in the absurdly named Balmoral Room with a reading from the Qur'an by a cleric named Ahmad al-Hilfi. The few non-Muslims among the 320 delegates maintain a respectful silence during the benediction. On a stage facing this assembly of Iraqis are their leaders, displayed like vegetables for prospective buyers: Abdel Aziz al-Hakim, Jalal Talabani, Sherif Ali bin al-Hussein, Ahmad Chalabi, Iyad Allawi, Izzedine Salim, His Eminence Sayed Muhammad Bahir al-Ulum, Safa al-Suhale, former

General Hassan al-Naqib and Massoud Barzani.

Chalabi, in what looks like a tailored suit, delivers a speech in Arabic. He promises, to polite applause, 'a democratic, federal state in all Iraq', an end to the 'fascism and dictatorship' and a country where all Iraqis – 'Arab, Kurd, Assyrian, Jewish, Christian' – will enjoy freedom and equality. He praises Syria's President Bashar al-Assad and calls on him to follow the Iraqi people in their opposition to Saddam Hussein. Hoshyar Zebari introduces each speaker in turn, and each speech is as general and inoffensive as Chalabi's. Clearly, whatever work is being done is not taking place in the conference room. In the corridor, coffeeshops and suites, the united opposition parties are annihilating one another.

Hussein Sinjari is sitting in the coffeeshop on his own. During the 1991 rebellion, he was based at Massoud Barzani's headquarters in Salahuddin. We saw him almost every day, and he was pretty straight with us about the KDP's progress on the battlefield. When the rebellion began its collapse, he remained candid. The only thing I could fault him for was not warning us that they were packing up all their communications equipment and maps to abandon Salahuddin to Saddam. We saw him drive away just before Saddam's helicopters bombed the village. I did not know what happened to him after that, although Don McCullin met him by chance once or twice in London. McCullin called him 'the Pelican' for his skinny legs and the way he fretted.

We take coffee together, and he says he has left the KDP. He is no longer a Kurdish nationalist. Now he is an Iraqi democrat. His newspaper, *al-Ahali*, is funded by the National Endowment for Democracy in the US. His organisation, the Iraqi Institute for Democracy, sponsored a 'Democracy Festival' in Northern Iraq last September. 'After the dictatorship falls,' he says, 'I'll do it as an annual event to involve young women and men in politics. When they see this bunch of people, they don't want to get involved. That is why you don't see the young here.' He's right. I would put the average delegate's age at sixty, and most of the leaders are well above that. Come to think of it, there are not many women either.

'Seventy percent of Iraqis are under twenty-five,' Hussein says.

No delegate is under twenty-five. 'When you see young people, they are security guards. They are not delegates. Or they're the sons or the servants of leaders.'

The young took over the Middle East with the revolutions of the 1950s, beginning in Egypt. The last young officer to seize power was Libya's Colonel Muammar Gadafi, who's grown greyer with the years – like all the Arab regimes which transformed themselves into dynastic republics. Old men don't make revolutions, and the delegates here are very old men. The US's Sunni favourites, al-Naqib and former Iraqi foreign minister Adnan Pachachi, while both honourable opponents of Saddam long before Washington was, are in their eighties.

Hussein has other complaints. 'There is no national Iraqi party. They are Kurdish, like the PUK and KDP, or Chaldean or Assyrian or Turcoman or Shiite. It's very difficult to build up a national democratic movement. That is why the US is doing it for us. The only national party is the Iraqi Communist Party, and it's a joke. The Baath is the Arab National Socialist Party. We need national political parties.' Chalabi sees the INC as a national movement with Arab – both Shiite like himself and Sunni – as well as Kurdish members. But most of the delegates here don't trust him. In the bar, I overhear two delegates.

One says, 'Whoever we choose should be decent.'

The second answers, 'So, that lets Chalabi out.'

When I mention this to an independent delegate, he says they all resent Chalabi because he's more intelligent than they are. (Chalabi's enemies accuse him of defrauding his investors in the Petra Bank that he once ran in Jordan, and that a Jordanian court found him guilty; his defenders point out that his judges were a secret military tribunal, an unusual procedure for a civil banking case.)

Back in the Balmoral Room, Labour MP Ann Clwyd is giving a speech. A pugnacious-looking blonde of a certain age, she was a rare voice for Iraq's Kurds in Britain's Parliament long before her party's leader, that nice Mr. Blair, discovered the uses to which their agony could be put. She is pro-war, but she is no hypocrite. She was screaming to heaven for the Kurds when Saddam was committing Kurdish genocide in the 1980s; and she has long campaigned against the American and British governments to indict Saddam Hussein for crimes against humanity. Her voice today is one of caution, 'You've had many uprisings and have heard many promises. Please make sure those promises are kept.' A man behind me, one of the delegates, says to another, 'She's warning us.' Near the end of her short speech, she pauses and looks at the delegates. 'Please,' she says, 'let's have a lot more women.'

After her, Hoshyar introduces the old general, al-Naqib, who struggles to the microphone and uses what is left of his voice to condemn Saddam. In 1991, when he was still young enough to walk without a stick, he had hopes of returning to Iraq and organising resistance within the armed forces to Saddam. I used to go to tea or dinner at his house in Damascus, where his daughter told me a shocking story. While her father was Iraq's ambassador to Spain, Saddam sent his two boys, Uday and Qusay, to stay with them in Madrid. The boys told her, with pride, that their father allowed them to enter security compounds and shoot prisoners. This was when they were in their early teens. It was not long afterwards that General al-Naqib defected and took his family to Syria.

Hoshyar thanks His Excellency the general and invites the next speaker, his party leader and nephew Massoud Barzani, to the podium. Massoud, in a suit and tie rather than the Kurdish mountain clothes he wears at home, addresses the delegates in Arabic. He grew up in Baghdad with his mother during his father's Soviet exile and received most of his education in Arabic. He praises the delegates for their commitment to democracy and emphasises the necessity for Iraq to become a federal state if it is to survive as a state at all. Sherif Ali, the prince who would be king of new Iraq, does not appear to be listening.

All around the aisles are American men, coming in and out of the double doors past the private security guards, occasionally calling some delegate or other for a *tête-à-tête*. One stands by the dais listening. With wire-rim spectacles, pale skin, a head that is almost shaved and a khaki trenchcoat, he could have stepped off the set of *The Quiet American*. I ask someone his name and am told, 'Christopher Straub.'

After lunch, Jim Muir interviews Ahmad Chalabi in the corridor live on BBC television. 'This conference,' Ahmad says, 'is an Iraqi idea. Iraqis organised it ... The United States is anxious that this is not seen as a war against Iraq, but as a war in which it has Iraqi allies.' The interview ends, and Jim asks for another. It seems the first was for BBC World, and the next is for a domestic channel. Jim is one of the BBC's best reporters, fluent in Arabic and Farsi, and lives in Tehran. He asks Ahmad new questions. Ahmad, his turquoise tie reflecting the lights, is happy to answer, 'We are looking for a united message for the overthrow of Saddam Hussein and the introduction of democracy in Iraq ... [and] to fill any gap in sovereignty ... We are looking for an executive committee to run the opposition. We are against a government-in-exile and in favour of a provisional government on our territory ... The Americans are our friends. This is an Iraqi conference.' Jim thanks him and says to the camera, 'Now, back to the studio.'

Ahmad, Jim and I sit down to talk without microphones. Ahmad's themes are consistent with his on-camera message. This won't be a war against Iraq, he says, but a war for democracy. 'America is like all other nations,' he admits, not that anyone in the White House would. 'It pursues its own interests. This time, its interests coincide with those of the Iraqi people.' Oil, we mention, is an American interest. 'The US is now the biggest buyer of Iraqi oil. Saddam will sell them all they want. That's not what this is about.'

Next, a press conference on the mezzanine by Ann Clwyd and Charles Forest of INDICT. INDICT has gathered evidence and lobbied for an indictment of Saddam Hussein for crimes against humanity and war crimes. The third person on the panel is Peter Galbraith, the US ambassador to Croatia under Bill Clinton and a long-time Kurdophile. Forest says INDICT is funded by Congress under the Iraq Liberation Act. The group seeks to persuade some country to indict twelve leading members of Saddam's regime, but they have failed so far. They had hoped the Swiss would indict Barzan Takriti, Saddam's half-brother and murderer of thousands of Kurds in 1988, who became Saddam's ambassador to Switzerland. INDICT filed a suit under Swiss law. 'The process had not even begun,' Forest says. 'Barzan was returning to Switzerland in September, but the Swiss cancelled his visa. They say they no longer have jurisdiction. Countries pass the buck. The result is that these people can travel.'

A journalist asks whether they can be tried by the International Criminal Court.

'The ICC,' Forest replies, 'has jurisdiction only for cases after it came into effect.' Moreover, the US does not recognise the court.

Over coffee with some of the INDICT representatives, I ask why no one ever indicted Saddam. They say the US, despite funding some of their research, never wanted to see Saddam or his henchmen before an international tribunal. At Senate hearings in January 1993, Senator Claiborne Pell of Rhode Island promised to make the issue of indicting Saddam his 'first priority'. Warren Christopher, Clinton's secretary of state – who was even then bungling the Israeli-Palestinian negotiations – promised Senator Pell that he would examine the evidence against Saddam. 'Then,' one of the representatives confides, 'nothing happened.'

Why not?

'Look at the National Security Archives website, and go to the video clip of Donald Rumsfeld and Saddam Hussein in 1983.'

Later, I do. Rumsfeld shakes Saddam's hand and embraces him, then sits beside him and gives him a present from then-President Reagan. This encounter reopened diplomatic relations, which Iraq severed during the 1967 Arab–Israeli war. It opened the Iraqi market to American industry, not least to the helicopters and dual-use pesticide factories in which Saddam would manufacture gas to massacre Iranians and Kurds. Could they indict him without indicting themselves?

All evening and night, they sit in the café of the Metropole Hotel's open lobby and knead their worry beads. Moustaches waltz down marble stairs. Trenchcoats take suits aside and, in the corners of long corridors, whisper promises beyond range of other suits to whom they have made other promises. It is three o'clock in the morning, and I have been here for about eighteen hours. A Kurdish journalist says one of the delegates has just stormed out of a working committee meeting and bellowed, 'I cannot work with these people!'

The black and the white turbans of tribal and religious sheikhs pass through the doors of the working committees. They are either old men or the sons of dead men, there by right of inheritance and tradition. Tonight, they speak the language of choice, of elections, of what the people want. In another time and place, they would use other words – the words of an earlier benefactor. These men would have been in Istanbul telling the Sultan that their people believed in the pan-Islamism of the Sultan-Caliph. They might have gone to Moscow to promise the solidarity of the Iraqi working class with their Soviet comrades. Tonight it is Washington, and the words are 'democracy', 'elections', 'free markets' and 'constitution'. Whatever it takes.

This is the Metropole Hotel in London in 2002, but it could be the Damascus Sheraton in 1983. That was where Syria organised the Lebanese opposition's tribal and sectarian chieftains to achieve regime change in Beirut. Lebanese Communists, Baathists, Arab nationalists, socialists, Islamic fundamentalists and tribal warlords read a script by President Hafez al-Assad that none of them believed. Yet it was the magic incantation that enabled them, with Syria's and Iran's aid, to expel the US Marines and, later, the Israeli army from Lebanon. They seized the symbols of power, at the cost of turning Lebanon into a Syrian colony.

Upstairs, almost invisible to the mortals in the lobby and the conference room, the US envoy and Bush's proconsul for Iraq, Zalmay Khalilzad, plays the role Syria's then-foreign minister Abdel Halim Khaddam did for Lebanon in 1983. The slogan, then as now, is 'salvation'.

Hiwa Osman and I have a last drink. He's a young BBC producer, whose understanding of this story is deeper than that of most other television producers. For one thing, he's Kurdish. For another, he's the son of Dr Mahmoud Osman. The war has yet to begin, and disillusionment is taking over. 'Khalilzad sat between Talabani and Barzani all day,' Osman complains. 'He was hearing about federalism and Kurds from every speaker. But Khalilzad never said 'federalism' or 'Kurds'. It's worrying. He did not mention that chemical weapons are the issue. The Israelis, Kuwaitis and Saudis have protection from the United States. The only people who do not have any form of protection against them are the Kurds who, outside his control, are most vulnerable.'

Sunday, 15 December 2002
London

Up early, short of sleep, back to the familiar pace of Middle East politics at the Metropole with my Iraqi opposition press credentials. Khalilzad has descended from his suite on the fourteenth floor to deliver, like Hermes, messages from Olympus.

'On behalf of the United States,' he begins, 'I see that, today, free Iraqis are here to take an important step to liberate their country from a brutal dictatorship.' Khalilzad, an Afghan immigrant made good, pauses for an interpreter to repeat his words in Arabic. 'I see many old friends,' he continues, 'committed Iraqi patriots. The Iraqi people and the United States have many of the same goals, an Iraq in which all Iraqis will enjoy civil rights regardless of ethnic background. We too see an independent Iraq that quickly resumes its righteous [*sic*] place in the community of nations, free of sanctions.' Another pause for the Arabic.

'A reformed Iraqi army should continue to have an important role in a free Iraq ... We hope the Iraqi military will be taught of the liberation of their country and to protect Iraq's independence afterwards. And that it will refuse to use chemical weapons on its people.' What about on other people?

'As President Bush says, "Iraqi resources are abundant".' That phrase falls a little flat on the delegates, who do not propose to share those abundant resources (i.e., oil – the US probably does not want Iraq's water or dates) with the friends of President Bush.

'The UN has given the Iraqi regime one last chance. The current signs do not encourage optimism.' If Saddam took that last chance and conformed to the UN resolutions on weapons inspections, would the US call off the invasion? Is that what the war is about? For these Iraqis, deposing Saddam has no connection to weapons. If they seize power, they will amass whatever arsenal they can.

'Many argue that Iraqis are not ready for democracy,' Khalilzad says, without mentioning who the 'many' are. I have not heard anyone on either side of the debate over war make that case. This argument has just enough straw for Khalilzad to blow it down. 'We in this administration do not accept this.' He goes on to say there will be 'no Saddamism without Saddam', one of the opposition's suspicions.

'America is a friend to the people of Iraq,' he ends. 'God bless the people of Iraq.'

A cynical Kurdish delegate invites me downstairs to the coffee shop, where he gives voice to his complaints. He asks me not to use his name. 'In this conference,' he says, '320 delegates have to discuss fifty speeches in two days. It's impossible. The original idea was to have 50–100 key people. Then Chalabi jumps in. He works with [Iraqi independent] Kanan Makiya and others to push for the line that the new Iraq should not be dominated by [political] parties. He says liberals, democrats and independents should take part in running Iraq and in a conference. He pushed for 1,000 delegates with the Pentagon.' He repeats what everyone else here believes, that the Pentagon backs Chalabi; the State Department, the Kurds; and the CIA, the Iraqi National Accord of Iyad Allawi. He adds a new thread: that the National Security Council is supporting Makiya and one of the few women delegates, Rand Rahim. 'Condoleezza Rice,' he says, 'worked with Makiya and Rahim.'

There are so many American bureaucrats here that only an expert would know which government departments they represent. Perhaps the Bush administration is using the British model: the Foreign Office, the Arab Bureau, the Indian Office, the War Ministry and Downing Street had their plans and their surrogates for ordering post-Ottoman Iraq. Why not State, Defense, the CIA, the NSC, the White House and the Vice-President's office?

'Bush finds out this conference could go nowhere,' the Kurdish delegate says, 'and appoints Khalilzad to take it in hand. Four departments [of the US government] sign a letter to the Iraqis to unite them when they are at each other's throats. Zalmay comes in and organises the conference.' He stirs his cappuccino. A waitress brings me a second espresso. Her name, she says, is Jana. She is Iraqi, born in London. Her mother is Turkish. She has never been to Iraq and knows nothing about its politics. When we ask her opinion about this gathering of fellow overseas Iraqis, she admits she doesn't really care.

My Kurdish friend blames Chalabi for making a mess of the conference, for delivering a weak and divided opposition into America's embrace. He says Chalabi must be excluded from the leadership. Why? 'Because he's corrupt,' he says, 'all the reasons we know.'

Who should lead Iraq?

'Ask any Iraqi here,' he answers, 'and he'll tell you he wants General Tommy Franks and not any Iraqi leader. Only Tommy Franks can keep the Turks and Iranians out.'

He accuses Chalabi of manipulating the conference by issuing a lengthy position paper yesterday. The document proposes a constitution for Iraq when Saddam falls. Kanan and Sam Chalabi have worked on it for months, and I know from discussions with them that theirs was a sincere if naïve effort to provide a framework for democracy. My friend refuses to see it that way. 'They presented the position paper to introduce chaos,' he says. 'There are 333 pages in English to be discussed by 320 delegates, a majority of whom do not speak English, in forty-eight hours.'

After lunch, there is a press conference given by Dr Hamid al-Bayati (SCIRI's London representative), Nabil Musawi (of the INC) and Hoshyar Zebari. Hoshyar says this morning's sessions were for independents and liberals to meet among themselves. 'There are two criteria for the success of this conference,' he announces. 'First, a unified vision shared by all. Second, an agreed formula for forming co-ordinating committees.'

An Arab journalist asks if delegates will vote to choose a leadership.

'An election will not be needed,' he says.

Noticing my surprise, one of the Arab journalists says, *sotto voce*, 'It could be interpreted as a government, and Chalabi might win. The Americans don't want the leaders to be elected.'

On the question of funding, Hoshyar says, 'All costs are contributed from our own resources.' (I like Hoshyar, but I doubt that he missed the desk outside the conference room where delegates complete US State Department chits for reimbursement of their travel and hotel expenses. A State Department official there told Hussein Sinjari he would receive his cheque within a month.)

Returning to the question of elections, SCIRI's al-Bayati says, 'We cannot just form a government without the people of Iraq.'

Someone asks whether the new Iraq will impose the death penalty.

Al-Bayati answers, 'That will be part of the constitution, and that is up to the people of Iraq.'

Back in the coffeeshop, an Iraqi sits down at our table and interrupts my conversation with Hiwa Osman. He says he is a nuclear engineer and claims he studied in Italy, worked in Iraq and fled to the West in 1999. Then he says Saddam tested a nuclear device south of Suleimaniya in the Hamrin Mountains. Iraq's technology, he says, came from Russia. Hiwa, who hates Saddam and believes him capable of any crime, looks doubtful, and turns away.

The man orders coffee and continues, 'He uses a substance called "red mercury" to enable the use of small amounts of uranium. Iraq is now selling tons of this stuff to Iran. Saddam divides the bomb into nine pieces. Each explosion is thirty minutes apart ... The first test was in 1989, September. I don't know why seismologists around the world did not detect this.' Hiwa says he has a good idea why not.

Failing to make much of an impression, the man tries another tack. 'I have evidence that Saddam Hussein is linked to al-Qa'ida.' For £12,000, he will sell me a videotape of Taha Yassin Ramadan, one of Saddam's inner circle, with the 11 September hijackers. But that's not all: he will also supply the names of 6,000 scientists working on nuclear, chemical and biological programmes in Iraq. The man looks around the coffeeshop at the delegates and says, 'I don't trust these people. Some are with the regime.'

Hiwa is not interested in buying this man's 'evidence' for the BBC, but I dutifully take his number for someone at ABC to call him. My expectations are already low when he says that Osama bin Laden himself attended a conference in Baghdad in 1993.

Later, in the bar, Hussein Sinjari describes his meeting at five this evening with Khalilzad in the Windsor Suite. The US envoy received a group of independent delegates, he says, and each one pressed his case for better American treatment. They are all worried that America will back down at the last minute, as it did during the 1991 rebellion. 'Khalilzad said, "We will not make that mistake again", Hussein says. It is interesting that a representative of the younger President Bush would implicate his boss's father in a mistake.

Hussein says Kanan was upset during much of the meeting. 'He wants technocrats and independents on the committees. Otherwise, he tells his friends, they will walk out.'

Back in the conference hall, a Chaldean delegate delivers a speech. When he begins speaking, the Assyrian delegates walk out. The Chaldean Catholics and the Assyrian Orthodox are Christians, dwindling minorities in a Muslim country. They hate each other far more than they do the Muslims.

The politicking gathers pace all night in the hallways, bars, cafés and in Khalilzad's Windsor Suite – everywhere but in the conference hall.

Sam, Kanan and Dr Goran Talabani, a neurosurgeon, Iraqi Kurdish independent and distant cousin of Jalal Talabani, are in the bar. Entering with Laura Hubber of *The San Francisco Chronicle*, I ask what is going on. At the moment, it's all about numbers and percentages of seats for the next conference – to convene in Iraq. The US, Kanan says, is promoting a consultative council of forty appointees. 'The key thing is they don't want a leader to emerge,' Sam says, unhappy at the way things are going. 'Khalilzad does not want to give a tactical advantage to any side. It's a fight that's removed from what is happening on the ground ... The fighting is over seats that don't mean much, but we don't want to be disadvantaged at this stage.'

Relations among the allies are cooling at the moment. Ahmad Chalabi paid court to the *mullahs* in Tehran recently. Rather than reassure Iran's Iraqi clients in SCIRI, Ahmad has outraged the al-Hakim brothers. Sam and Kanan say Ahmad's closer relations with Iran neutralise SCIRI, which no longer has sole use of the Iranian card. They say Iran is implying – the *mullahs* rarely speak in a direct fashion – that SCIRI's military wing, the Badr Brigade, might be integrated into a larger Iraqi force.

Kanan is furious with the State Department for interfering in this conference. 'Mr Warwick', he says of Tom Warwick, an American diplomat, 'decides like a policeman who is an Iraqi independent and who isn't.' It seems that Warwick prevented some of the delegates from attending a caucus of independents. Then, according to Kanan, he arranged for State Department Arabists to translate Kanan's and Sam's constitutional document into Arabic. (I can almost hear Edward Said's exasperated voice asking why they didn't write it in Arabic from the beginning.) Kanan complains, 'We wanted to produce a document to go to the conference, because we knew this was going to happen. They [the State Department] did not want this. They were providing a vehicle for the backward people to govern. We took over their co-ordinating group and made a structure they didn't want.' He says the constitutional document represents three months' work, but State calls it only one of many working papers.

Goran supports the INC rather than either of the Kurdish parties. He doesn't like what is happening at this conference. 'The agenda of this conference is pre-arranged,' he observes. 'Two days, thirty-seven speakers, all the same rhetoric. It means there's only a little time left to discuss the real issues.'

Our little group around a table in the Metropole bar grows to include Trudy Rubin of *The Philadelphia Inquirer* and Hugh Pope, Istanbul correspondent of *The Wall Street Journal*. John Rhode from the Defense Department stops by our table and puts a hand on Kanan's shoulder. 'This is a good man,' he says. 'I've probably just killed your career.'

When Rhode walks away, Kanan returns to his document. 'I showed it to Condi Rice,' he says. 'She read it twice. They supported it.' He talks about moving things forward, about a council of Iraqi leaders and asserting some independence. It cannot be easy, when all the armed forces that will topple Saddam are American and the US finances most of the opposition groups.

'There is an American need to have a vague result here,' he says. 'But there is an Iraqi need to give Iraqis a sense that they are a part of this.'

His disagreements are not only with Khalilzad, who is resisting Kanan's proposal for a technical committee of independents to work under a political council; they are also with SCIRI. The al-Hakims, he says, want to keep their percentage of seats, set in 1992 at 40 percent. The Shiites are at least 60 percent of Iraq's population, but there is no reason to suppose that the al-Hakim family and SCIRI represent all of them. Kanan says SCIRI is holding out for 40 percent of this conference and any committees it creates – a clear majority over each of the other parties. 'Khalilzad is trying to find a way out of this,' Kanan says. 'The State Department is not. State has a notion that these parties do not represent anything. They have this notion that political movements in Iraq will come forward.' He believes the State Department lacks vision. 'The State Department is in the business of appeasing people. A democratic Iraq is a truly structural change. It can be Oslo.'

Oslo, I remind him, did not work.

'It can in Iraq,' he replies. 'That idea [of a democratic Iraq] finds a resonance in the US government. If this idea finds a resonance, I, as an Iraqi, want it. It's far riskier than putting up a military dictatorship.' Then he takes me through a history of his beliefs, an evolution common among his generation of Arab intellectuals, 'I used to believe in the unity of the Arab world. I've given up on that. I used to believe in a socialist revolution. I've given up on that. Now, I just want to help Iraq.'

Many others who passed through the stages of Arab nationalism, when Nasser ruled Egypt, and international socialism, when Dr George Habash rallied Palestinian commandos in the name of class struggle, took other courses. Some remained nationalists or socialists and divorced themselves from the currents flowing past. Some abandoned politics and the ideals that failed them. Others turned to the last idea remaining, the idea that was always there to be scorned by nationalists and socialists alike: that deliverance would come with submission to the will of God. Kanan did not go as far in adapting to his time as the religious fundamentalists. He has kept the secularism of the nationalists and the democracy of the socialists, but 'helping Iraq' does not carry the persuasive force of returning to God and building His kingdom on earth. Ask John Ashcroft and some of the other born-agains in Washington.

I end up late in the bar with Siyamend Osman, a Kurdish

independent who worked for Amnesty International for twenty years. He has documented some of the worst crimes of the Saudi royal family and their police forces, which Washington ignored. He belongs to no political party, but he is close to Kurdish and Iraqi politics. He was at the meeting of 130 independent delegates, when Khalilzad said the US made a mistake in betraying the rebellion of 1991. 'It's the first time I've heard a serving US official say this,' he says. Is it important eleven years later? Nothing else at this conference or about Khalilzad impresses him. 'We are sceptical about your intentions,' he says he told Khalilzad. 'If you want democracy, why do you support people who are not democratic?'

Monday 16–Tuesday 17 December 2002
London

The conference drags on for two more days, the second unscheduled. Press conferences are announced, postponed, cancelled. The delegates argue and fight for seats at the next conference, to meet in Erbil on 15 January 2003 – a curtain-raiser for the war – to give the US what one delegate calls 'Iraqi cover' for the invasion. Iraq's exiled politicians take their disputes to Khalilzad on the fourteenth floor, where Tom Warwick decides who will and will not be admitted to the proconsular presence.

The parties slander one another in the Metropole's coffee shops and bars. 'If you want to make money in Washington,' a pro-Chalabi independent delegate says, 'just say you are against Chalabi. You can sell your product to the State Department.' Massoud Barzani threatens to withdraw from the conference on the grounds that Chalabi and Abdel Aziz al-Hakim, both Arab Shiites, are conspiring against the Kurds. Barzani also distrusts his Kurdish rival Jalal Talabani, who has done much to build alliances with the Arabs. Talabani is worried, so I am told by a friend of his, by Barzani's *rapprochement* with Iran. Mohammed Khatami, the Iranian reformist president, recently received Barzani with full honours. 'Talabani played down the Tehran meeting,' the friend says, 'but he was upset.'

Everyone is sending messages. Chalabi has opened an INC office in Tehran. This tells SCIRI it is not the only Iraqi group with Iranian support. It says to Washington: 'You are not our only friend'. Barzani's pilgrimage to the *mullahs* sends the same signal to the US and tells Talabani that the Barzanis have the most important ally in the region. Iran lets the US know that it cannot be ignored in Iraq.

Six of the main leaders – Chalabi, Barzani, Talabani, al-Hakim, Iyad Allawi and Sherif Ali bin Hussein – meet together for many hours to work out an agreement they must submit to Khalilzad and then force on the 320 delegates fighting off sleep in the main conference room.

No agreement, no final statement, no anything is ready by the time the conference is scheduled to end on Monday night. Khalilzad continues to receive squabbling Iraqis in the Windsor Suite, but patching up petty differences leads nowhere. Suddenly, on Tuesday morning at 0130, a dozen or more men march into the Metropole Hotel. They are bodyguards and officials accompanying the Pentagon's man, Deputy Undersecretary of Defense Bill Luti; Luti works for Undersecretary of Defense for Policy Doug Feith. It's as though the sheriff has kicked open the saloon doors to tell the brawling cowboys the party's over.

The BBC crew in the lobby asks Luti what he's doing here. He says he's come to 'facilitate' the progress of the conference. Hiwa Osman asks me, 'Where does that leave Khalilzad?'

Luti apparently goes upstairs, where the Big Six are meeting. Someone must have told Khalilzad. At three in the morning, Khalilzad storms out of the hotel. Hiwa, a kind of Scarlet Pimpernel here, slips past the security men guarding the meeting. Later he says Luti told the US's Iraqi allies, 'We are going ahead. This is your last chance. If you come up with a united committee, you will be part of a future government. If not, we'll do it on our own.'

Long after the sun rises, when the delegates have slept, there is a final communiqué from the 'united' Iraqi opposition. The delegates have 'chosen' sixty-one members to convene in Erbil on 15 January in preparation for the new order in Iraq. Later, the number of delegates is increased to sixty-five. Then to seventy-five. Three are women.

Exhausted, I take a late train home to Paris.

Friday, 17 January 2003
London

Chris Isham, the head of ABC News's Investigative Unit, has flown over from New York. I've taken the train up from Paris. Chris and I met in 1983 in Damascus, when he was producing a documentary for ABC in Syria. We've been friends ever since. When he became head of investigations at ABC, he transformed a moribund team into the most aggressive investigators in television. The reporters and producers he trained either started or improved similar units at the other networks. There is a kind of pride in having worked for Isham and his I-Team that reminds me of those *Philadelphia Inquirer* and *New York Times* journalists who tell you of their glory days under the legendary Gene Roberts.

Chris and I did a series of investigative pieces together in the 1980s on a terror state that Washington did not want to hear about – Iraq. Our pieces documenting Saddam Hussein's possession of biological weapons, murders and expulsions of Kurds, and the consistent mass torture of his subjects, met with indifference and often outright denial from the Defense and State Departments. Saddam noticed, however, and put me on the blacklist. I could not get an Iraqi visa until he threw away the list and let any journalist enter – including *The Independent*'s Patrick Cockburn, who had written horror stories about this charnel house of a country – after the 1990 invasion of Kuwait.

We're staying at the Metropolitan Hotel (not to be confused with the Metropole, where the Iraqi opposition met last month) on Park Lane. Chris and I have an appointment with Ahmad Chalabi at his Knightsbridge office. Zaab Sethna, Ahmad's elegant public relations director, takes us to his quarters. An Indian Parsee raised in England and educated at Georgetown, Zaab came to the INC from the US-financed public relations firm, the Rendon Group, that had been assigned under the Iraqi Liberation Act to help the INC. I think Zaab liked Ahmad more than the firm, or Ahmad paid him more, or both. He's intelligent, friendly and good with the Western press. On his debit chart are the facts that he is not an Iraqi and speaks no Arabic.

Ahmad, in shirtsleeves, invites us into his office. There, Arab and Kurdish Iraqis are conducting a post-mortem on the London conference. Someone is complaining about the imperiousness of Zalmay Khalilzad.

'Khalilzad has the Afghan model on the brain,' Chalabi says, taking a chair in front of a computer screen. 'The problem with America is it has a great army and its politics are shit.'

Siyamend Osman is sitting near Ahmad. Kanan has yet to return to Brandeis, where he teaches. Latif Rashid of the PUK is here from his office down the corridor. Goran is also here. Sam comes in after us and takes a chair. The only journalists are Chris Isham, someone whom I have never met named Gavin Smythe from *The Financial Times* and me.

These days the names Percy Cox and Gertrude Bell, the two Britons who created Iraq after the British invasion of 1917, come up again and again. Many of the speeches at the Metropole spoke of them, and Ahmad mentions them now. 'There's a new Gertrude Bell in the State Department,' he says. 'Tom Warwick. He was for prosecuting war crimes in the Balkans. Now he's for putting war criminals into the presidency in Iraq.' That means, Ahmad continues, that the State Department wants Baathists in a post-Saddam government. The CIA, he says, still seeks a *coup* to leave the Iraqi military in power.

He recounts the final hours of the Metropole conference on the unscheduled extra day and says Khalilzad told him, 'We are going to do this with or without you.' His response, he says, was, 'I warn you not to try to intimidate anyone here.' It seems, according to Ahmad, that Khalilzad wanted to pick all sixty-five delegates to the next conference in Iraq. The opposition resisted. But the delegation, he says, 'has no structure, no articles of association, no funding.' It is scheduled, nonetheless, to meet in northern Iraq next month.

Kanan, although an independent, is spending most days with the INC while he's in London. He says he had a meeting recently with President Bush in Washington, and that Bush spoke for ten minutes and then asked questions about Iraq. One was, 'How will the American army be received?'

Kanan says he told him, 'Mr President, the Iraqi people will greet you with sweets and flowers.'

Bush asked, 'Would it be the same if the bombing is so severe?'

Kanan says he answered, 'Does it have to be severe?'

Bush tried to reassure him, saying, 'The Army Corps of Engineers will rebuild everything that is destroyed.' I think he meant Bechtel and Halliburton.

The Iraqis here talk about postwar Iraq, their obsession. Siyamend says, 'It is Defense Department policy to take over the country and dictate what will happen.' Kanan agrees. Ahmad sits on a desk, plants his black trainers on a chair and says, 'He [Bush] used the Japanese and German models, but said he wanted a shorter occupation. That was at a meeting with Dick Cheney, Steve Hadley and Khalilzad.'

Goran recalls a meeting of Massoud Barzani, Jalal Talabani and Khalilzad during the London conference. Khalilzad declared that he would choose the delegates for the next meeting. Jalal Talabani asked Khalilzad whom he would pick. Barzani whispered to him, in Kurdish, 'Traitors and spies.'

Sunday, 26 January 2003
Paris via Frankfurt to Tehran

After a late and lively night out with my friend Goldie, closing Chez Paul in the eleventh *arrondissement*, I struggle to get up. I finish packing, hiding my chemical suit and gas mask at the bottom of a canvas bag where Iranian customs might not notice them. I send a few emails and call my children in Britain. I call Sophie, a young woman I met in London, and we speak as if I were leaving for the Somme. A taxi arrives on time to take me to Roissy and my first ABC News jaunt since 1993. I wait a few hours to change planes at Frankfurt airport, where I used to waste whole days. It is a shopping mall for transients – no familiarity allowed; no one stays; and the traveller is among strangers no matter how often he stops there. I have my last beer, my last pork sausages and my last European papers.

The front page of today's *Independent on Sunday* from London screams, 'STOP. THINK. LISTEN. STOP THE RUSH TO WAR. THINK OF THE CONSEQUENCES. LISTEN TO REASON.' In Britain, only *The Independent*, *The Guardian* and *The Mirror* oppose the war. The rest urge their readers to support the US-led invasion of Iraq and disseminate without scrutiny Washington's case for war. Even *The Observer*, the only paper to condemn Britain's fiasco over Suez in 1956, supports an Anglo-American invasion of Mesopotamia. *The Observer* was right about Britain's invasion of Egypt, which ended Britain's imperium in the Arab world. On Iraq, there will be time to judge.

The plane serves taste-free chicken and indifferent wine. In the seats on either side of me are beautiful Persian women, who in a few hours will hide their short skirts and tight sweaters under black shrouds. Theirs is the black of mourning for hidden bodies, shameful in the Islamic Republic. They drink their last legal beers and vodkas and watch near-naked cheerleaders bounce across an overhead television monitor. The girls onscreen look like stupidity made flesh, embodiments of the West that the *mullahs* resist and for which millions of young Iranians yearn.

The plane lands at 0120 Monday morning. The time in Tehran is three and a half hours later than Greenwich Mean Time, eight and a half hours ahead of New York. Or, as the joke goes, it's Iran, turn your clocks back 500 years.

I am on my way alone to Iraq. My plan is to find hotel rooms, drivers, translators and the rest of the infrastructure ABC will need to cover the northern front. I'll return to Paris to wait for the right moment to enter Iraq again with Fabrice, Qassem and the rest of the crew. That, anyway, is the plan.

Monday, 27 January 2003
Shohreh Hotel, Tehran

The ABC office manager, Afshin Abtahi, meets me at the airport. He is more rock band lead singer than Iranian office manager: about six-foot-two, wearing blue jeans, a loose cotton shirt and a ponytail. On the drive in, he says he studied at an Islamic seminary and served as a Revolutionary Guard. Religion was his form of rebellion against his middle-class family. We arrive at the Shohreh Hotel in north Tehran at about four in the morning. Latif Rashid is there, about to leave for Iraqi Kurdistan, and says we'll meet in Suleimaniya in a few days. My suite at the Shohreh is better than any I have had in post-revolutionary Iran. The sheets and towels are clean, it has lots of space with a small kitchen and is comfortable if a bit tacky. It is not difficult to sleep.

I am up for an early breakfast in the fifth-floor restaurant with Sam, Kanan, Goran and a few other exiles on their way home. They have been in Iran for almost a week, meeting with the Islamists of SCIRI, Iranian Pasdaran (Revolutionary Guards), intelligence officers and politicians. The Iranians impressed them with their detailed knowledge of Iraq – superior, they say, to Washington's. The US government, meanwhile, is blocking a meeting in Iraqi Kurdistan of the sixty-five Iraqi opposition delegates chosen at the London conference in December. After breakfast Sam, Goran and I wander through the bazaar, chased by young men trying to inveigle us into their carpet shops. We go on to the Golestan Palace, where the last Qajar *shahs* awaited the demise of their dynasty. Goran insists on lunch in a little tea shop within the palace complex. We eat well: saffron rice and grilled meats, then cinnamon tea and water pipes.

We visit Jim Muir, who lives below his BBC office in a big house in north Tehran. Upstairs, he rents out space to other Western news agencies. The women here are not wearing *hijabs*, and the atmosphere is relaxed. Jim gives us tea and chats about Iran. Two BBC teams in succession have jeopardised the survival of his bureau. One came on tourist visas and used hidden cameras. The other staged some story that the government did not like. Neither informed him or his bureau what they were doing, a violation of journalistic protocol. The BBC somehow involved Afshin Abtahi, ABC's Tehran office manager, and got him into trouble. The teams left, and Afshin has had to bear the consequences.

Jim introduces his cameraman and video editor, Kaveh Golestan, and the bureau stringer, the beautiful Miranda Eeles. They are in the midst of editing a television story. Jim jokes with Kaveh about Millfield, Kaveh's English school. That explains Kaveh's public-school accent, if not his droopy moustache. He is teaching Miranda film composition while he edits her feature. Jim and I go downstairs for dinner with his Italian girlfriend, Cristina.

I have known Jim since 1975, when he moved to Beirut with a wife and child to risk his life as a freelance journalist in what became a battle zone. Equipped with a Cambridge Arabic degree, he covered the civil war for several British papers. After some time, he went to work for the BBC – first for World Service radio and then television. Since coming to Tehran, he has learned Persian. After dinner we watch a film on DVD, *Bend it Like Beckham*. Sam Chalabi drops by with Elizabeth Rubin, who writes for *The New York Times Sunday Magazine* and *The New Republic*. I don't know Elizabeth, whose brother Jamie was Madeleine Albright's flack at the State Department. During the movie, Sam whispers, 'We leave at nine tomorrow.' That means I won't have a long wait in Tehran. Back at the hotel, I call Sophie in London. No answer.

To bed at two o'clock. Sober.

Tuesday, 28 January 2003
Shohreh Hotel, Tehran

Snow is falling on the north Tehran hills, and rain sweeps the poorer streets of the plain in the south. Tehran is much like Los Angeles, with the hills of Bel Air and Hollywood in the north, the poor to the south, highways, concrete and traffic keeping the two apart. Our 0900 departure from the hotel takes place at 0930, and the twenty-minute journey to the airport lasts an hour. Ahmad Chalabi and his daughter Tamara are coming from their guesthouse. Despite the delays, we reach the airport in time for the flight to Urumieh. This makes no difference, because Iran Air has cancelled the flight due to fog, rain and snow. I go inside to ask about the next flight and am told it leaves at 1330. While we wait at the airport, Zaab Sethna repeats a rumour that the US will deploy troops in Northern Iraq on 1 February. He calls Aras Karim, a young Kurd who is the INC's operations chief, who says our departure is postponed until tomorrow. The drive back through the rain takes an hour and a half. No city in the world has worse traffic than Tehran.

On the Shohreh's fifth floor, Sam, Kanan, Zaab, an Iraqi writer named Abu Samih, an old friend and associate of Ahmad's named Mudhar Shawkat and I have lunch. The food and the dining room are not much, but Tehran below us looks enchanting in the snow. The Iraqis are talking about Syria and the massacre of Muslim fundamentalists in Hama by Hafez al-Assad in 1982. They recall the history of the Baath Party, its philosophy of Arab renaissance and its three founders, Michel Aflaq, Salah al-Din al-Bitar and Zaki al-Arsuzi. Could they have known where their ideals would lead Syria and Iraq? We discuss the war between Iraq and Iran that lasted from 1980 to 1988 and killed more than 1 million people. Mudhar says that although he had been arrested and tortured as a student by the Baath in 1968, he returned from exile in England to join the Iraqi army during the Iran-Iraq war, 'I fought for Iraq, not for the regime.' This leads to an argument with Abu Samih, a Shiite for whom fighting for Iraq was the same as fighting for Saddam. Mudhar is from a wealthy Sunni family, some of whom were prime ministers before Saddam's time.

In the evening, Miranda takes me to Jamshidieh Park, a forest on the high slopes of north Tehran. Wrapped in her *chador*, she takes me along a snowy path for miles uphill. Courting couples, far from the Revolutionary Guards and other protectors of virtue, hold hands as they wander hidden corners of the park. A few are throwing snowballs at one another and laughing like children. Some sit on benches like couples anywhere. Miranda leads the way, talking all the while about her life here, the stories she's done for the BBC – including some on prostitutes for pilgrims at shrines – and her attempts to master Farsi. Near the summit are a series of wooden chalets, apparently built in the Shah's era, which are Persian, Kurdish and Turkish restaurants. We go into the Kurdish one. A fire burns in a kind of inglenook, and a waiter is the only human presence. While we eat Kurdish *kebabs* and rice without wine, Miranda's scarf falls from her face from time to time.

She has a beautiful face, but it's her voice that – however inadvertently – seduces. This is, despite the *mullahs*, the sensuous land of Omar Khayyam. Back in the forest, Miranda, beside me, whispers in the wilderness.

After dinner, I'm back at the Shohreh in a college BS session. Sam and Kanan are debating politics in the sitting room of their suite. Sam is thirty-nine and Kanan, in his fifties, is about my age. We all grew up on political discussion rather than talk of clothes, lifestyle and 'relationships'. Kanan has been all over the spectrum: Arab nationalist, communist and now, more or less, neo-conservative. He spent hours today with the devout Shiites of SCIRI. Sam and Kanan discuss whether to call Iraq an Arab state despite its many Kurds, Assyrians, Turcomen and others. Do such terms matter? Later, I watch German television news: General Ariel Sharon has won thirty-six Knesset seats in today's elections and will, therefore, form the new government of the Jewish State.

Wednesday, 29 January 2003
Shohreh Hotel, Tehran

Ahmad invites his INC group to lunch at the Shandiz Restaurant. Afshin and I join them to eat grilled meat, something for which the vast eating hall with its long picnic tables is said to be famous. Ahmad is in a heady mood, more confident of his position than ever. He is here to cement a relationship with the Iranians and with Iran's favoured Iraqi group, SCIRI. Ahmad says 300 US troops are going to an airbase at Harir in Northern Iraq to prepare the way for another 3,000. He tells Afshin he remembers him from a visit they made to Iraqi Kurdistan a few years ago. Afshin is not sure that Ahmad really remembers. Then Ahmad asks, 'Does your father still work in the bank?' Ahmad forgets nothing. It is as much the mathematician in him as the politician. He has an abrupt way of leaving lunch and dinner. He just stands up and goes to one of the cars waiting outside – which he does now at the Shandiz. The others, including his bodyguards, follow. They go to meetings. Afshin and I go to Afshin's house for coffee.

To reach an evening appointment with Abdel Aziz al-Hakim of SCIRI, Sam and I take an hour and a half to go from the hotel in north Tehran to the centre of town. We find the SCIRI offices on a darkened commercial street. Abdel Aziz's son, a man in his early twenties dressed in Western trousers and shirt, opens the door. He shows us into a little room carpeted like a mosque. We sit and await his father, who comes in a few minutes later. Abdel Aziz is wearing a long clerical robe, trim beard and the black turban of a *sayyid*, a descendant of the Prophet. He is the younger brother of Ayatollah Mohammed Bakr al-Hakim, the supreme leader of the Supreme Council.

The first thing Abdel Aziz says when he takes his chair and kneads his amber worry beads is that President Bush's recent State of the Union address was 'accurate' about Iraq. But he prefers, he says, to 'reserve comment' on Bush's observations about 'other countries'. 'Other countries' means one other country, his host for twenty years – Iran. This is the ritual of Middle Eastern political interviewing, the deciphering of obvious codes like 'other countries'. A servant places a tray of tea glasses, spoons and sugar on a coffee table. A guard of some kind takes his place behind the deputy leader. Other men, unintroduced, sit on chairs around us. I ask about Bush's stated rationale for war, the WMD.

'I think that weapons of mass destruction are a key determinant,' he says. 'There are others, especially after 11 September: to build democracies in other countries. In several countries in the Middle East, US policy would be appropriate to impose democracy.'

'Like Afghanistan?'

'Clearly, getting rid of the Taliban is a positive step, especially from the Shiite perspective.'

The Sunni Taliban massacred Afghan Shiites and nearly provoked a war with Iran in doing so. Al-Hakim is beginning, however, to sound like Rumsfeld. Does he really support US policy?

'One reservation I have is that the American system is not sensitive to local customs.'

He has another reservation. SCIRI, he says, opposes a US invasion. Opposed or not, he and his brother will take advantage of it. He says he told the US that an uprising by the Iraqis themselves would be better. 'You were there in '91, when fourteen out of the eighteen provinces fell.' Does he differ from other Iraqi opposition leaders on this?

'Most of the Iraqi opposition agree with this point of view. If you read the political statements of the opposition in the last few days, they say the primary responsibility rests with the Iraqi people and not with the US.'

The US claims that the Iraqi opposition wants an invasion. Why hasn't he made his position clear? He says he has no media access in the West. He has told Western ambassadors. 'I myself am willing to get into a debate with anyone who believes war is the right path.'

He insists on two principles, 'Sovereignty lies with the Iraqi people themselves. They should choose the structure of the state and who should govern.'

Sam adds, 'We are worried about it too.' He means the US might govern Iraq directly.

The conversation turns personal when I mention Lebanon. Al-Hakim says his mother is Lebanese. I ask about her. The family name is Bazzi, and they are from Bint Jbeil in South Lebanon. His mother's brother is Ali Bazzi, who was Speaker of the Lebanese Parliament. Bazzi's son Tareef was my Arabic teacher in Beirut. I tell Abdel Aziz that my bad Arabic is his cousin's fault. We part on friendly terms. Later that evening, someone who knows Abdel Aziz says, 'Abdel Aziz ordered the execution of Iraqi prisoners during the war.' The story is that he took charge of some Iraqi POWs in Iran. He let the Shiite soldiers live, while killing the Sunni officers. If this is true, the Sunnis of Iraq – until now, the ruling and wealthy minority – will not embrace the al-Hakims as national leaders.

From the SCIRI offices, it is another hour and a half in a Tehran taxi to the Gandhi Centre. These drives would, in any other city, take fifteen minutes. In Tehran, our car sits in one spot for forty-five. The Gandhi Centre turns out to be a modern-ish shopping mall with several cafés, where young boys and girls meet in what seems a more relaxed setting than is usual in Iran. The girls wear their *chadors*, but let them fall back on their heads to expose some of their hair the way California girls show a little breast. This was not happening in public when I was last here ten years ago. Illegal drinking at home and clandestine trysts have gone on for years, with bribes to the local Pasdaran to look the other way. What has changed is the public flouting by the young of the old revolutionary strictures. And, in this tea-drinking country, cafés are serving espresso and capuccino. Elizabeth Rubin, an unlikely daughter of the Revolution in her long, black shawl, meets Sam and me at a café. She says the Ministry of Culture and Islamic Guidance, Ershad, has just told her that it would no longer approve visas for American journalists. Why? They don't like Bush's State of the Union references to Iran. She told them to look on the positive side: he may have accused them of terrorism, but this time he didn't call them 'evil'. His policy of antagonising Iran reminds me of Reagan's, when US troops were forced out of Lebanon.

Sam, Elizabeth and I walk to the Alighapoo restaurant for dinner. The cellar hostelry is full of light and noise and families at big tables. A gallery at eye-level has private patios, and old Persian hunting prints adorn the walls. One live band after another plays Kurdish and Persian music on a small stage. More grilled meats, more rice, more bread, water and tea. I like Elizabeth, her sense of humour and cynicism about Washington and Tehran. She wants, as I do, to get into Iraq before the war begins. Wild Kurdish music prompts clapping from the diners, but they dare not dance – not yet.

Return to the hotel at 0100 and receive messages from Chris Isham and Chuck Lustig of ABC and from Miranda. Chris says he wants to come to Iraq and asks whether I can help with an Iranian visa. Lustig is responsible for ABC's foreign news coverage in New York. When I call him, he conferences with Marcus Wilford in London. They say there is a threat from the Iraqi government to kill Americans, including journalists, in northern Iraq. I'll go anyway, because neither they nor I take the report seriously. The Pentagon is pushing the networks to pull their people out of Baghdad and the north. General Richard Myers, Chairman of the Joint Chiefs, invited Peter Jennings to dinner to tell him that journalists who are not 'embedded' with the US or British military would not be safe. I assume he is dining the other networks as well. The Pentagon never welcomes coverage it does not control.

I call Miranda back. She invites me to come skiing with her in the mountains over the weekend. If I were not going to the airport again in the morning, I would. This time, we might actually get on a plane. I call Sophie in London, where she is finishing an edit of her film for a first showing to its backers tomorrow. I know it will be good, and I find myself wanting to be with her every time I hear her voice on the telephone. But I am three and a half time zones away.

Thursday, 30 January 2003
Tehran to Erbil, Iraq, via Urumieh

I am up for a 3 AM rendezvous with Sam, Kanan, Goran and Mudhar in the Shohreh Palace lobby. Kanan is wearing a khaki fishing hat on his bald head, but he doesn't look like a fisherman. Ahmad, Tamara and their bodyguards meet us at Tehran's domestic airport. Ahmad is wearing brown tweeds and some snow boots that he bought in Tehran. His daughter is uncomfortable in her *chador*, the price she pays to visit the Islamic Republic. A sign at the airport says, '*Hijab* is like a shell for a pearl.' Tamara's pearl doesn't need a shell. With bodyguards, we are twenty-six people.

The 6 AM flight to Urumieh takes an hour. At the clean, provincial airport, Iranian officials greet Ahmad like royalty. Flunkeys carry the luggage to vans outside, and local dignitaries invite the Chalabi entourage to drink tea. I realise I've left my camera at the airport in Tehran and ask the Urumieh airport manager to help me retrieve it. Kanan, Goran, Sam and I are installed in a new Toyota Land Cruiser. The others are distributed among similar four-wheel-drives. I assume we are heading straight to the border, but I'm wrong. Ahmad's hosts, the Pasdaran, drive us to their headquarters. On entering, we remove our shoes and sit amid armed Guardsmen for tea, bread, sweet water buffalo cheese and honey. One of the INC people complains that the previous night Zalmay Khalilzad called Abdel Aziz but did not call Ahmad.

At the abrupt ending of breakfast, we scramble for our shoes and rush out. Back in the cars we head through Urumieh, with its giant fruit sculptures at every roundabout, and up the snowy mountain. Ascending for over an hour, we reach the last Iranian town, Piranshahr.

We stop for a gargantuan lunch that a local restaurant has prepared for us, though I have yet to digest breakfast. When the Iranians like you, as they seem to like Ahmad Chalabi, they kill you with hospitality. It is not easy for Ahmad, who has been dieting for the last few years and has dropped about forty pounds. He avoids the bread. Aras Karim, his chief of operations, explains the border protocol. It is the drill for a head of state, not that many cross this border. The Revolutionary Guards will stand to attention, salute Ahmad and hand him over to the KDP on the Iraqi side.

At the end of lunch Tamara asks me, 'Have you ever had the hospitality of the Revolutionary Guards before?' In a way, I have, and she knows it: Hizbullah was working with the Guards when it kidnapped her uncle Ali Osseiran and me in 1987.

We drive along icy roads out of the rough breeze-block border town and into open country, past smugglers leading cigarette-laden donkeys up twisted trails. The Land Cruisers ascend a desert of snow, where you could drive all day without seeing a tree. We reach the border. Nine Iranian soldiers stand to attention, shivering in their flimsy camouflage fatigues, white tunics and white spats. They salute Ahmad, who shakes the hands of Iranian dignitaries and poses for photographers. The last pictures we see in Iran are giant posters of Ayatollah Khomeini and his successor, Ali Khamenei.

A fleet of white KDP Land Cruisers, numbered from one to ten on their windscreens, waits for baggage to be decanted from the Iranian cars. The KDP people check our names against a list before assigning us to cars. We are on our way. I am entering Iraq at last, but I am just another journalist. Ahmad, however, comes with grand plans. He is either Iraq's future president or a politician soon to be overtaken by events. The second we are over the border, Tamara pulls the Iranian black scarf off her head and shakes her long hair free.

I am in car number three with Goran. We drive along the Hamilton Road, an engineering marvel built by the British army to control the Kurds. It winds along the banks of coursing rivers, through gorges that shoot up to the sky, and onto soft meadows of late winter soil awaiting wildflowers. Our first stop is the village of Harir. Ahmad says the Pentagon told him that 300 Special Forces troops have just landed at the local airstrip here. In the valley below, beside a tarmac stretch, are white tents and a Humvee. 'Come here,' Ahmad calls to me from the front steps of the local KDP office. 'There are your compatriots.' If US troops are there, they are not visible from the village. I walk to the end of town to get closer but, without binoculars, I cannot see who is there.

Near sunset, we are in the mountain resort of Salahuddin, headquarters of Massoud Barzani, his tribe and his KDP. Fabrice Moussus, Qassem Dergham, Don McCullin and I made this our base in 1991, near the KDP's military communications centre and a half hour from the stench of the hotel in Erbil where Jon Randal of *The Washington Post* caught dysentery. The KDP dumps us at the Meedia Palace Hotel, unimproved since 1991. We sit, backs to the wall, in a dingy reception room facing coffee tables of bananas, sodas, apples and tea. We wait. We wait a little longer. If Ahmad left Iran like a king, he is entering Barzani's Iraqi Kurdistan like a pauper. No one is here to welcome him. This is like arriving at Claridge's in a boiler suit without reservation, credit card or cash. Ahmad sits, quiet and restrained. Mudhar becomes furious and shouts at the KDP guards, 'No one treats Ahmad Chalabi like this! Tell Barzani to receive him in his home at once.' A KDP official pulls out a telephone and leaves the room. Later, he returns to announce that our group of twenty-six is to be separated, some going to guesthouses and others to a hotel in Salahuddin and two – Zaab Sethna the spokesman and me the only journalist – down the hill to the city of Erbil. It is a hierarchical plan, like seating at a queen's banquet, and the journalist is as far down table as possible without eating in the kitchen. Actually, I suppose Erbil *is* the kitchen.

While arguments proceed, the KDP evacuates Ahmad, Tamara, Sam and Kanan to a Barzani guesthouse. Next to disappear are some of the delegates, and then the bodyguards. Zaab and I, left on our own, wake a barman to bring us a drink. Later, the bodyguards, mostly Iraqi-born ex-bouncers from London nightclubs, return. The hotel they were offered was disgusting. One compares it to a prison that Saddam put him in. A smooth-talking KDP public relations man, Fawzi Hariri, drives Zaab and me to Erbil, 'It's better than this, I promise.'

A half-hour down the hill, we check into the Chwar Chra (Kurdish for 'Four Lanterns') Hotel. My room is dark, and the bathroom is no place to take a bath. Fawzi recommends a restaurant, the Hawler, in the Christian quarter. Zaab and I take a taxi there for a late, hearty dinner of *kebab*, rice and bread. Since I left Paris, I have not eaten anything else. Now I am in my hotel room, wondering what the hell I'm doing here. I remember: advance work, making contacts, finding places to stay, renting local cellphones, hiring drivers and Kurdish translators. Getting things ready for my guys. In television news, we call it 'logistics'.

Here I am, standing by for a war that I don't want. It is like waiting for a terminally ill friend to die. This is my first war since I resigned from ABC News after Bosnia. I am back with ABC and back in a war zone, cut off again from my children and from a new girlfriend I don't want to lose. During my time in Bosnia, as in Lebanon and Israel and other places, my children missed me and worried about me. After a long stint in Lebanon, my wife left me. During the Bosnia war, two women in succession did the same.

This is my first night in Iraqi Kurdistan since 1991. The piece McCullin and I did then was published under the title 'The Road to Karahanjir'. If Fabrice, Qassem and Don get their visas, we'll be together again, on the road to Baghdad. The four of us, the old team, reunited. Qassem, Fabrice and I are in our fifties. Don is sixty-seven. Not so much the Wild as the Mild Bunch.

There are three ways into Iraqi Kurdistan, the only part of the country not under Saddam's control: through Syria, Turkey or Iran. The Turks closed their border to journalists a long time ago. The Syrian route is closed to everyone because CNN aired footage of its crossing. Iranian visas take weeks or longer. Once you're in, you have to wait for permission to leave for Iraq. Companies allegedly affiliated to Iranian government officials are charging $3,000 to speed the process. Fabrice, Qassem and Don are waiting for Iranian and Syrian visas, and they may yet smuggle themselves here from Turkey.

I want the story we had in 1991, but with a happy ending. This time, I would like to see the Iraqis defeat Saddam themselves. But they won't. The US does not want Iraqis to take part, and most Iraqis don't trust the US.

Friday, 31 January 2003
Chwar Chra Hotel, Erbil

Kevin McKiernan, the stringer ABC hired when he arrived in Kurdistan last September, calls to say the PUK has evacuated journalists from the Palace Hotel in Suleimaniya to a motel outside town. It seems there was a security scare. A few wouldn't budge. On a phone in the lobby I ask Kevin whether he could go to Harir to shoot some video of the airbase. He says no. The US is more likely to land troops at an airstrip next to Suleimaniya. Could he shoot the Suleimaniya airfield then? He whines that the PUK won't give permission. He should call Latif Rashid, I say. 'Listen,' he answers, 'I have people higher up the food chain than that. And they're not giving permission.' Latif, as the London spokesman for the PUK, might not be the most senior man in the politburo; but he is Jalal Talabani's brother-in-law and is staying in Talabani's house. Food chain or not, he is closer to Talabani than anyone else. But why tell this to McKiernan?

A Persian-American journalist from Chicago, Borzou Daragahi, interrupts. The Americans won't land at Harir or Suleimaniya, he says, but at Barmani way up north. Why? The Turks already have tanks at Barmani, and it's safer. Daragahi says the CIA and Special Forces are already in Salahuddin, Dohuk and Zakho. Funny, sharp and streetwise, he talks like a Damon Runyon police reporter. Iranian-born, American-raised, he lives in Tehran with his girlfriend. We have coffee, and he gives me tips on survival in Kurdistan. His strongest advice concerns communications. There are two types of satellite phones here, Thuraya and Iridium. He has both. When the US invades, he assures me, the army will shut down the Thurayas. But he'll be able to file with his Iridium. He has been coming back and forth for the last few months and is cynical about the Kurds, as all Iranians are. A little later he puts me on the telephone with Bob Reid, who is running the AP's war coverage from the US's Central Command (CENTCOM) in Doha, Qatar. Reid is one of the funniest guys I know. We worked together in Cairo, where he was AP's bureau chief, and in Beirut. He says the war is all bullshit, the press briefings in Qatar are bullshit and the Middle East is still bullshit. What's changed?

Fawzi Hariri sends a local businessman named Rizgar Kadir to the hotel to help me. Rizgar offers to procure anything I need: places to stay, drivers, telephones, cash. He drives me to the bazaar, a vast complex of lanes and shops below the mud-brick Citadel of Erbil. There I buy a camera to replace one I left at the airport. (The Iran Air manager at Urumieh's airport called to say the camera turned up at Tehran Airport, where the staff will keep it for me.) Rizgar remembers meeting me in 1991, when he was a nineteen-year-old *Peshmerga*. He was one of my KDP guards in Kirkuk, but I don't recognise him. (He says he was much thinner then.) It turns out his partner is my friend Sherwan Dezayee in London. They own two hotels here. CNN has reserved one to itself, but Rizgar can give me as many rooms as I need in the other. Back at the Chwar Chra, he finds me a driver named Muhammad Amin, who is about thirty and speaks a little English and no Arabic. He carries an English grammar book and is serious about improving. As we drive, he teaches me Kurdish words.

The road up to Salahuddin runs through miles of grassy meadows. Boys are selling bananas in cardboard boxes for much of the way. Because it is Friday, there are picnics, wedding parties and dancing. A billboard for Korek Telecommunications declares in English, 'We Minimize the World'. At the sight of power pylons, Muhammad says the electricity is on only fourteen hours a day. Better than in 1991, when it was off all the time. The road rises from the Erbil plain to swivel back on itself and around again all the way to the top. New pines in rock circles are replacing the thousands that Saddam destroyed during the Anfal campaign and which people scavenged for fires to keep from freezing during the winters of 1991 and 1992. For the most part, these hills are as rocky and barren as those in the West Bank, but they are higher.

Muhammad barely slows at a lazy checkpoint guarding Salahuddin. Before we left, he said he knew where the KDP guesthouse was. Now, he doesn't. We stop at one official-looking house after another, pass a checkpoint and find ourselves in a rocky KDP compound on hundreds of acres. Land Cruisers and Toyota trucks are parked at a likely-looking mansion. I walk through the gates, where a tall American with a ginger moustache is speaking on a Thuraya. Pacing up and down, he is conducting an animated, personal conversation,

'Did she really say that? No shit?' A second American steps forward, pistol visible in his belt, and waves me out of the CIA's front yard. Officially, they are not there. The Kurdish guards outside make calls and give us directions to the right guesthouse.

Ahmad, Tamara, Sam, Kanan and Mudhar are enjoying the luxury of Barzani's hospitality, compensation for the insult of their arrival. We go to Aras Karim's room, where books about the CIA and spy thrillers sit on a bedside table. Aras is, as usual, on the telephone. He has distributed Thurayas to his people in Kirkuk, Mosul, Baghdad and the south. It is risky for them, but they keep him informed.

Mudhar takes me outside, away from indoor recording devices. The sun is dropping, and we pace in a circle beside the guesthouse. He says the opposition is going to declare a provisional government. This is what the US told them not to do. There will be a leadership council, *majlis al-siadi*, with seven to eleven members. The provisional government will have twenty-one ministers with Ahmad as Prime Minister. This is the plan that Ahmad will discuss with Barzani at seven o'clock this evening. Tomorrow, he will seek support from Talabani. The al-Hakims of SCIRI already support the idea, he says. Zalmay Khalilzad arrives in four days, and they hope to present the US with a *fait accompli*. The problem, he believes, will be over federalism for the Kurds. Turkey, Iran, Saudi Arabia and the US do not want a federal Iraq. 'Don't use this, Charlie,' he asks. 'It's too delicate. Keep it off the record.' While we talk outside, Ahmad is inside telling Borzou the same thing, albeit in less detail, on the record. It does not matter to me. I cannot do any reports for ABC until the crew arrives. I suspect the Americans do not much care what these Iraqis do.

We hear more rumours of US troops arriving by air. It seems they were not at Harir when we stopped there. Barzani gives Ahmad a banquet, while I have dinner in the Chwar Chra with Borzou.

Back in my room, I watch Tony Blair with George Bush in Washington on CNN. They say war will begin in 'weeks, not months'. How many weeks?

Saturday, 1 February 2003
Ashur Hotel, Lake Dokan, Northern Iraq

John Hemmings of Reuters, Borzou and I have a quick breakfast of stale bread, boiled eggs and tea in the Chwar Chra's basement. I check out of the hotel, and Muhammad Amin arrives to take me to Salahuddin. Erbil is a city of busy open boulevards, houses the colour of sand and dreary eucalyptus trees. There is much traffic on the first day of the working week. Erbil is the capital of Iraqi Kurdistan, one of several cities in the world – Damascus and Jericho are two others – with a fair claim to have been inhabited longer than any other. We pass a new, nearly-built mosque that is playfully modelled on Hagia Sophia in Istanbul on the way to Fawzi Hariri's house in the Christian Quarter. Fawzi is the son of Franso Hariri, the popular mayor of Erbil until his assassination by an Islamic fundamentalist a few years ago. The killer may have hated Christians or the (secular) KDP to which Franso belonged. Franso's death brought Fawzi back from London, where he was working for British Airways, to become the KDP's press relations director. I sense that Fawzi, who has a David Niven moustache and speaks precise British English, would rather be in London. We drive past some of the institutions the Kurds have built since they expelled the Baath Party in 1991: the Human Rights Ministry, the Centre for Battered Women and the Ministry of the *Peshmergas*. Back in Salahuddin, I catch up with the INC and follow them to PUK-land.

It is a long drive through alpine scenery to the line which the PUK and KDP drew across Kurdistan to end their civil war in 1996. I am in a new Mercedes with Zaab and Goran. Goran says his family name, Talabani, means 'Bitter [*tala*] Heights [*ban*]' in Kurdish. It has no connection to the Arabic *taliban* (student), he says; the Talabanis are more a tribe than a family.

The frontier between KDP and PUK territories is not the usual hostile face-off of armed roadblocks, as between the Israelis and their occupied Palestinian subjects or the opposed militias during the Lebanese civil war. Somewhere on the plain lies a field of rocks and boulders that an artist has coloured with doves and amoeba-shaped blues, crimsons and sunny yellows. For half a mile on both sides of the road, peace symbols, slogans ('Peace for Kurdistan') and vivid designs deny the ground to fighters and their arms. The artist, whose signature 'Ismiel Khayat' rides up one of his 'canvases', must have spent a year transforming the battlefield into this stony monument to pacifism. We wait here for the PUK to receive us from our KDP escorts.

If Ahmad's reception by Barzani's KDP left a foul taste, the welcome by Jalal Talabani's PUK is a wedding feast, with Ahmad as the groom. The PUK caravan of unmatched cars takes our party – Ahmad's delegates, advisors, bodyguards *et al.* – past the town of Khoi Sanjak, along rough roads through magnificent mountain passes and over a fertile plateau to the Dokan dam. At Lake Dokan, Jalal kisses and hugs Ahmad and some members of the entourage. The PUK serves tea in a reception room overlooking the lake. The two parties, Talabani's and Chalabi's, sit in a rectangle of chairs to listen to Jalal laugh and tell jokes. Talabani is always smiling. Everyone calls him Mam (Uncle) Jalal. He is big, good-natured, without pretension and eats too much. Massoud Barzani is more or less his opposite: quiet, withdrawn, ascetic, almost shy. Barzani, younger than Talabani, leads the movement and the tribe he inherited from his father. Talabani, originally a member, left the KDP to form what he called a more modern, non-tribal party. He tends to attract the middle classes, the educated and those who have lived overseas. The Barzanis depend on feudalists, farmers and herders.

After the welcome, we go to the lakeside Ashur Hotel for a banquet lunch. Talabani, at one end of a long table, tells stories. He says Kurdsat, the PUK's international satellite channel, broadcasts eighteen hours a day. 'You can have three hours a day on our television,' he says to Ahmad. Ahmad answers, 'Good. I'll take it.'

'But,' Talabani says, 'the INC must pay for it. We need the money.' He laughs, as does everyone else. His laugh is the loudest. When the fruit comes, he talks about his meetings in Washington with the Bush administration. He met a right-wing, Christian fundamentalist there.

'I said he must like this government. He said, "No. How can you like a government that has a communist like Colin Powell in it?"'

Talabani lays it on. He has heard how Barzani received the INC yesterday, he says. He makes a point of treating them with more respect and warmth. The INC and PUK were driven out of Erbil together in 1996, when Barzani turned to Saddam for help in the Kurds' civil war. That was when the INC lost a lot of people, because the CIA skipped town and left them to die. The few who escaped were taken to Guam and then to the States. It was a decisive moment for Ahmad, who stopped trusting Bill Clinton and began cultivating Washington's neo-conservatives. Talabani takes his guests outside for coffee beside an empty swimming pool. Sam and I walk down to the lake. He takes off his clothes, save for his boxer shorts, and dives in. He lasts almost a minute in the icy water and emerges blue and shivering.

When he dries and dresses, we go back to the pool. Talabani is telling his guests that he is opening a 'Speaker's Corner' in his capital, Suleimaniya. 'People can come there and curse me,' he says. Khosrat Rasul, his senior military commander, adds, 'They already do.' Once again, Talabani laughs. I remember Rasul, a brave man, from the battles in Kirkuk in 1991. He led the PUK forces into the city and fought the Iraqis, until General Schwarzkopf let them use their air power against the Kurds.

A few of us drive up the mountain to see the holiday lair of Ali Hassan al-Majid, who directed the genocide against the Kurds in the late 1980s and earned the name 'Chemical Ali'. From the front porch of his small, round, vulgar house, he must have watched the Kurds then like some Roman proconsul at Carthage. The view is unobstructed, thanks to his removal of forests and burning of houses. 'They made a desert and called it peace,' Tacitus wrote of Rome's ethnic cleansers. Zaab says it reminds him of Berchtesgaden. Rasul owns the house now and will lend it to Ahmad if he wants it.

Tamara tells me today is Sam's fortieth birthday, so I take a taxi down to Dokan town to find him a present. There are primitive shops on both sides of the only street, but all they sell are food and shoes. I find one dusty bottle of whiskey on a back shelf and buy it. We give Sam a big dinner in the hotel and sing 'Happy Birthday'. He seems to miss his fiancée, Saba, in London. We drink whiskey until late, all apart from Ahmad, who does not drink. He, Kanan and Mudhar recall their student years at Baghdad College. This was a Jesuit high school where a friend of mine, Jim Callaghan, taught until the Baath expelled the Jesuits. The college educated Iraq's mostly Muslim elite, whom the Jesuits did not try to convert. All three men loved the school. Mudhar had one bad experience, he says. He was assigned to demonstrate his command of English grammar and vocabulary in an essay the teacher set, 'It is wrong to base your success on the misery of others. Explain.' Mudhar wrote on the nuclear bombing of Hiroshima. That was too much for his Boston Jesuit teacher.

'He did not give me an F,' Mudhar says. 'He gave me an O. No one ever heard of an O. But it was much worse than an F.'

They remember the principal, Father Powers, SJ. A few years back, Kanan says, he had a call from an old man in Vermont. It was Father Powers.

'He said, "Call me Ray." I couldn't. He was Father Powers.'

Ray Powers told Kanan he had left the order, married, had two children and become a baker in Vermont.

'They were all Irish-American Jesuits from Boston,' Kanan says. 'They are why I went to MIT.'

I, too, am Jesuit-educated, but the only Catholic among these Muslims. Ahmad, despite his nostalgia for Baghdad College, condemns the Jesuits for supporting Arab nationalists at Georgetown University. He does, however, credit them for having been expelled from France.

Later, in the room, the television covers the landing of the US space shuttle *Columbia*, live; suddenly, the *Columbia* disintegrates over Texas. The crew, including an Israeli pilot, are dead.

Sunday, 2 February 2003
Palace Hotel, Suleimaniya, Northern Iraq

At the Ashur Hotel this morning, a Pasdaran delegation interrupts our breakfast. Ahmad stays behind with them, while the rest of us proceed in a long line of cars to Suleimaniya. We check into the Palace Hotel, a modern seven-storey, glass-and-marble structure that seems to be the highest in this growing city. The INC takes the whole sixth floor, and I have Room 106. Not bad: small and functional with a clean bathroom, tiny balcony overlooking People's Park and a big bed.

Tamara, Sam and I go to Suleimaniya University to meet its president, Kamal Koshnau. Koshnau, under a photo of Jalal Talabani, is proud of the university's 'academic independence' from the political leadership. Founded in 1968, the year the Baath returned to power, it moved to Erbil in 1981. Koshnau boasts that, when the university was rebuilt here in 1992, the teachers helped lay the bricks. The university has 7,000 students, about the same number of women as men. It is the largest of Iraqi Kurdistan's three universities. The others, in KDP land, are at Erbil and Dohuk. While Koshnau speaks, a television screen without sound shows a documentary. There are black-and-white shots of Gamal Abdel Nasser, smiling and waving in an open car just after the Egyptian revolution of July 1953. The new generation hoped he would expel the British imperialists – which he did – and unite the Arabs in one state – which he did not. Arab nationalism died with Nasser in 1970, superseded by the political Islam that the US used against him. Arab nationalism never did much good for the Kurds, who were no more Arabs than they were (as their neighbours insisted) Turks or Iranians.

At lunch in the hotel, the INC gang gossips about its Kurdish and American allies. I doubt they trust either of them. The hacks are gathering, too; many are at tables in the Palace lobby, near an espresso bar which makes pretty awful coffee. Michael Howard from *The Guardian* has returned to Kurdistan and to his tribal roots. Raised in Britain by his English mother, he has a Kurdish father whose family name, Hawar, became 'Howard' in London. He says KDP border guards just forced him to pay $150 to enter the country from Syria. Damn them! Michael's father supported the Kurdish movement all his life, and his grandfather sent money to Mullah Mustafa during his Soviet exile after 1946 – and still the KDP shakes him down!

Unlike his newspaper, Michael favours the war. We argue, as we have in London. The question is always 'How else can we Iraqis get rid of Saddam?' My answer is always, 'Do it yourself'. You did it in 1991, almost. This argument with the pro-war Iraqis never cuts the circle open. They do not believe they can do it on their own. I do, although it may take a little assistance from the world in the form of a countrywide no-fly zone and better weapons. If the US allowed Saddam to be indicted for war crimes and his regime to be declared culprits in genocide, the UN would be legally obliged to assist the Iraqi people in Saddam's overthrow. That is a legal argument, but no one cares about law anymore. If the Iraqis depose Saddam themselves, they can govern themselves. If the US occupies Iraq, I tell Michael again and again, Iraqis will regret it and fight back. Howard is sitting with a large man whom he introduces as the news director of Kurdsat: Azad Seddiq is a chainsmoker, dark-skinned, friendly, well-informed, a little fed up. He and Michael argue about the INC. Azad says he does not like Chalabi and asks, 'What support have they got?'

Michael answers, 'The Pentagon.'

'Puppets?' Seddiq says. 'That is very bad. They have no support from the Iraqi people, but support from America. It's bad.'

For most of the day, the ABC stringer Kevin McKiernan and I leave messages for each other. In the evening, he comes to the Palace Hotel from the Ashti, a smaller, dingy place down the road where he and several of the other hacks are staying. I expected a skinny twenty-five-year-old, the kind you often meet in war zones trying to make some money and a reputation. But McKiernan looks sixty-five, a giant with a white brush moustache and shaggy white hair to match. In a safari suit, he looks like a parody of the veteran overseas hack circa 1965. He has been here since September and knows the place well. For me to obtain local cellphones, he says, I'll need permission from the Ministry of Cooperation and Affairs. (Iraqi Kurdistan does not have a Ministry of Foreign Affairs, because it is not a state.) As for drivers, he promises to arrange everything.

I hope for a night off, but a driver arrives to take me to dinner at Barham Saleh's house. Saleh is the PUK prime minister, appointed to the post by Talabani. Leaving the hotel in a Land Cruiser, with armed guards front and back, I realise I don't know any of them. I don't really know where we are going. Could this be a kidnapping? The drive is too short for me to worry. Saleh lives in a small, two-storey house that belongs to his mother and has a few guards outside. Ahmad and his minions are already upstairs, gathered around a coffee table. Waiters serve delicious stuffed grape leaves, rice and, inevitably, *kebabs*. It is all polite welcomes rather than substantive talk. Saleh's English, like his hospitality, is impeccable. He lived in Washington for many years and is probably a few years younger than I am. His mother's stuffed cabbage and grape leaves are so good they are almost Lebanese.

Back at the hotel Sam, Kanan, Mudhar, Tamara and I go up to Goran's suite. Perhaps because he doesn't drink, Ahmad rarely joins these late-night bull sessions. Mudhar takes off his jacket. When he turns around to grab a chair, we see a holstered revolver on his belt. Tamara asks him what it's for.

He answers, 'You can have all the bodyguards. It doesn't make any difference. You can rely only on yourself. And I told myself, I will never, ever let myself be tortured again by one of those Baathist bastards.' Mudhar and I are becoming friends.

Many whiskeys later, I am back in my spartan hotel room, alone and waiting for an operator to connect me to London. This is old-time journalism: out of touch and in the thick of something I don't understand, waiting for a war I don't want.

Monday, 3 February 2003
Palace Hotel, Suleimaniya

Ahmad is vanishing for 'secret' talks with Massoud Barzani, Jalal Talabani and Abdel Aziz al-Hakim somewhere on the KDP side of Kurdistan. This gives his family and colleagues a respite from banquets. He hopes to return with an agreement on the provisional/transitional government with seven or eleven elders and a cabinet of twenty-one. The driver McKiernan sends is a pleasant young man named Irfan, but he has a withered right arm and a bad limp. A Kurd, he speaks neither Arabic nor English. His old saloon car is not much use on the road. I cannot use him for long; he would be a danger to us and to himself in a conflict.

Covering this war will be easier, it seems, than the last one here. The communications are better. The Kurds have what amounts to a state, and what the state does not provide, Kurdish businesspeople do. There are two mobile telephone networks, one on each side of Kurdistan. Both are on the British system, dialled from abroad with the British +44 code. For anyone in London, it is a local call. But neither half of Kurdistan can call the other. In 1991, it was cleft sticks over the borders to Iran and Syria. Now, the networks have satellite dishes to transmit video and live footage of their correspondents looking brave. If these fail, Kurdsat will make its facilities available. Hiro Talabani, Jalal's chainsmoking wife, tells me at the station's studios above Suleimaniya that she will help ABC any way she can. Her station has two satellite paths, one of which Kurdsat uses for its international transmissions for about twelve hours a day. The other is always free. She makes coffee in her office for me and Azad. Azad, who hosts a weekly interview programme, says Suleimaniya's 'Speaker's Corner' opened in Azadi ('Freedom') Park today. As expected, the first speaker got up and denounced Jalal Talabani. Hiro thinks it is very funny.

Spent most of today talking politics with Kurds, who – unlike their brethren under Saddam's rule to the south – are outspoken and relaxed. Michael Howard returns from Halabja with the first battle story of the war. He was in the PUK's headquarters when a shell from the Ansar al-Islam group landed nearby. One *Peshmerga* took some shrapnel in his arm. Michael, some hours later, is still excited. (We all get excited when shells hit and we live.) I experiment with the hotel's Indian food. The grilled meat and rice tastes more Kurdish than Punjabi, but it's not bad. Someone says the chef is Iranian. No chutney, but this could be the best restaurant in town.

Tuesday, 4 February 2003
Palace Hotel, Suleimaniya

Today Mudhar says he is in touch with Sunni officers of the Iraqi army, who want to maintain contact with Ahmad. We discuss his war plans, and he says the INC is building an armed force to go into Baghdad. 'We must be in Baghdad,' he says. He assures me that, when the advance begins, my ABC crew and I can follow. It would be something to be the first journalists into Baghdad. Apart, that is, from those who are already there. McKiernan's driver Irfan arrives at nine o'clock, but I have no work for him. Most of my appointments are within walking distance, and I like to walk. I ask him to return at three o'clock to take me to Chamchamal, a town on the road to Kirkuk. The checkpoint outside Chamchamal is the extent of PUK-held territory, and I need to do some reconnaissance there to find a good position to film any US bombardment of Iraqi positions beyond. Fabrice, Don and I were there in 1991, and I went back there a year later. Azad and I go to lunch at a popular restaurant on Suleimaniya's main street. Azad is smart, cynical and funny. He is barely thirty, looks forty and loves his food. He hates the Baath Party, but distrusts the US. He asks if I will do an interview with him on Kurdsat. Why not?

There is no driver at three for my trip to the front line at Chamchamal. I call McKiernan, who doesn't know where Irfan is. We agree to fire him. I postpone Chamchamal to tomorrow and content myself with a long walk in the bazaar. People crowd the marketplace for fresh meat and vegetables, but there is not much on sale that is locally made. There is a surfeit of cheap bananas, which are not grown here. Everyone says the Oil for Food programme is destroying Kurdish farmers, who cannot compete with what amounts to free food from abroad. The town is livelier than during my last trips in 1991 and '92. The barbers do brisk business, teahouses are full and the appliance shops sell the same computers, washing machines and refrigerators you see in Europe.

We have dinner at Khosrat Rasul's house, where pictures of his children stare at us from the wall. Someone tells me three of his sons died, all from accidents, none in the wars. Khosrat himself has been wounded many times and has a bad eye from an Iraqi chemical attack. He is a warrior turned politician, always in a dark suit rather than the uniform he wore when I first encountered him during the 1991 uprising. Eighteen men, Tamara and a Swiss woman journalist take their places at Khosrat's dining table for a feast of stuffed vegetables, rice and *kebabs*. I am seated between the bearded Nibros Kazimi, an American-raised Iraqi who works for the INC in Washington, and the Swiss woman. She writes for the *Frankfurter Allgemeine Zeitung* and is married to the Swiss ambassador to Tehran.

Nibros says, 'I've spent five years in Washington fighting the American administration. There is no institutional difference between Clinton and Bush. They do not want Iraqis involved in Iraq. They do not listen. They will be defeated by Muslim fanatics.'

Barham Saleh, also there, is believed to be Khosrat's rival for power. After Khosrat fought in the 1996 civil war with the KDP to save Suleimaniya from Barzani's forces, Talabani made him Prime Minister of the PUK area. A few years later, Talabani told him he was going to reunite the two halves of Iraqi Kurdistan, making Barzani's nephew the prime minister with Khosrat as his deputy. Khosrat resigned at once, unwilling to serve under a youngster with no military credentials. Talabani then appointed Saleh Prime Minister. The reunification did not take place, and everyone says it was Talabani's ruse to get Khosrat to resign.

After dinner, Ahmad scoffs at Tony Benn, the former British Labour Party minister and retired MP who is interviewing Saddam Hussein on television. We watch it in Khosrat's cavernous sitting room. I like and admire Benn, but the interview is embarrassing.

Wednesday, 5 February 2003
Palace Hotel, Suleimaniya

Mudhar, a driver, an armed INC guard and I drive to Chamchamal, a ramshackle village built around the mound of an ancient and crumbling citadel. We drive past the PUK checkpoint for half a mile until we are within sight of the first Iraqi army post almost a mile further on and get out of the car. This is empty land, with grass and rock on both sides of a road that disappears between two hills. Kirkuk and its oil are twenty miles away. The main town on the way there is Karahanjir. In 1991, the Kurds of Karahanjir arrested Don, Fabrice, Gwynne Roberts and me. They were in a panic. Minutes before we arrived, Iranian Mujahideen-e-Khalq irregulars had shot up the town: Kirkuk was falling back into Iraqi hands, and Saddam had unleashed these Iranian stooges on the Kurds. Convinced we were Mujahideen, they announced they were going to execute us. Qassem Dergham, that master fixer, calmed them and persuaded their officers we were not Iranian.

Mudhar leans on the car and lights a cigarette. This is his first sight of an Iraqi soldier since he escaped from Baghdad in 1986. A long queue of cars waits to pass the Iraqis and come into the Kurdish zone. People say the soldiers, who receive almost no pay, demand bribes to let them through. Above is a ridge, known as Bani Makan (Kurdish for 'High Plateau'), where the Iraqis are dug in. From there, they dominate the entire plain from here to Suleimaniya. If they have rockets, they could hit the city from here. But Iraqi soldiers are deserting, probably as frightened of the US Air Force as Kurdish civilians are of them. Mudhar inhales his cigarette, stares at them and shakes his head. This may be the way we'll go south, through Kirkuk and down to Baghdad, when war begins. Mudhar and I go back into Chamchamal and drive up to the empty citadel for a clear view across the valley. Fabrice filmed part of the Kurdish advance on Kirkuk in 1991 from here, before we joined their assault all the way to Kirkuk itself. We retreated along the same road.

At lunch at the Ashti Hotel, Michael Howard and I resume our argument about the American invasion. He is with a young man from the Ministry of Cooperation and Affairs named Hajhir Aref, who is working as Michael's interpreter and driver. Back at the Palace, the NBC crew has arrived from Iran and taken the whole sixth floor. McKiernan wisely takes more rooms here for ABC. At the UN, in a performance watched on a lobby television by some of the INC people and other Iraqis, Secretary of State Colin Powell presents a sound-and-light show to prove that Saddam Hussein possesses chemical and biological weapons, in violation of UN resolutions, and the means to deliver them beyond his borders. His performance contradicts former UN weapons inspector Scott Ritter, who wrote that Saddam had destroyed his WMD. I believe Ritter.

Barham Saleh welcomes the foreign press corps with a night-time banquet on the top floor of the Palace Hotel. In what could be called the Moonlight Ballroom, the prime minister promises visiting journalists free access, no censorship and any help we need. Then he says we will meet again in Baghdad. Michael and I order a bottle of whiskey and argue late into the night. Nobody wins.

Thursday, 6 February 2003
Palace Hotel, Suleimaniya

The BBC World Service reports a Pentagon announcement that 110,000 US troops are now in theatre. The Palace is so full of hacks and politicos that it looks like the old Commodore in Beirut. NBC, BBC, *The Guardian* and a legion of freelancers are down at breakfast, talking and talking. There are no newspapers to read, although Kanan has an old issue of *The New York Review of Books*. After breakfast, most of us go to the coffee shop in the lobby to have espresso (which you cannot get in the breakfast room). Nibros Kazimi asks, 'How'd you like the speech?' He means Powell's UN lecture.

One of his colleagues, who asks me not to use his name, answers, 'First of all, he could have made that speech a year and a half ago. Powell is a self-promoter. He is the one who pushed for the weapons of mass destruction path as the excuse to get Saddam. He did not want to know about al-Qa'ida. They told us to be quiet. George Tenet is the politician. He sat there and told Congress, 'We can't rule it out'. But we've told him about it for a year.'

'They're your friends,' I say.

Nibros says, 'No, they're not.'

At lunch in the garish restaurant of the Abu Sanah Hotel on the edge of town, Kurdish music blares. Goran recalls how the crowds in Suleimaniya lifted up Jalal Talabani in his car to celebrate his break with the KDP in 1966. Talabani was thin then. Now, they would have to choose between Talabani and the car – nobody could lift both. There are many stories, some of which Goran retells, of Kurd fighting Kurd. Goran's father, a KDP commander, fought against his cousin – Jalal Talabani – after the party split; the old tribals stayed with the Barzani family, the young progressives taking their chances with Talabani.

Most Kurdish war stories begin well – fierce fighting, beating the British or Iraqis in some minor engagement, and then ... the story stops. You ask: what happened next? After a while, you stop asking, because the end is always the same. The speaker laughs and says, 'And then? Then we lost and ran to the mountains.' (I've been reading the collected nonfiction of Jorge Luis Borges, who wrote that 'no one in the history of the universe has been defeated more often than the Cossacks'. He should have met the Kurds.) And still they dance and fight and drink. No one looks more warlike than a Kurdish mountaineer in his baggy trousers and turban, with a bandolier over his chest. You see them everywhere, but at this time of year they are all holding nosegays. Dana Adams Schmidt, one of the first American journalists to spend time in Kurdistan, titled his book on them *Journey Among Brave Men*. They seem to be brave and cowardly in equal measure, massing for fights and then running away. McCullin and I joined a massive offensive in 1991 at Altun Kupri that simply melted away without anyone firing a shot. We still don't know what happened. I don't see how they can lose this time, although I said the same in 1991.

Goran says Zalmay Khalilzad is inviting Ahmad to Turkey for a meeting with Turkey's foreign minister and the Iraqi Kurds. Talabani is going; Barzani is sending his son. Ahmad has yet to respond to the invitation. While Baghdad and Washington exchange insults, the discussion on Iraq's future continues in Turkey. Khalilzad told the Kurds and Abdel Aziz al-Hakim that the US would not accept a provisional/transitional government, a federal Iraq or Iraqi interference in the US's coming military administration. In the evening, Zaab says Ahmad will not meet Khalilzad in Turkey. He does not want to receive the message the American gave to the others. Ahmad will visit Iran. The Iranians, Zaab says, oppose the deployment of Turkish troops in Northern Iraq and the US's rejection of an Iraqi provisional government. Ahmad has to find support somewhere.

My crew – Fabrice and Qassem – have no visas for Iran yet. The INC is compiling a list for Iranian visas, and I add their names. I also add McCullin as well as P. J. O'Rourke, who called from New Hampshire to say he wants to come. They say it will take a week, and the visas will be issued in Paris.

Friday, 7 February 2003
Palace Hotel, Suleimaniya

Lunch at the house of Omar Fattah, a tribal leader. Jim Muir and I are the only journalists. Most of the INC group attend, with a dozen of Fattah's retainers. No one here likes the US-Turkey deal: the US sends troops through Turkey to Iraq, and Turkey occupies the border areas inside Iraq. I take notes of a long conversation with Ahmad while we wait for lunch. He says the Kurds are not the only ones against a Turkish intervention, 'One hundred thousand Iraqis would be on the streets of Baghdad to oppose the Turkish occupation of the north.'

What, I ask, about Khalilzad's insistence that there will be no Iraqi administration?

'We'll see,' he says.

Aren't the Americans just using you?

'Who's using whom?'

As a mathematician and former banker, Ahmad sees postwar Iraq's problems in economic terms. He says the country imports $14 billion a year to meet its current needs, and the cost of reconstructing postwar Iraq would be about $50 billion over the next ten years. Kuwait's war reparations from 1990–91 eat 30 percent of Iraq's oil revenues. 'It would be dumb,' he says, 'not to get the US to convene a conference in Washington on debt, reparations and sanctions.' It is vital that Iraq reclaim its share of OPEC oil production quotas, which since 1991 have gone to Saudi Arabia, Venezuela, Indonesia, Iran and Nigeria.

But, I say, oil policy would be up to the US, not the Iraqis, if the US occupies the country.

'This occupation crap,' he says. 'The US will be getting itself into serious trouble.'

Again and again, as in London, he says there must be no interruption of Iraqi sovereignty if the adventure is to succeed. 'Some people are set on this idea [occupation]. They're the usual bozos who say Arabs are incompetent – they love the Arabs, by the way – and say the only thing the Arabs understand is tyranny.'

Ahmad believes that Iraqi politicians cannot be seen to support a foreign occupation of their country. 'Given the historical record, the people who win the election will be those who oppose the US. And the US will help them win. This is the danger and the fear. Our ally here is President Bush. He said he is not going to replace one dictatorship with another. We are not going to throw out the Baath and the baby.'

Outside, the snows are melting, laying bare the dull brown mountains. The Iraqis' desire for liberation from tyranny blocks their view of what is next: US occupation, the exclusion of Iraqis from decisions and Bush-Cheney-Rumsfeld's long-term plans for the Mideast. If Ahmad favours a US invasion, it is because he believes he can outsmart them, 'We are using the Americans; 150,000 American soldiers are going to get rid of Saddam for us.' Invasion, however, means occupation. One cannot come without the other. I remind Ahmad that Amin Gemayel, President of Lebanon from 1982–87, thought he was using the Americans. (He believed the US would protect him from Syria, Iran and most of the people of Lebanon. It didn't.)

Ahmad says, 'We are not a minority of Maronites. Look at us. We are on excellent terms with Iran and the people of Iraq.'

Ahmad blames the Kurds for the US's approval of a Turkish invasion: 'If our Kurdish brothers had listened to us and not dealt with the Turks on their own and as local potentates, this would not have happened.' On the BBC this morning, Khalilzad claimed that Turkish intervention in Iraq would be for humanitarian purposes. A Turkish general contradicted him, announcing that Turkey would invade to 'protect our interests'. Turkey's interests among the Kurds are not humanitarian.

Omar Fattah, at lunch, appears to offer Ahmad support. He is a small player, but, with a few thousand loyal tribesman, a player nonetheless. I do not doubt that if someone other than Ahmad rose high in the political firmament, his loyalties would transfer to him. Ahmad probably knows this as well.

Dildar Kittani, the woman-with-a-clipboard that every war seems to cough up, comes to the hotel from the Ministry of Cooperation and Affairs. She has a car to take Borzou Daragahi, his photographer Hassan and me to a press briefing at the PUK's security headquarters. 'I know this place,' Borzou says when we arrive. 'It's where they take the political prisoners.' The chief's office is already crammed with journalists – Jonathan Landay of Knight Ridder newspapers, Chris Chivers from *The New York Times* in his lumberjack clothes, freelancer Domeetha Leuthra, Roberto di Caro from *L'Espresso*, Jim Muir in his rectangular spectacles, McKiernan and a dozen others. Like most Kurdish offices, this one has a television playing without sound. The broadcast shows Venezuela's president, Hugo Chavez, who just survived an attempted US-backed coup. Chavez, watch out. After Saddam, you could be next.

The chief of internal security, Dr Khosraw Mohammed, asks us not to film him and to refer to him as an 'official source or something like that'. Azad, pulling a Marlboro Light from his safari vest, translates for Dr Mohammed, who details a long history of Islamist groups in northeastern Iraq: Jund al-Islam, Ansar al-Islam, etc. 'These groups have sent their representatives to Afghanistan,' he says through Azad. 'They came back in August 2001 and declared themselves as Jund al-Islam [Soldiers of Islam].' He gives the names of various Jordanian and Kurdish leaders of different organisations, saying that a Mullah Krekar founded a reform faction and then sought refuge in Holland. His group became Ansar al-Islam of Kurdistan. Then came 11 September 2001 and the US invasion of Afghanistan. Hundreds of fundamentalists, many of them Arabs, fled through Pakistan and Iran to Iraq. He says, 'They thought Iraqi Kurdistan was a safe haven.'

The television leaves Venezuela for Iraq during the war with Iran in the 1980s: artillery firing, Saddam's speeches, the US Navy protecting Iraqi shipping, Iranians lying dead from chemicals sprayed on the battlefield and mass funerals. Dr Mohammed continues, 'Some 650–700 Ansar guerrillas, of whom about 150 are Arabs, have settled in villages there.' (That is, along the Iranian border near Halabja.) 'We have strong evidence that Ansar has relations with al-Qa'ida. The assassination attempt by Ansar on Barham Saleh was directed by al-

Qa'ida. Three persons were involved. Two were killed in the attempt, and the third is in prison here.' The third's name is Qais Ibrahim Qadir.

While Dr Mohammed gives details of the would-be assassin's itinerary and meetings with al-Qa'ida operatives, the television switches again: Rumsfeld is meeting Silvio Berlusconi, part of the 'new Europe' in favour of his war in Iraq. Berlusconi offers words, not Italian troops, putting himself on Washington's good-guy list without antagonising the majority of Italians who oppose the war. His legislative programme – preoccupied with bills to keep himself, and his lawyer Cesare Preveti, out of prison – leaves no time on the calendar for votes on war.

Dr Mohammed explains why he is telling us about the Islamists. 'You know the area is heading towards change,' he says. 'We are part of the Iraqi opposition and are taking part in the effort to liberate Iraq. This is part of it.' He is trying to establish the connection between Saddam Hussein and Osama bin Laden that has eluded Washington from the beginning of its Iraq crusade. If he succeeds, Washington will be grateful.

Saturday, 8 February 2003
Tower Hotel, Erbil

Another morning of tea and coffee with the Iraqi opposition leaders and the hacks at the Palace. An Iraqi from the opposition confides, 'I don't like to say this, but the Iraqi people deserve Saddam. Why? Even with what he has done, many of them, they still support him. They don't like democracy. They like the one with the stick.'

Muhammad Amin, the driver from Erbil, comes to Suleimaniya to drive me back to the dreaded Tower Hotel in his hometown. In the fields, sheep and goats graze where farmers should be planting. There is mile upon mile of untouched land with barely a tree to hold topsoil or give shade. The asphalt road rolls up and down PUK-land, left and right, more or less keeping to the centre of the valley. A blood-drenched hare lies crushed beside a sign reading 'Koya 22 Kilometres'.

Nearby, as on almost every other road in Kurdistan, a boy is selling bananas from a stack of imported boxes.

We stop for a rough lunch at a kind of truckers' café with naked cement floors and walls. After a postprandial tea, we drive over the summit to Khoya, or Khoi Sanjak, cast like seed on the plain. Here begins the foresting of Kurdistan – young cypresses and clumps of fresh pines. The road opens onto a dual carriageway, and in its central reserve baby conifers sprout no higher than a man's knee. The kerbs are painted in alternate yards of yellow and white. Khoya is a gaggle of new single-storey houses, a new mosque, old stone-and-mud houses and low walls down to the river. At the far end of town, a mother goose parades her goslings under the eucalyptus. The Kurds lounge about in paramilitary uniforms, or baggy trousers and turbans, or shabby European work clothes.

In the early afternoon we reach Erbil, capital of KDP-land and, technically, all of Iraqi Kurdistan. Muhammad drops me at the Tower Hotel, beside the ancient citadel that was, for centuries, all that there was of the city. The Tower is rundown at best, like some old downtown travelling salesman's hotel in the Midwest – except that commercial travellers here would be selling sheep. None of the staff speaks English, and only a few of the oldest retainers know any Arabic. I take the whole top floor for ABC, eleven rooms in all, and move into Room 901. When the crew arrives they can take the other rooms for themselves and we'll still have leftovers for guests. I call Qassem, who is in Beirut trying to get the KDP to help him into Iraq via Syria. He is going to liaise with Fabrice in Paris and with Bruno Roeber, a producer in London whom I don't know. I call Don McCullin in Somerset and give him Qassem's fax and telephone numbers in Beirut. He might be able to come to Iraq with Qassem through Syria, our 1991 route over the Tigris. We now have the KDP begging the Syrians to let us in that way and the INC asking the Iranians to get them in over the mountains; if they were not stateless, they would not have to ask.

The news: Kofi Annan gives a speech at William and Mary College to say that Iraq 'has not yet satisfied the Security Council it has eliminated its weapons of mass destruction'. He's in a green academic gown, perhaps receiving an honorary degree. His words should please

Washington, until he adds, 'As the United Nations, we have the duty to exhaust all possibilities before resorting to the use of force.'

Rizgar Kadir, co-owner of the Tower, and I have dinner in his second-floor restaurant. There is the standard Kurdish fare, *kebabs* and rice. Rizgar is the Milo Minderbinder of Erbil, dabbling in anything that makes money. Imports are no longer profitable. The Turks, who used to let goods through after levying a 'tax', have stopped them at the border. Several container-loads of his Pepsi Cola have been waiting on the Turkish side for weeks. Because the Kurds are raising such hell over the possibility of a Turkish intervention, Turkey is making life difficult for them. Imports from Jordan and via Baghdad have dried up as well. 'The Iraqis are bad,' he says. 'I remember the Anfal and Halabja. But we can live with the Iraqis. We cannot live with the Turks.' And if the Turks invade? 'I will fight them. I can raise a force of thirty men against the Turks right here.' He means right here in the dining room, where there are about thirty Kurds of fighting age. In Kurdistan, fighting age ranges from ten to eighty.

NATO announces that Germany and Holland will supply Patriot missile batteries to defend Turkey. But against whom? Saddam could no more attack Turkey from the south than he could Washington. Barzani is back in the country, visiting Talabani at Dokan, and Rumsfeld is in Germany. On the television, Germany's foreign minister Joschka Fischer rejects Rummy's demand for German war support. Rumsfeld says, 'Let me be clear: no one wants war.' Surely someone wants war. There are more than 100,000 US troops here for something. Fischer tells Rumsfeld of the US case on Iraq's WMD, 'I am not convinced.' UN inspectors Hans Blix and Mohamed ElBaradei have gone to Baghdad, and we'll see if they are convinced.

Most of the lights in Room 901 do not work. I take a bulb from a fixture in the front room to replace the one over my twin bed. Then I read more Borges. This is a squalid, grubby place, and I am not the first to sleep on these sheets.

Sunday, 9 February 2003
Tower Hotel, Erbil

Can there be a more morbid setting for breakfast than the cave that is the third floor of the Tower Hotel? Beige curtains hide the sun, the better to disguise the unappetising morsels of food on a long buffet table and the islets of empty tables floating above a red carpet of non-Euclidean squares and dots. The word 'squalid' approaches the feel of this place, but it misses the target. If P. J. O'Rourke gets here, he'll know what to call it. Something like 'room for a hangover'. I take a plate from a wet stack and cover it in cucumber, warmish yoghurt, processed cheese and olives topped with a stale loaf of flat Kurdish bread. No tea or coffee in sight. I look for someone who might bring coffee and make the error of glancing into the kitchen. It looks like the Sorcerer's Apprentice has just left. The floor is two inches of muddy water, and a haggard old woman is scrubbing something in a sink. I retreat to the breakfast room and give up on coffee. Someone has emailed me an article by Edward Said on Arab society and culture from *al-Ahram Weekly*. It fits the mood here: melancholy and portentous.

Before the crew arrives, I have to make sure we have all we need to cover the war. Ibrahim Haji Saleh, satellite director at the KDP's television station, has given me an early-morning appointment. Muhammad takes me to his compound in the middle of town. It looks like a militia base – bungalows, small offices, men outdoors in the sun. Haji Saleh gives me a printed price list for the station's facilities, cameras, crews, editing equipment, uplinks, live shots, satellite time. 'I'm not technical,' he says. 'I'm a journalist.' He offers help and tells me to see the technical director, Abdel Karim, in Salahuddin. We go to Korek Telecommunications opposite the Chwar Chra Hotel to buy SIM cards for myself and the crew. A young woman at the reception sends me to see the manager, who opens a briefcase filled with SIM cards for rent. I pay him $1,340 in cash, and he gives me five telephone accounts and hours of time. The pleasant efficiency of it all reminds me of the private companies and NGOs working in the West Bank and Gaza, where young people at companies like Palnet Telephones were trying to make their country work. I wonder whether, as in Palestine, it could all be taken away.

Muhammad and I have a quick buffet lunch at the Chwar Chra Hotel. He practices his English with the dictionary and teaches me more Kurdish words. My Kurdish has a longer way to go than his English. Outside, he smashes his car into a lamp post. To find a repair shop, he drives to a neighbourhood that I have to call Car Wreck City: ruined cars everywhere, body parts, old engines and open-front shops working on them. People live in shanties and survive by fixing cars. Cars line the unpaved roads, and they are stacked on roofs. The smell is oil and petrol, the sound is banging metal. Mostly the garages specialise in Volkswagens and Toyotas. Muhammad goes from one shop to another in search of the right fender for his black BMW. After an hour, he finds one. It is a perfect fit, and he leaves the car there to be repaired. But he cannot take me to Suleimaniya.

Monday, 10 February 2003
Tower Hotel, Erbil

Muhammad, in his repaired BMW, drives me at dawn to Banislawa. It looks like a Palestinian refugee camp and houses 50,000 people. Saddam dumped them here, in what he called a 'collective town', to make way for Arab settlers around Kirkuk. The rain has been falling, and ponds are forming in every unpaved road. There has been no effort to make the place permanent. Like the Palestinians in Lebanon and Jordan, these refugees believe they are going home one day. Unlike the Palestinians, victims of similar ethnic cleansing, they are probably right. Hussein Kalari, the camp's *kaimakam* – an old Ottoman title, roughly meaning 'mayor' – receives Muhammad and me in his office upstairs in the largest building in the place. The electricity is off, and what light there is drifts through the clouds outside.

'When they came here,' he says of the Kurds displaced from Kirkuk, 'they had nothing.' They don't have much now. A Japanese NGO helps with their small hospital. There are nine local schools for 10,297 students. Kalari himself is from Kalar, a town at the edge of the PUK zone facing the Iraqi front lines. He is serious, interesting, informed. 'At the opposition conference in London,' he says, 'there were talks on these people going back to their homes and on the Arabs there. Our problem is with the regime and not with the Arabs.' When the displaced Kurds return, he says, it will have to be in an orderly manner. The Arabs to whom Saddam gave their houses and farms have been living there since 1987. Many of them were coerced into leaving their own homes to become Arab pioneers on the wild Kurdish frontier and have nowhere to return. Although most of the 50,000 people in Banislawa came in 1987, at the beginning of Saddam's Anfal, more are still arriving. It seems astonishing that Saddam, trying to forestall an American invasion, would use his final months in power to continue displacing Kurds. Others are just leaving rather than fall under US bombs meant for the Arabs. Kalari says 170,000 Kurds have been exiled from Kirkuk province to the province of Erbil.

I assume he, like most other Kurds I've met, wants the war. But he doesn't, 'Any country whose military wants to come into our country, we consider as an invader. And we don't want any invader ... America's plan is not in our hands. The Americans decide.' Outside, I wander around the camp. Again and again, it reminds me of its Palestinian counterparts: breeze-block houses, the overwhelming presence of children, the 'permanent impermanence' of the place, the unreliable electricity supply, the handouts, the lack of jobs for the men, women who somehow smile and make strangers welcome. They are people displaced for another, better-armed people, like Indians on reservations. The US may invade, allowing them to return home. Is that why it is invading? Would the US do anything to allow Palestine's refugees, who have been in their camps four times longer, to go home?

I spend the rest of the day wandering in Erbil, in the slums up on the old citadel, in the bazaars and in an Ottoman palace falling to ruin. In the evening, at the Chwar Chra Hotel, I hear American slang with a Kurdish accent at the bar. I know the voice: it belongs to Subhi Shaker. Stopping on my way to the restaurant, I have a drink with this roguish Kurd. He was always talking about 'guys and gals', having a 'cool time' and 'takin' it easy'. We met in 1991, during the rebellion. Then, he called himself Subhi Rawanduzi, perhaps because his family was from Rawanduz. An out-of-work engineer, he offered to interpret for us, and he was great. We helped him escape to Turkey and on to Germany. He usually sends Christmas cards from Stuttgart to prolong thanking us. His favourite journalist is Gwynne Roberts, the Welsh documentarian who proved in 1988 that Saddam used chemical weapons at Halabja. Gwynne was with us in 1991 when we met Subhi, and they have remained friends.

Subhi slaps my back and offers me a drink. He is moving to Toronto, having had enough of Germany. His memories of the battles for Erbil and Kirkuk are more vivid than mine. He reminds me that, when the Iraqi army was coming north, I wanted to head for Iran. It was his idea, he says, to try Turkey. He tells everyone at the bar how brave I was under fire. That does not accord at all with my recollection. All I remember was running from a helicopter gunship and hiding under a bridge until it stopped bombing a Kurdish village.

When the Iraqi army came north, we all ran. I remember that Qassem had organised a fleet of cars for a press exodus ahead of the Iraqi advance. I did not want to leave without any of my colleagues, some of whom were stuck in Erbil without transport. When we left the KDP headquarters in Salahuddin, watching their jeeps evacuate with maps and Racal military radios, an American journalist told me I could not take Subhi along. She said it would create problems for the rest of us at the border. I exploded. Subhi was my friend, this was my convoy and he was coming with me – she could walk. She had not organised a single car, had not requisitioned an ounce of petrol or paid for any driver. She was there on sufferance, and I was not leaving anyone behind on her account. Subhi was grateful for my loyalty and probably worked harder than anyone to get us out safely as a result. In the mountains that night, he was the one who rented mules to carry our luggage and equipment into Turkey. Truth is: if not for us, he would not have made it to safety in Germany; if not for him, we might have died in the Iraqi onslaught. The only journalist who stayed on in Kurdistan was Jim Muir, who did the right thing by hiding out with Jalal Talabani.

Subhi and I have dinner with Michael Howard and Hajhar Arif, who have just come from Suleimaniya. Sadi Piri, newly installed

PUK representative in KDP-land, joins us. Subhi offers drivers and contacts. He is pleased that Fabrice, Qassem, Don and, especially, Gwynne Roberts are coming. He wants to work with us again.

After dinner, he takes me to his cousin's compound beside Erbil. The cousin is Salem Baradosti, a good-looking young man who studied architecture at La Sapienza in Rome and speaks beautiful Italian. (My Italian is terrible, but I can tell the difference.) Salem's father is Karim Khan, chief of the Baradosti tribe, which trades between Syria and Iraq. Before the rising of 1991, they were known as the 'Jash' – Kurdish for 'donkey', and a play on the Arabic word for 'army', *jaish*. The Jash were Kurdish auxiliaries in Saddam's army, traitors and accomplices in the genocide of their own people – Kurdish *kapos*. When the Jash turned against Saddam in March 1991, the rebellion began. Barzani and Talabani had a few thousand loyal fighters between them, but about 100,000 Jash – largely from the Baradosti and Surchi tribes – fought to force the Iraqi Arab army out of Erbil, Suleimaniya and the other Kurdish cities.

The tribes trust their leaders to choose the winning side. In 1991, Saddam was losing. They did not know the US would change tack and give Saddam permission to use helicopters, with their potential for dropping gas canisters, against them. The Barzanis as well have a history of, if not quite collaboration in arms, then of occasional cooperation with Saddam. Since 1991, the Baradostis, Surchis and other Jash tribes have fallen into the new order of Kurdish semi-independence.

A servant brings us tea, and Salem Baradosti offers to let me hire any of his fleet of Land Cruisers with drivers. The drivers have combat experience, and he has vast stores of petrol. If we need cash, he can bring dollars over the border from Syria at a commission of 1 percent. That's pretty good. In Suleimaniya, a *hawala* – money transfer – costs 5 percent. Rizgar at the Tower takes 5 percent as well. Salem, who dresses more the Roman playboy than Kurdish tribesman, moves back and forth between Syria, where his father lives, and Iraqi Kurdistan. His compound includes a palace where men sit on floors waiting to speak to their chief's son. Before I go, he gives me his satellite telephone numbers.

Tonight, lying in my dingy room trying to read in bad light, I listen to the BBC World Service. Osama bin Laden is calling for suicide attacks on Americans in Iraq. He takes a swipe at Saddam Hussein as well, calling him an 'infidel'.

Tuesday, 11 February 2003
Palace Hotel, Suleimaniya

I leave Erbil at 1030 with a driver named Tariq. Shops are closed and the streets free of cars for Eid al-Adha, the feast of sacrifice that ends the pilgrims' month of Haj. At the demarcation between PUK and KDP lands, beside the painted rocks, Sam and Kanan are standing next to their car, waiting for a PUK escort before going on. I send my taxi back to Erbil. There is no point waiting for the escort, so we drive on towards Suleimaniya in their car. Just past Dokan we see a convoy of white SUVs heading west. Ahmad is on his way to a late lunch at the Ashur Hotel. We turn around to follow. Meanwhile, Sam and Kanan describe their evening in Salahuddin with Barzani and Hoshyar Zebari. Disenchantment with the US is setting in among the KDP, who fear a US-approved Turkish invasion, and among the INC, which thinks the US is cutting it out of a credible postwar role. Ahmad arrives at the Ashur like a rock star – bodyguards, groupies and paparazzi clinging to him. After the usual huge Kurdish banquet, we drive up to a new INC house on the lake. They now have two houses. I call the new one, which is as big as a hotel, the 'Big House'. Up on the hill is Ali Hassan al-Majid's old palace, the Round House.

In Suleimaniya, Sam, Tamara, Kanan, Mudhar, Jim Muir and I have dinner in the Palace's top-floor restaurant. Below is a view of Suleimaniya, almost a modern city with blinking electric lights all the way to the hills. After a long conversation, Kanan laments, 'We started out fighting Saddam, and we'll end up fighting the Americans.'

Wednesday, 12 February 2003
Palace Hotel, Suleimaniya

Morning news: Alan Greenspan's economic forecast and a new threat from Osama bin Laden depress the world's markets. NATO meets to discuss Turkey. After breakfast, Kanan, Sam, Mudhar and a few of the other INC people argue about the Iraqi opposition's disagreements with Zalmay Khalilzad in Turkey. The INC people say the KDP and PUK – who were the only Iraqis there – briefed them on the Ankara meetings. Khalilzad is said to have proposed a US military government with an Iraqi board of advisors, a judicial commission chosen by the US to write a constitution, a constitutional convention with elected delegates to ratify the constitution and US advisors in each ministry.

'Maybe they'll design the flag,' Kanan says. 'It is an unmitigated disaster from the point of view of the United States itself. Here you had an Iraqi opposition, doing something no Arab opposition group had ever done. It worked hand in glove with the US. It openly took money. It isolated itself in the region.'

A telephone rings. Someone from the PUK calls to say Ansar al-Islam just executed the three hostages it took the other night. No one comments. Ansar is a Kurdish problem; they are worried about Iraq.

'We broke the language,' Kanan continues. 'We said Palestine is not the be-all and end-all. We said dictatorship is. The INC's declared position is for democracy and federalism and has been for many years. It worked closely as part of an opposition of Kurds, Assyrians and others. It has its failings, sure. It sits on 20 percent of Iraqi territory. The whole of this legacy is being tossed aside. And these people [the INC people around us] are going to have to oppose the United States the day after [meaning after Saddam]. And the US is driving us to use that old crappy language of anti-colonialism and anti-imperialism. So, I think they've decided to lose the opposition.' Kanan's distress is visible, as if a lover had discarded him.

Where will the US look for Iraqis to govern Iraq, if not the existing Iraqi opposition to Saddam?

'The US is going to use the existing structures of power. The regime will remain intact – the institutions, the organising structures. They're back to the politics of '91 with the exception that they know now a *coup* doesn't work. And it's the same people who wanted a *coup* in '91.'

He has coined a phrase for what the US may be seeking, 'Saddamism without Saddam.'

The US, he believes, does not care. 'I told the president and Condi Rice, "Let the Iraqis make their own mistakes. The Americans should not run the streets."'

Mudhar interrupts, 'They will be surprised at how much support we have.'

'The people who were with them for years will not accept to be cast aside,' Kanan continues. 'Khosrat Rasul on an equal footing with some guy who's just come on board in Washington? Ahmad goes back with the Barzanis to 1975. SCIRI paid a huge price in blood to fight this regime. The principle of the US dictating how things would be run is unacceptable. We are partners, allies and friends. We do not dictate to them. We should sit down together and discuss together. But they have shown us disrespect.'

What did these men expect? The US cannot regard them as anything more than instruments of American policy for American goals, even if that is not how they see themselves.

'It's not too late,' Kanan says. 'I see the Salahuddin meeting as a way for us and the US to come up with a plan, a compromise.'

Mudhar says, 'We have worked with the American administration for such a long time that we do not want to find ourselves in opposition to what a lot of people would describe as twenty-first century colonialism. All the Iraqi people will stand together against this plan.' Kanan says he will write an op-ed piece on US policy and send it to *The New York Times*.

We spend most of the morning in discussion, first at breakfast, then in the lobby coffee shop on what we would have called the car-bomb side of the Commodore Hotel in Beirut. Outside, a truck with a mounted anti-aircraft gun guards the hotel. Inside, journalists and politicos mingle at round tables, grouped by language as much as anything else. Jim is with Kaveh Golestan and other Farsi speakers. Azad Seddiq is with some Kurdish journalists and Minister of

Cooperation and Affairs Abdel Razzaq Mirza, whom I met at Latif Rashid's house in England. Abu Samih, the writer, and some of the other Shiite Arabs take another table. Jonathan Landay asks Zaab for an interview with Ahmad. Domeetha Luthra comes over from her Apple laptop and reminds Zaab he promised her an interview with Ahmad. When she returns to her table, Zaab's expression indicates she won't be interviewing Ahmad anytime soon.

Mudhar, Landay, Zaab and I drive over to Ahmad's new safe-house in town. He is having a late breakfast of buffalo cheese, honey and tea. Workmen are buzzing about to make the concrete bungalow cosy. Flames burn in the fireplace, and there is a strong smell of paint remover. Ahmad, dressed in a grey jacket and blue tie, is relaxed and, as ever, buoyant. It is as if he is immune to Kanan's pessimism over Khalilzad's plan, 'I haven't heard the plan directly. In fact, I haven't heard from the Americans since the middle of last month.'

Friends in Washington have told me that Dick Cheney complained that Ahmad's visit to Iran on his way to Iraq meant he was too close to the *mullahs*. Insofar as Ahmad understood Khalilzad's plan, what did he make of it?

'Unworkable. There is the issue of the returnees. There are millions of such people who will want to go home. Will they want to stop them? Will they want to evict the people who are living there now? And there's the oil. Who owns the oil? Will the revenues be used to pay for the occupation? Iraqis should always be responsible for Iraq.'

I repeat Kanan's misgivings to him. Again and again, he says, 'The Americans don't want allies. They want agents.'

Later, Prime Minister Saleh conducts a press conference at home to put a different interpretation on the US proposals: not as bad as first reported, with room for cooperation between the opposition and the US. Meanwhile, the press corps is growing. It's impressive that so many manage to sneak or bribe their way in from Syria, Turkey and Iran. One Turkish television reporter hid in the undercarriage of a truck and jumped out on the Iraqi side. I find him in the lobby to congratulate him. Everyone is speculating on a start date for the war. I take Umran Safter, a CNN Türk correspondent, to dinner at the Abu Sanah Hotel. She studied Arabic in Damascus and, unusually for a Turk, is something of an Arabophile. We return to the Palace and drink whiskey late with Jim and Zaab at the Indian restaurant.

Thursday, 13 February 2003
Palace Hotel, Suleimaniya

Breakfast chitchat. Fred Francis of NBC tells us which divisions are coming from which US bases and where they are going. He claims that the Pentagon plan calls for an invasion of part of Iraq before the bombing starts. Before? He works at the Pentagon and has better US military sources than I do. Perhaps he knows something. Trudi Rubin of *The Philadelphia Inquirer* joins our breakfast along with Mudhar, Zaab and Kanan. I met Trudi in Jerusalem in 1974, when we went to interview the ancient Rabbi Katzenellenbogen in Mea Shearim. The rabbi made her wear a scarf to hide her hair, and she hated it.

After breakfast, Mudhar and I have coffee and talk about Iraqi history. His family, the Shawkats, were Circassian, and an ancestor had commanded the Janissaries in Baghdad. The cousin of his great-grandfather, Mahmoud Shawkat Pasha, was an Ottoman prime minister and a defence minister at the turn of the last century. In 1909, he was part of the movement to overthrow Sultan Abdul Hamid. Mudhar believes he was assassinated in 1913 on the orders of the Sultan, possibly in revenge. Naji Shawkat, his great-uncle, served as prime minister in 1932 and 1933. Another cousin, Hikmet Suleiman, was prime minister in 1936. Mudhar's grandfather headed the Fatoua movement, 'something between the army and the boy scouts', at the end of the 1930s. He was also the minister of education. Another Shawkat, Saab, was the royal physician until the revolution of 1958. Mudhar's father, Ghassan, studied agronomy at MIT and stayed out of politics. Mudhar himself was born in Baghdad in 1950. After studying at Baghdad College, he took his undergraduate degree at Mosul and his PhD from Newcastle. Arrested by the Baath and tortured in 1968, he stayed away from the country until 1980. He returned, he says, for the war with Iran. He joined the army, serving six years. Politically suspect, he fled – first to Iran, then to Britain. He now lives in British Columbia.

Ahmad attends another lunch in search of tribal support. His host today is Hama Haji Mahmoud, known to most people as Kaka (Brother) Hama. His tribe controls a large area around Halabja, but his modern guise is Chairman of Iraqi Kurdistan's Social Democratic Party (SDP). (In Lebanon, the Druze feudal lord Walid Jumblatt heads the Progressive Socialist Party: distinguishing tribe from party can be as difficult as it is pointless.) Kaka Hama has what seems to be the typical townhouse for a Kurdish politician, a large cement bungalow with vast reception rooms and lots of staff. A ceiling fan revolves on this cool late-winter afternoon. Bouquets of plastic roses and tulips sit on a desk next to a small SDP flag. Kaka Hama's legs stretch wide apart, as if he were still in tribal trousers. His double-breasted brown suit does not hide a gut borne of years of plenty. We await lunch in his sitting room, altogether a score of his men and a dozen of Ahmad's, almost all in dark suits with a few of the Kurds in baggy trousers and turbans. The chairs and stuffed sofas are pushed against pale blue walls. Some of the men pinch worry beads while their leaders talk to each other in Arabic. The issue today is Ansar al-Islam.

'The PUK brought Ansar to this area,' Kaka Hama says. 'The PUK asked us, "Why are you fighting them?" We don't want them here. They were brought here because they fought against the KDP.'

It seems that, when Barzani's KDP expelled the Islamists, Talabani let them set up in Kaka Hama's tribal area near Halabja. This led to fighting between the Social Democrats and the fundamentalists. Kaka Hama says the Ansar people are not to be trusted, 'Three days before they massacred forty-two PUK people, the PUK sent them guns and money. For two months, I said this on Kurdsat.' He also says the Taliban trained Ansar Kurds in Afghanistan. The fundamentalists call his people *kafir* (infidels) because of their socialism.

At lunch in the dining room, Kaka Hama plunges his huge hands deep into slabs of meat and pulls out chunks for his guests. The meat and rice are greasy and tasty. Ahmad says Zalmay Khalilzad is warning the Kurds not to allow any *Peshmergas* into Kirkuk. Nor are the Kurds to stage a 'spontaneous' uprising there. The US does not want displaced Kurdish families returning, either. It seems, Ahmad says, the US promised Turkey a strip of Iraqi Kurdistan. 'There is no information

Outside the ancient citadel of Erbil, 2002. The statue commemorates Ibn Mustafa, a great Kurdish poet.

Camera crews and US soldiers, Northern Iraq, 2002.

Women returning from prayer in New Halabja, Iraqi Kurdistan.

Kurds gather in Erbil to oppose a threatened Turkish invasion in March 2003.

A woman in the bazaar, Suleimaniya, Kurdish Iraq.

A Kurdish wedding party gathers by the road between Erbil and Salahuddin for a picnic in March 2003 – a tradition that continued despite the onset of war.

Peshmergas from Jalal Talabani's Patriotic Union of Kurdistan train on the outskirts of Suleimaniya, in March 2003.

Wreckage from the 1991 Gulf War in the desert near Nasiriya, twelve years later.

Ahmad Chalabi (fifth from left) is hosted by sheikhs of the Ghizzi tribe, near Nasiriya, in 2003. To his left is his daughter Tamara; next to her is Chalabi's special advisor, Mudhar Shawkat; at far right is US military liaison Col. Ted Seel.

A crowd in Nasiriya cheers Ahmad Chalabi's arrival in April 2003. Saddam Hussein's regime had just been deposed in that region.

Ahmad Chalabi addresses 5,000 Nasiriya citizens from the balcony of the former governor's residence. Although he proclaimed a free Iraq, Chalabi stopped short of declaring himself a candidate for its leadership.

Ahmad Chalabi after addressing the crowd in Nasiriya in April 2003. Next to him is his trusted bodyguard Hussein, a former nightclub bouncer. In the foreground are members of the FIF.

A religious sheikh who accompanied Ahmad Chalabi and his entourage to Nasiriya in April 2003, where the sudden appearance of a crowd of a jubilant Shiites caused unnecessary alarm.

Col. Ted Seel, US political and military advisor to the Free Iraqi Forces (FIF), in April 2003.

on how many Kurds are coming or when,' he adds. 'Nor anything on whether the Turks will be part of a US force, or independent. The Turks requested that the Kurds commit in front of the Americans that they would not do anything against them.' Kaka Hama does not like what he is hearing. Ahmad's rendition of Khalilzad's directives to the PUK and KDP echoes the one I heard from Hoshyar earlier. Hoshyar doesn't like it either.

Ahmad is almost giving a speech, 'As allies and friends of the US, we'll work together to liberate Iraq. But we are not agents. We are going to elect a leadership of opposition in Salahuddin to coordinate the liberation and administer change. I don't want a vacuum of sovereignty for any period during the change. We agreed this in Dokan ten days ago with Jalal, Massoud and al-Hakim. Their spokesmen say something different to the press and appear to support direct military rule by the US. That is very dangerous for the future of Iraq and very dangerous to the gains the Kurds have made in the last few years.'

Kaka Hama responds with a speech of his own, 'Turkey has always been upset at having Mosul Vilayet taken away in the First World War. Turkey is ready to seize on any weakness in Iraq and take what it thinks belongs to it. And the Americans are being nice to it. One of the problems is the relationship between the KDP and PUK. They don't trust each other. Each suspects the Turkish intervention is a trap being laid by the other side. The US can thus manipulate this. Iraqis should determine the future of the country. We thank the Americans for their help and support, but we do not support those who want to take a single inch of our land. When they tell us not to go to Kirkuk and Mosul, what guarantees will the US give us that the Turks will not go there?'

He says displaced Kurds have the right to return home. The PUK and KDP cannot stop them. Then he gives Ahmad what he wants. 'We will coordinate militarily with the INC, when they establish bases. Please feel that our troops are your troops. We have people in both Kurdish areas and inside government-controlled territory. They are ready to begin marching at zero hour.'

It is almost four o'clock when we return to the sitting room. More politicking. Ahmad invites Kaka Hama to a meeting with the four main parties – INC, KDP, PUK and SCIRI – before the opposition conference begins in Salahuddin. Sam, Kanan and Mudhar are leaving for Salahuddin tomorrow to coordinate with the KDP and PUK. 'The Iraqi opposition has fought the regime for a long time,' Ahmad reminds his audience, 'even when the United States supported the regime. Hence, no one should brush aside that opposition and take decisions for the country on his own. The powers will respect us if we stand for our rights and will disrespect us if they find us cowardly and compromising in terms of what we have fought for – our belief in the future of Iraq.'

Back at the Palace, Zaab says, 'The Kurds have rejected the provisional government idea at America's request.' So much for Iraqi unity.

That night, they screen a film for the journalists called *Jian* (*Life*), in the hotel mezzanine. The director, a tall, gaunt man named Jano Rosebiani, sits in the audience. *Jian* is the story of a young Kurdish teacher who returns from exile to build a clinic in Halabja. The village and its people remain scarred by the chemical attack of 1988. It is peopled with wonderful characters, including the melancholy Mullah Rostom. He lost his wife and his eight children to Saddam's poison gas and does not speak. Instead, he sits on a flat roof playing the flute. When the local religious fundamentalist condemns him for making music, in violation of a very strict form of Islam, the woman next door beats the fundamentalist with her broom. The neighbours cheer her on. One man explains to the visiting teacher, 'They have turned God into a dictator.'

The hero, insofar as the film has one, is Sherko the shoeshine boy, aged eight or so. He asks the visiting teacher, 'Mamosta [Teacher], are there chemical attacks in America?' A woman blinded by poison gas says, 'It smelled like apples and oranges.' When the teacher visits a hospital, we see for the first time real victims of the sarin and VX gases that the Western world denied Saddam had used. They are badly disfigured, some unable to move. At the sight of them, the Kurdish girl next to me cries.

Kanan says the White House called him this evening. They are asking him not to publish the op-ed piece, 'Saddamism without Saddam', which he has written for *The New York Times*. His White

House contact told him, 'We are working on the policy.' Kanan agrees to delay publication for twenty-four hours.

Friday, 14 February 2003
Palace Hotel, Suleimaniya

Whatever is happening here or at the UN does not hit me as hard as my son George's call from London tonight. He says that Orlando Sesti, the youngest child of my friends Sarah and Giugi Sesti, died in a car accident. Two other boys were killed with him, and a fourth was injured. George is devastated. They were good friends. I love the Sestis, who were my neighbours in Tuscany, and cannot bear this for them. Orlando was the same age as my younger son Edward, twenty-two. He was an original, wild, creative and woman-loving kid whom I've known since he was ten.

It is the end of dinner at the hotel's Indian restaurant. Most of the hacks have left, and only Jim Muir and I are there. I think of Orlando and of his family, and I weep inside. Jim and I go outside in the rain for a walk along the boulevard. We see that the KDP, expelled from here in 1996, is reopening its offices. The sign above the building, in huge letters, says, 'Kurdistan Democratic Party – Forth Brunch'. Any other night, I would laugh.

Saturday, 15 February 2003
Palace Hotel, Suleimaniya

Breakfast at the INC safe-house in a quiet Suleimaniya neighbourhood with Ahmad, Tamara, Nibros and Zaab: buffalo cheese, honey and tea. Ahmad shows us the new blanket Tamara found for him in the bazaar: Tom and Jerry on a red field. It makes him laugh. He reads passages from a new biography of Gertrude Bell, *The Desert Queen*. The Naqib, a religious leader in Baghdad, told Miss Bell on 6 February 1919:

> You are the governors and I am the governed. And when I
> am asked what is my opinion as to the continuance of British

rule, I reply that I am the subject of the victor. You, Khatun, have an understanding of statecraft. I do not hesitate to say to you that I loved the Turkish government when it was as I once knew it. If I could return to the rule of the Sultans of Turkey as they were in former times, I should make no other choice. But I loathe and hate, curse and consign to the devil the present Turkish Government. The Turk is dead; he has vanished, and I am content to become your subject.

Ahmad reads some more of their conversation and laughs when he comes to the Naqib's thoughts on his own people, the Shiites:

But I tell you to beware of the Shi'ahs. I have no animosity against the Shi'ah sect. They love and respect me, and I am regarded by them as their Sheikh. But turn your eyes on the pages of history and you will see that the salient characteristic of the Shi'ahs is their *khiffah* [volatility]. Did they not themselves murder Musa ibn Ali whom they now worship as a God? Idolatry and mutability are combined in them. Place no reliance on them.

As it happened, the British didn't rely on the Shiite majority. They imposed a Sunni government and ignored the Naqib's view that the Hashemites of Hejaz would not be welcomed as Iraq's kings, 'Our politics, our trade, our agriculture are all different from those of the Hejaz.' The Naqib, as Ahmad read, told Bell he 'would rather a thousand times to have the Turks back in Iraq than see the Sharif or his sons installed here.' The next year, Britain installed the Sharif's son as King Feisal. Within a month, the Shiites, Sunnis and Kurds rebelled against the British.

We drive to the new house in Dokan, where more furniture is in place and carpenters are assembling cabinets for the INC staff. At a press conference down the hill, Talabani declares his opposition to the US proposals for governing Iraq.

Asla Aydintasbas, a Turkish journalist who lives in New York, comes to lunch at the Ashur Hotel with Zaab, Tamara and Hussein the bodyguard. Hussein tells fascinating tales of his three-year exile from Iraq. He was arrested and held in airports and prisons in Saudi

Arabia and Yemen, hiding in safe-houses all over the Middle East and Armenia, trying to stay in touch with his family in Baghdad. He says the Yemeni prison was filthy, the Saudi one clean and modern. In the Saudi prison, however, he was required to pray and read the Qur'an. Before he fled Iraq, he was a Republican Guard. In London, he worked as a nightclub bouncer. I must have seen him guarding the door to China White in Soho. Somehow, he ended up with Chalabi. So did another bodyguard, Samih, who lives in Wembley. Although Iraqi-born, Samih has a North London accent and plans to return to Britain when this is over. He, too, was a bouncer.

After lunch, Ahmad and I talk for hours at the Big House by the lake. Mostly we disagree about an American invasion. I return to Suleimaniya in the dark and have another Indian dinner at the hotel with Jim and Zaab. The television news broadcasts demonstrations against the war, an estimated 8 million people in sixty cities. After dinner, I call Sophie and George, who were both on the London march.

Sunday, 16 February 2003
Palace Hotel, Suleimaniya

On Sunday morning here, the last peace march is taking place in Sydney, Australia. No war has brought so many onto the streets before troops have been committed to battle. What would millions marching through Vienna, Berlin, Paris and London have achieved in 1914? But they did not question then. They had the vote, apart from the half who happened not to be men. They did not take part in political decisions; their role was to serve and to obey.

People are less docile now, many of them, and there are enough veterans of the protests that slowed and ended the American war in Vietnam to remind the rest that stopping a war is possible. It took from 1963 to the late 1960s, about five years, for the anti-war campaign (aided by disgusted American soldiers who joined the protest movement) to reach the critical mass that cost Lyndon Johnson the New Hampshire primary and led to the Paris peace talks. The movement against the war in Iraq started fast and is gaining speed. But the momentum is not affecting leaders who are determined, whatever the pretext, on war.

Peace Day in Europe, the US and Australasia was a success in terms of mobilising mass opinion, a failure at changing the outcome. How long will people accept the futility of political action? When will they seize power?

The INC delegates have gone to Salahuddin to negotiate with Barzani and will then settle into their two Dokan houses. Without them the Palace is emptier at breakfast time. This morning, the only person in the breakfast room is Borzou. I sit at another table to read, and he comes over to say he is writing a piece for his 'other clients' (including *Newsday* and *The San Francisco Chronicle*) on Chalabi and the INC. He doesn't like the INC. He says they are always whispering, conspiring and sneaking around corridors. They don't confront anything, he says, and they're cowards. What do I think? Not much, I say. What I do not say is that I like them and wish them well. It is not my place to call them names, even if I am opposed to the war they want.

I take my clothes to the laundry in the bazaar. Every time I let the hotel laundry handle them, things disappear or are returned torn. Perhaps an outside laundry can do better.

Turkish coffee with Jim, Asla and Tamara in the lobby café. Jim is driving to Erbil with Kaveh Golestan for the opposition committee conference in Salahuddin. The meeting is postponed from 15 to 19 February. I assume it will be delayed again. Asla says she is looking for Turcomen to interview for her Turkish newspaper, *Saba*. Tamara is in town to collect her clothes from the local safe-house to take to Dokan. A big television by the window blasts Arabic music videos, while rain floods the streets outside. The PUK soldiers manning the curbside anti-aircraft gun are wet and bored. Their job is to protect the Palace Hotel, if not from Saddam or Ansar al-Islam, then from its disgruntled guests. John Hemmings of Reuters says he has rented a house for $350 a month. The place is rough, but near an internet café. He runs a high-speed cable connection from it to the house. Now he needs to buy furniture. Reuters must be planning for a long war – or a long wait.

Osama bin Laden has issued a statement through the Lebanese daily *al-Hayat* urging Muslims to wage *jihad* against the 'Crusaders' who are sabotaging the world. He calls Bush 'this century's pharaoh'. The BBC says people in the US are buying supplies, chemical suits, duct tape and water in preparation for an attack by Iraq. Why don't they hide in those fallout shelters they built in the 1960s against the Soviet menace? President Bush's radio address assures Americans that he is 'standing watch twenty-four hours a day in the war against terrorism'. Condoleezza Rice tells Fox Television that the US does not need another UN resolution to invade Iraq, because it has the authority to wage war under Resolution 1441. That is not what Tony Blair told the British. Then, again, who cares what he tells the British? He'll go along with or without a resolution, with or without evidence of Saddam's chemical and biological weapons programmes and with or without the support of the British public.

Monday, 17 February 2003
Palace Hotel, Suleimaniya

Dildar Kittani, the clip-board woman from the Ministry of Cooperation who trawls the corridors of the Palace looking for journalists to help, interrupts my morning's reading in the lobby café to ask me about Kevin McKiernan. In confidence, she says, she believes he works for the CIA. I say I doubt it. He's a little old, doesn't speak Kurdish and does not seem to be recruiting anyone. I explain to her that ABC hired him on contract to do camerawork for them, because he arrived in October when the network had no one here. She seems to understand, but I cannot be sure.

For lunch, I go with Ahmad, Tamara and Zaab to Khosrat Rasul's house for a mass Kurdish banquet, all the foods, the stuffed vegetables, the rice of different types, the roast lamb, the *kebabs*, spread on an Olympic pool of a table. They are in fulsome mood, these Arabs and Kurds, allied for now in the battle against Saddam. For a few minutes, Ahmad and Rasul retire to a corner for whispered discussions. We meet a Kurdish war veteran named Mam Rostom, who wears the

baggy trousers and loose shirt of the Kurdish mountaineer. They say
he is a real soldier, close to his men, honest and tough. When lunch
is over, he drives away in an old Land Cruiser.

I spend the afternoon wandering through the bazaar. Mariwan the
'barbar' gives me a shave. When I return to the Palace, McKiernan
approaches me in the lobby. We sit at a table in the café. He is angry.
It seems Dildar went to his hotel this morning to announce that
I told her he did not work for ABC. That is *not*, I say, what I told
her. He does not believe me and moans for some time, ending each
sentence with, 'I don't understand how you can say such a thing!'.

Luckily, Dildar is in the hotel. I ask her to join us; she pleads
other duties, but I insist, and she sits between us. I ask whether I said
McKiernan did not work for ABC. She says no. McKiernan looks
shocked and angrier. She must have told him something; why else
would he be doing this? She could hardly tell *me* I said something I
had not. She complains we are putting her in an impossible position
and leaves. I say that ends the matter; McKiernan persists. What
more does he want? I say I never said it; she says I did not say it; he
believes I said it. I tell him if he wants to accuse me of lying, he can
resign right now. (ABC has been asking me to fire him, but I have not
until now had the heart to do it.) He withdraws the accusation, but I
see we are not going to work together.

In the evening, Wendy Steavenson, a freelance journalist for *The
Daily Telegraph*, and I plan to have dinner at the Abu Sanah. We are
outside the Palace hailing a taxi when Mam Rostom staggers out.
He blocks us from getting into the taxi. I ask the driver to wait, and
Rostom orders him to leave. This is for our safety, he says. The driver
obeys Rostom, there with his bodyguards, rather than me, and drives
off. Rostom forces us into the back of his Land Cruiser and jumps
in beside Wendy. He asks me in Arabic why I take taxis, saying the
drivers could be bad people. I say they have always been fine. We
argue back and forth on taxi safety until he whips out a .45-calibre
pistol and shoves it against my temple. He asks, 'What would you do
if one of them did this?' I have taken fifty taxis here, I say, and so far
the only person to do 'this' is him.

His driver drops us at the Abu Sanah, and my only fear now is that

Rostom will stay for dinner. He seems to have a more than avuncular interest in Wendy. He does not stay, thank God, but warns us not to take a taxi back. Over a long dinner of many *kebabs* and Iraqi *arak*, Wendy says she spent two years in Tbilisi. It gave her a lot of hangovers, a love of the Georgians and a book called *Stories I Stole*. We go back in a taxi.

Tuesday, 18 February 2003
Palace Hotel, Suleimaniya

Marcus Wilford of ABC in London says all ABC crews who are to be 'embedded' in American units are being 'called up' tonight. War is coming. Noam Chomsky emails to say he believes it might yet be prevented, but I don't see how. I hire Hazhar Arif, who worked for Michael Howard until he left, to drive and interpret. He seems like a good kid. He tries to drive Asla, Wendy and me to Dokan for dinner this evening in his black Mazda. The raging snowfall makes the road invisible and impassable. We call Ahmad, Tamara and Zaab to cancel and turn back. An hour later, we are at the hotel's Indian restaurant again, eating chicken *tikka* and drinking Turkish Efes beer. My main preoccupation now is obtaining visas for my crew. It will be impossible to cover the war without them. There is no word from the Iranian embassy in Paris. David Westin, the president of ABC News, is having dinner with Iran's UN ambassador in New York to ask for his help. ABC is also trying Turkey, where rumour has it the border may open to journalists. Syria isn't letting anyone over the Tigris, apart from the enterprising hacks without equipment who pay border patrols to look the other way. Sam, Mudhar and Kanan are still in Salahuddin with the KDP.

Wednesday, 19 February 2003
Palace Hotel, Suleimaniya

BBC News this morning: Israel kills eleven Palestinians in Gaza when it invades the Strip again. I spend the morning at the Ministry of Cooperation. Abdel Razzaq Mirza introduces me to some people from a battered women's protection organisation and, later, Minister of Public Works Sadi Dezayee. Mirza is informative on the PUK area's infrastructure and economic problems. More interestingly, he makes a passionate case for war. He says all Iraqis want the US to invade, 'They want it because they know the cost is cheaper than continuing this regime. This is not poetry. How many lives have we lost in Iran, in the marshes, in Kurdistan, even in Tikrit? ... If Saddam Hussein goes on, how many wars are ahead of us?'

In the afternoon, Wendy and her driver-interpreter Omer take me through the bazaar to the Chai-khana Shaab (People's Teahouse). It is a loud, vibrant place where men squeeze into concrete banquettes and chairs to play cards, dominoes and backgammon, or to talk. Mostly, it's talk. There is a tiny bookshop in one corner and a big stove with teakettles bubbling nearby. Wendy introduces me to a fascinating character, Hama Ali Khan – film director, writer, storyteller, poet. He is also, I see in his face, a drinker. Here he drinks tea and shares his rich imagination with his friends. We drink tea and listen to Ham'ali (as he says we should call him), who is free of inhibition. Later, when the teahouse is closing, he says he is going on for a real drink. I go back to the hotel and have dinner at the Indian restaurant. My companion is a book of English short stories I found in the bazaar.

Thursday, 20 February 2003
Palace Hotel, Suleimaniya

Jonathan Landay tells me a bit about himself over lunch today at the Ashti Hotel. His father was the Westinghouse Broadcasting correspondent in London in the 1960s. Jonathan went to the eccentric Hill House School behind Harrods and then a boarding school in Surrey, until his father was posted back to the States. He met his wife when she was working as a translator in Yugoslavia. They now live with their one son in Washington. She is half-Croatian and half-Serb, a real Yugoslav, now without a country. Landay's job with Knight Ridder is Pentagon correspondent. He misses his wife and son, but plans to be home for the boy's birthday in April. Sounds optimistic.

Hajhar and I go to the Komolaiti Club in Azadi Park for a drink. It's a social club for the PUK elite, a big, stucco cylinder where small children roam the dark restaurant wreaking havoc while their parents eat. Meanwhile, negotiations go on: the US, Turkey and the Kurds; Turkey and the Iraqi oppositionists; the opposition among themselves; and, far away, France, Russia, Germany and Belgium, who attempt to delay and to distance themselves from the war.

Friday, 21 February 2003
Palace Hotel, Suleimaniya

Jonathan takes me with him to the PUK's Suleimaniya Security HQ to meet Ali Kadir Jadir. A forty-five year old tank mechanic and master sergeant in the Iraqi army, Jadir deserted his unit in Kirkuk in late January. A PUK guard brings him to a small office off the courtyard to speak to us. He is not exactly a prisoner, but not quite free either. He sits next to one of the metal desks. Jonathan gives him a carton of Rothman's cigarettes to thank him for speaking to us. Through his interpreter, Jonathan asks Jadir if he is speaking to us voluntarily. He smiles and answers yes. 'Feel free to smoke,' Jonathan says. 'We're journalists, not interrogators.'

Jadir, with some but not much questioning from us, recounts his story in Kurdish. 'I was in Battalion 34,' he begins, leaning an elbow on the desk beside him. He pauses long enough between statements for the interpreter to translate. 'From 1974, I have been in the army, but not continuously. This is the fourth time I've deserted. *Wallahi* ['By God'], I was a professional, and it was not easy for them to replace me. They let people in this job retire at age fifty-five.'

He says he was trained to maintain Soviet-manufactured T-55 and T-62 tanks, models more than twenty years old. He says the army has not received anything newer.

'It is rare to get spare parts. Our unit has twenty-eight tanks, and 128 personnel. That is the standard. Out of the twenty-eight tanks, only four work properly.'

Don't they have spare parts?

'Sometimes. From the Taji military plant outside Baghdad. Once in two or three months. The main problem is that we were not given the proper amount of oil, because the officers would sell our oil supplies. They would sell new spare parts and give us used spares. They would sell it to the industrial plant near Mosul. It greatly affected our abilities in the field. When we asked the officers how to handle the situation, they would say, "You have to do your best to make it work".'

He and the other mechanics cannibalised old tanks to keep the newer ones working. 'Or we would send them to Baghdad for repair and they would not come back. The most we have is four [working] tanks, because we ran out of batteries and electronic spare parts. Of course, the tanks of the Republican Guards are different. The Republican Guards have T-72s that are quite developed. The Republican Guards have all their tanks functioning. Their tanks are cared for more than ours. Even their personal weapons are better. So are their clothes, food and salary.'

Will the Iraqi army fight?

'The Republican Guards will fight seriously. The regular army won't fight. My friends in the unit are looking forward to the day when the Americans will start the war and they can surrender. Most soldiers would like to come to Kurdistan. Big numbers have already deserted.'

Jadir deserted on 28 January, about three weeks ago. Thirty-five of his colleagues had already fled. He says fewer soldiers will risk being shot fleeing, when they can just wait and surrender.

'When we were working during the day, we would say, "We are doing all this work and we are not respected". We asked why the Americans are not coming to destroy the Iraqi government. We would speak in front of our friends, not the informers. We knew who they were in our unit. Every unit had military security and military intelligence. The only thing they can do is to flee. Their faces will become black [meaning 'they will be shamed']. I think three out of four will seek revenge on those people.'

Jadir had pretended to be an Arab. 'When I rejoined the army after the October [2002] amnesty, they discovered I was a Kurd. They summoned me to battalion command. I said I was not a Kurd from Kirkuk, but from Suleimaniya. So, I would avoid the mistreatment they would give to people from Kirkuk. I was under close surveillance, because I was a Kurd. I think they wanted to get rid of me.'

The telephone in my jacket pocket rings. Fabrice says he is on the road from Adana to Diyarbakir in Southeast Turkey. Don, Bruno the producer, Andy Lewis the tape editor and soundman Bob Harle are with him on a bus in Turkish Kurdistan. They should be here soon. That is good news. For one thing, we can do interviews like this on camera.

Jadir continues, 'I was the only Kurd in the unit. The rest were Arab. Except for the officers, they were all Shiah. The officers were from Sharkat and Gayara, between Mosul and Baghdad.'

Were you mistreated?

'In one instance, they arrested me for seven days. There was some fighting with smugglers in Qushtapa. A soldier was killed. They suspected me, as a Kurd. During the interrogation, my officer said I was a professional tank repairman and they needed me.'

Jadir isn't smoking the cigarettes Jonathan gave him. I ask the PUK guard, who seems to be on friendly terms with Jadir, to bring some tea. The room is freezing, the kerosene stove in the corner unlit. When the tea comes Jadir stirs in several spoonfuls of sugar and speaks about his colourful military career. He seems to have been a deserter for as long as he was on duty. He volunteered at age seventeen in 1974, when the Kurds were in full rebellion under Mullah Mustafa. The army trained him as an electrical engineer. In 1975, when Saddam crushed Barzani's forces, Jadir was transferred to the Second Battalion of the Second Division in Kirkuk. He repaired cars for the infantry until 1979, when the army moved him to al-Rasheed Camp in Baghdad to work on radios.

'After a year, they said they don't want Kurds to develop such skills, and I was transferred to the Tenth Division. I was with them until 1981, when I deserted. The war [with Iran] had begun. In 1982, the government gave an amnesty [to deserters]. An officer asked me to go to a place in the no-man's-land between Iraq and Iran. There was a vehicle there that needed to be repaired or brought to base. I asked him to send soldiers with me. We found ourselves in a minefield. There were explosions. There were nine of us; three died. The marks can still be seen on my face.' (Jadir's face is pocked, as though from an adolescent skin disease.) 'After that, I was given two years and six months' sick leave in the military hospital. I stayed in the same division until 1989. I deserted again. I was arrested in Kirkuk and sentenced to two years in prison.'

He was released when Saddam announced another amnesty, to celebrate his invasion of Kuwait in the summer of 1990. 'I was taken to Kuwait where my unit was based and given three days' leave. They told us, "Whoever comes back one day late will be executed, and we'll arrest his family". After my three-day leave, I did not rejoin the army. I was in Kirkuk, and the uprising began. Ali Hassan al-Majid, the defence minister, arrested Kurds in Kirkuk. A cousin and I were in a house there. We were both deserters. He's a doctor now in the *Peshmerga*. We went to Laylan and walked to Bani Makan by night, where we met *Peshmergas* who had just taken control of that place. They respected us. We told them al-Majid arrested many people. I stayed in Chamchamal to 1993. As we didn't have any job in Chamchamal, I decided to go back to Kirkuk to surrender and [re]join the army, hoping things would not be as bad. I was sent back to my old unit, then based at the Saddam Dam north of Mosul. There was a decree: Kurds are not allowed to be in the army in this area. I was sent to Amara, to the First Division. We were three Kurds together; they asked us to set ambushes at night and harmed us. We were given too many tasks. We were put on duty most of the time. We decided to desert.'

He deserted again in 1993, but was back in the army in 1995. Jadir reminds me of those inflatable punching-bag men, who bounce back every time they are hit. I wonder how many armies would let him desert and re-enlist as often. Certainly, not the US.

He deserted in 1995, but this time he was arrested. On his release, if I understand him, he was re-arrested, in 1999. At the end of his term, he went back into the army. That was last October. Why, I have to ask him, did he keep going back to the army?

'I was afraid of losing my family,' he says, 'and I didn't have another job.'

Conditions for the average soldier are terrible, he says. 'If I speak about food, it's not proper and enough, because the officers steal the soldiers' share. The soldiers are all hungry. In the morning, they give us tea and lentils. At lunch, rice and broth. It's not enough. Dinner is tasteless soup. Uniforms were coming to the unit, but the officers sold them in the market. Ordinary soldiers had to buy good ones for themselves, while the officers were provided with good uniforms and boots.'

He believes some of the units will fight for Kirkuk. 'They are very afraid of losing Kirkuk. Senior officers said they will explode the oil wells if they lose Kirkuk, so no one would get the benefit from the oil. They said we would repeat what we did in Kuwait.' (The Iraqi army set the Kuwait fields alight in 1991, and they burned for months.) 'I don't think they will do it,' Jadir says. 'It's just a threat. Part of the propaganda to raise morale. They want to persuade the soldiers how strong the Iraqi army is. They don't know the soldiers know better how weak the army is.'

Landay asks about WMD, and Jadir says no one ever mentioned chemical or biological weapons, 'Iraqi officials have to find somewhere to hide rather than think of using chemical weapons.' He was back in his tank unit for only three months before he deserted again. 'I am sure it will be the last time,' he laughs, and we laugh with him. 'The last of the last.' Now, he says, he wants to join the Kurdish regional army – presumably, the PUK's. I wonder whether he'll desert them too.

Jadir says the PUK should free him soon. 'It's a sincere task of any government security official to interrogate me before setting me free. I will assist the Kurdistan Regional Government by providing information.' He says no Americans have come to ask him about the Iraqi army in Kirkuk. Landay asks how they are deployed. Jadir says each division has three tank units. 'We were far from each other. I heard from the others that they had more technical problems than we did. The Republican Guards near Kirkuk are on their way to Baghdad.' He says many of its officers are deserting. He gives us details, far more than ABC's viewers would absorb, names of each division and unit near Kirkuk. Most of the units, he says, are well below strength and won't fight. 'People are looking forward to the attack,' he says, 'both Kurds and Arabs.'

Jadir turned himself over to the PUK in Chamchamal, easier perhaps for him as a Kurd than for an Arab soldier. A smiling, relaxed man, he hopes his wife and two children – fourteen-year-old daughter and eleven-year-old son – will escape from Kirkuk to Chamchamal today. '*Inshallah* [God willing], I will see them soon.'

The BBC reports that the US is offering Turkey $26 billion to let it open the northern front. The US says it has sent about 3,000 troops to Romania to await deployment in Iraq. Back at the Palace Hotel, I check emails in the government's Internet room. Subi Shaker in Erbil writes to say he must rush to Toronto: his father has just died. I write back with condolences.

I go up to Dokan with Asla for dinner at the Round House, perched atop a hill like a vulture's nest. At dinner are Ahmad, Tamara, Zaab and a Kurdish INC official, Kamran Khoshnan. Abu Muhammad, a kindly Turcoman who was Ahmad's *major domo* during his previous tenure in Iraqi Kurdistan, has arrived from Denver and is preparing dinner. He has the dignified bearing of a Jeeves and, according to Ahmad, 'speaks five languages – all of them badly'. Ahmad puts Mozart's *Requiem* on the CD player. They complain about Khalilzad's *diktats* to the opposition. Zaab says, 'We don't want him to screw up Iraq they way he did Afghanistan.' Ahmad discusses Kurdish history, Mullah Mustafa's wives and children, the Kurdish dialects and tribes. Among other things, I learn that Massoud Barzani grew up in Baghdad, virtually a prisoner of the regime, during his father's Soviet years. His education was in Arabic, and he is less hostile to Arab Iraq than are most other Kurds. I doubt Khalilzad or any other American would-be administrator of Iraq knows the tribes, families or human make-up of this made-up country as well. The British studied the country in every detail before they conquered it, and still they failed.

Saturday, 22 February 2003
Suleimaniya to Tower Hotel, Erbil

Hans Blix announces that Saddam's al-Samoud missiles have a range of 180 kilometres – thirty kilometres longer than UN resolutions permit. He gives the Iraqis eight days to destroy them. Thus, the US may launch a war for thirty kilometres of air.

Ham'ali Khan comes by this morning for coffee at the hotel. He is one of this city's great characters. Sometimes he is like the Ancient Mariner, who won't let me go until he has his say. Other times, I ask to hear more – this morning, about his stage career. 'I translate *Hamlet* from Persian to Kurdish,' he says. He directed it here in 1991. A bit old to play the Prince, he would have been a good Polonius. The play went to the Fajr Festival in Tehran. 'I act Hamlet in Arabic in Baghdad when I was student. I act in Eugene O'Neill plays. And Osvaldo Dragùn's *The Story of the Man Who Turned Into a Dog.* I play Mozart in Pushkin's *Mozart and Salieri.* I act Steinbeck, from the novel *Of Mice and Men.* The director was Karim Osman. He's dead now. They kill him in the war between the PUK and KDP. I was in play by Nazim Hikmet, *The Skull.* I act in forty-five plays and fifty films.' Then, uncharacteristically modest, 'I'm not famous in Baghdad like I am here.'

He made a film about Saddam's ethnic cleansing of Kurdistan, *al-Anfal.* He played the title role in the film *Qazi Muhammad,* about the fall of the Mahabad Republic. His list of credits goes on, while I try to finish breakfast. 'I act in Samuel Beckett's *The Scream.*'

The Scream?

'That was the Kurdish title. And I was in *The Chairs* of Ionesco. I learned English from films. I watch two or three a day.' He pulls out a bunch of DVDs, including *Gangs of New York.*

He pats his pockets, looking for something. 'You didn't smoke?' He needs a cigarette. I don't smoke them, but I could use one too. Or something. 'Every person here has 500 stories, because every person in this area didn't live for peace for one minute. War. War. War.' He lists the wars from the time the British arrived. It takes some time. 'This area lives from war to war.'

Ham'ali leans towards me and confides in a whisper that he needs a job – as translator, maybe. Though his English is not good enough, he has too many talents to waste them. I will try to think of something else. He says, 'I have two brothers and one sister in Germany. They say,

"Come, *kaka*." In 1987, I tried to go. I was in the mountains. I went to Tehran. I came back. A friend from Karbala, name Qassem, he died by the way, because he cannot breathe in the triangle of Pakistan, Iran and Afghanistan. I write a poem to him, "The Bells". A man bleeds to death. They translate it into Arabic.'

Then he tells me about a woman he saw for the first time in twenty-eight years. A former lover and a popular Persian singer, she now has a husband and four children. She came to the opening of one of his films. 'She cry when she see me, because she think someday I'll be great because I read too much. I like Dostoevsky, *The Brother Karamazov* ...' Ham'ali is a Kurdish Dmitri Karamazov. 'I like *Peace and War*, Gogol, Turgenev. In America, I like Steinbeck and Hemingway. I read them in Persian and Arabic. I like Pasternak, Solzhenitsyn, Fitzgerald, Faulkner. This woman, she was crying' – he imitates a woman's voice – 'I am very happy to see you, a famous man now. One of my children is named Ham'ali.' She then urged him to make a film about Kawa the Blacksmith, 'a very famous legend'. Did I want to hear it? Later. Then he asks if I know the real problem of the Kurds. 'All of this, these tears, the Anfal, come from Islam. They come by their souls and cut the heads of children and say, "You must learn the Qur'an."'

McCullin and the ABC crew call from Diyarbakir, where hundreds of hacks are gathering amid confusion and disinformation. The Turks say they will let them cross the border to cover the Iraqi opposition conference in Salahuddin. The condition for entry is that they return to Turkey when the conference ends. The journalists fear the Turks will keep their passports to make sure they come back.

Hajhar Aref from the Ministry of Cooperation drives Asla and me to Erbil after lunch. Asla calls the Turkish prime minister's office from the car. Someone tells her the US aid package for Turkey is not what it seems. The US, the official says, is offering $3 billion in debt relief and a $3 billion grant in aid. The other $20 billion must be negotiated as a loan from the International Monetary Fund. 'They are very frustrated at Washington's disinformation,' Asla says. 'It makes it look like the negotiations are only about money.' Aren't they? She says the Turks are discussing political, military and economic relations. The US, she says, is asking to send 80,000 soldiers to Turkey. The Turks want to set a limit to the number of foreign troops on its territory to 10,000 at any one time.

'An American I spoke to in Washington last night said we might finally reach an agreement, but there will be scars for some time,' she says.

Asla seems as plugged into Washington as she is to Ankara, perhaps because one of her strings is *The Wall Street Journal*. The *Journal*, she says, could not quite believe that George Bush told the head of Turkey's ruling Islamist party, Tayyip Erdogan, last December, 'You believe in God Almighty. I believe in God Almighty. God Almighty has given us a duty to spread freedom and democracy around the world.' That was how the Turks remembered it, and Asla wrote it up. The *Journal*, however, changed the God reference to, 'You are a man of faith and I am a man of faith ...'

There is now a KDP checkpoint blocking the way to the Tower Hotel. More people should want to get out than in, and a checkpoint seems unnecessary. We negotiate our way into the hotel, where security men check our bags. This is another new development. In our absence, the hacks have arrived in force. I go up to Room 907; I am keeping Suite 901 as an office-edit room, lending one room to Asla and two to the CNN Türk crew, who are homeless.

Asla and someone from the PUK take me up to the lavish new KDP guest palace for the INC in Salahuddin. It is between two identical mansions, one for the Islamists of SCIRI and the other for the PUK. It seems that, on arrival, there was some confusion as to who was staying where. The SCIRI people found their palace minibars filled with alcohol, and the INC rooms all had prayer rugs and compasses pointing to Mecca. The two delegations swapped houses, and the INC ended up in the middle palace with the booze. All the palaces are grand and lavish, gilt everywhere, as if for oil sheikhs. Abu Muhammad is overseeing the local cooks and waiters, who are preparing dinner. Among the guests tonight are Adham Barzani, Massoud's Islamic fundamentalist cousin, and four of his retainers. Adham's father was Sheikh Ahmad Barzani, Mullah Mustafa's brother. He calls his party 'Hizbullah'. Although the KDP is a secular party, relations within the family and between the two parties are good. Adham says, 'My

Islamic beliefs are the old Barzani beliefs.' Ahmad Chalabi says the arrangement is more practical than that – Hizbullah was the conduit for Iranian arms to the KDP in 1994. Those weapons helped the KDP expel the PUK from Erbil.

Adham condemns the Turks, who he says want to occupy Iraqi Kurdistan and put an end to Kurdish autonomy. He says he is calling for a *jihad* against the Turks. None of the other Iraqis, including Massoud, goes that far. He gives me an appeal he has written to the 'People of Kurdistan, Political parties and the Kurds' friends.' It reads, in part:

> ... the Turkish military regime, in a very fearless and headstrong way, threatens the achievements and freedom of our country. It plots to occupy our land and to enslave the Kurds again. It wants to announce itself as the heir of Saddam's gloomy history, without considering the will and the wish of Kurdish people which rejects all kind of occupation or living under the sovereignty of a cruel regime ...

The 'revolutionary' Hizbullah announces its support for Massoud, invites all parties in Kurdistan to do their national duty 'to counteract the plots of Turkey regime ... '. The two final points of the document are:

8. We ask the struggling forces within Northern [Turkish] Kurdistan to increase their activities in order to make Turkey busy, so in this case it cannot invade the Southern [Iraqi] Kurdistan.

9. At the end we as revolutionary Kurdistan renew our pact and promise our people that we will support the Kurdistan territory to the end if there is Turkey's invasion. We are also ready for preparing a defending national force for supporting our people against any invader.

When Adham leaves, we move out of the formal sitting room to a small table in the foyer under a massive glass chandelier. Ahmad says, 'This is Massoud saying, "I will resist somehow".' Massoud does not say this himself, lest the Turks close his border and cut his supplies, so he leaves it to his cousin. But he is sending signals.

Ahmad continues, 'Barzani is thumbing his nose at them. He just arrested the Turcoman security chief and accused him of planning to blow up a hotel. The KDP also claimed seven Turcomen were going to blow up a hotel. All of this Turcoman stuff is a bullshit issue.'

Asla, always ready to defend her nation, asks, 'Why?'

Ahmad answers, 'It is blown up beyond all proportion.'

'It is true the Turks are, for the first time, taking up the Turcomen,' she says. 'For the first time, Turkish Star TV had hours of Turcomen here telling their stories.'

'Who made them suffer? This issue ... When you have 17 million Shiah suffering for years, deportations, killings, and the Kurds, chemical weapons, etc. And we sit here at the INC talking about cultural rights ... The Turcoman issue is blown out of proportion, because Turkey wants some way to put a nail into the situation. Turkey is setting itself up for a conflict about legitimate fears. Now, I will oppose having a Turcoman in the leadership council because of what Turkey is doing. I will not accept to divide Iraq on an ethnic basis.'

Kanan says, 'Then you have two Kurds, one from the Majlis [SCIRI], yourself and one Sunni on the leadership council of five.' Turcomen and Christians are not represented.

'I'm prepared to say a Turcoman has the right to be President of Iraq,' Ahmad answers. 'He can be Prime Minister or anything he wants, as under the monarchy.'

Kanan repeats something he has written and said before, that Iraq should not define itself as an Arab country. Ahmad loses patience.

'Kanan,' he says, 'don't say Iraq is not an Arab state. You can't ask 80 percent of the population to deny they're Arabs.'

Mudhar diverts the conversation. 'Let's not make Turkey our enemy. We'll talk to them. Don't take positions.'

Ahmad says, 'I'll take positions.'

'Abu Hashem,' Mudhar says, 'don't side with this guy or that guy. You're above everyone.'

'You think I want Iranian troops to come here? I talked to the Turks when I was in Turkey. What I don't want is all this ball-busting.'

(If Turkey invades, Hoshyar Zebari told me in London, Iran will invade as well.)

Asla says, of the Turks, 'They're coming, because the Americans are coming and they don't want Kurdish independence.'

Ahmad says, 'Turkey has a phobia about the Americans' plotting with the Kurds to make Kurdish separation possible in the near future. It could be a pole towards which Turkish Kurds will gravitate. If it goes on, this will cause such terrorism in Turkey. If we assume there is an American-Kurdish plot, if we assume all Iraqis are weak-kneed and hate each other more than they love their country, fine. The biggest guarantee against a Kurdish state is not Turkey, it is Iran. I think Turkey will be responsible if there is a Kurdish state inside Iraq. They dealt with Kurdish leaders as if they were independent. I would say to the Kurds, I would go on TV and say, I now call for a referendum and will let you choose self-determination. It would force Turkey to invade and occupy and have 7 million more Kurds.' That may not be the scenario Turkey wants.

The conversation jumps from one topic to another. Abu Muhammad directs the tea and coffee service, while everyone goes on talking and talking.

Ahmad says, 'The Arabs of Iraq are tired of fighting the Arabs' wars, against Israel, against Iran. Do you think the Arabs of Iraq want to give 1 million more dead to make Turkey feel good? We are a people who want to live in peace ... Gertrude Bell said we need the Kurds in Iraq to balance the Shiah. She said we must not let the Kurds be independent, because independence would violate our [Britain's] agreement with Turkey. We are sitting here eighty years after this, after us having created this monster Saddam, coupled with threats from the Wahhabis [in Saudi Arabia] whom they supported for sixty years, and the place they decided to do something is Iraq. As Iraqis, will we force the Kurds to stay in Iraq? Or will we negotiate the terms on which we can accept to have them be part of Iraq? No separate Kurdish army, no Kurdish customs, etc? Turkey wants me to say I will fight the Kurds and Turkey will help me to fight you [Kurds] and prevent you from having a say in Iraq. They have said it to me.'

Asla says, 'I think the turbulence is in the State Department, who have not empowered the INC to speak for Iraqis.'

'Listen,' Ahmad says, 'the CIA said, "They [the INC] are bastards, they are corrupt." Turkey's vision of Iraq almost coincides with the INC's.'

'No,' Asla answers.

'I said, "almost",' he responds. 'I don't like it that Iraq should be jabbed around because Saddam is in power. All I am doing is what De Gaulle did to the Americans and the Brits.'

Kanan tries another tack. 'Let the Turks come. This will bind the Kurds to the new state. What is wrong with that?'

'Nothing,' Ahmad says. 'I want to have a common market with Turkey, a Baghdad Pact. I want to have the best possible security cooperation with Turkey. Turkey is the ideal partner.'

Kanan asks, 'Will you go to Silopi, then?' (The Turks have invited Ahmad and the Kurdish leaders to meetings in Silopi, the first Turkish town north of the border from Zakho.)

'Silopi?' Ahmad says. 'I don't want to go to Silopi, because that is where they bring the Kurds to whip them.'

Sunday, 23 February 2003
Tower Hotel, Erbil

I come down for breakfast to see Hoshyar and Latif Rashid giving a press conference on the second floor. They read statements from each of their parties condemning the proposed Turkish intervention. Nothing as harsh as Adham Barzani's statement of last night. Among the hundred or so journalists are Patrick Cockburn from *The Independent*, Allen Pizzey of CBS and a few other old friends. I let Hajhar Arif return to Suleimaniya, because he keeps disappearing when I need him. Not good for a driver, but somehow in keeping with an honourable tradition in Kurdistan: Victorian travellers complained about Kurdish muleteers' absenteeism during crises.

I hire a local driver and an interpreter, Jella – pronounced 'Jeela' – Desai. Her sister is called 'Jalla' and works for UNESCO. They come from a good Erbil family and grew up in Canada. We go to lunch at the Chwar Chra, where newly installed security guards keep us waiting outside. The hotel manager comes down to vouch for us. It seems delegates to the opposition conference have taken over the Chwar Chra, expelling the resident journalists. Allen managed, however, to hang onto the suite CBS is using as an office. Jella, Jalla and I join him and his crew for lunch. His soundman is George Ionnides, whom I have known since the October 1973 Arab-Israeli War. A Greek who grew up in Beirut, he speaks perfect Lebanese Arabic. I've often believed he can do anything. He charms people – soldiers, officials, hotel owners – when he needs to. I buy cards to keep up the credit on the mobile telephones and a car charger for the batteries. Sherwan Dezayee of the KDP arrives today from London, via Turkey, and we meet for tea at the Tower. He says he saw hundreds of hacks waiting in anger on the Turkish side of the border.

In the evening, I call the Sestis in Italy. While Orlando's brothers Cosimo and Petroc tell me about the funeral, I cannot stop the tears. They say my son George read a beautiful poem in the chapel next to the house. They took the coffin from the chapel along the lane down to a small cemetery in the valley. Everyone who knows the Sestis, myself included, loves them. This is too horrible.

I see another Sherwan Dezayee, cousin of the first and manager of the Tower, in the evening. And I meet a Turcoman leader. He says he is pro-KDP and all Turcomen will march in demonstrations against a Turkish invasion. There is nothing worse for a minority in the Middle East than to have an outside benefactor interceding on its behalf: French support led to the Armenian genocide by Turkey, Venizelos's invasion of Turkey finished off the Greeks in Anatolia, Israel's support of Lebanon's Christians cost them the country and the Turcomen here know the Kurds, as well as Arabs, would take it out on them if Turkey invaded. Allen, George, wry CBS producer Kurt Hoefle, Patrick, Jim Muir and I have drinks in the CBS suite and go on for dinner at the Hawler. They have grilled carp, and I eat excellent large, flat *kibbe*, Mosul-style with *arak*. I come back to the hotel and talk until three o'clock with Asla, who frets over Chalabi and company.

Apart from the empty rooms I'm saving for our crew, the Tower is full. I can almost hear Rizgar downstairs counting 100-dollar bills.

Monday, 24 February 2003
Tower Hotel, Erbil

When I wake this morning, I look down from the ninth floor at the Sheikh Muhammad Roundabout to see it bordered with new banners. The ones facing me say, 'Forever Kurdish-Arab Fraternity'. Translated, that means: No Turks.

Bruno Roeber calls me at 0930 to say that he, Fabrice, Don, Bob and Andy are leaving Diyarbakir today on a Turkish bus with all the other hacks. Their Turkish government escorts should drop them in Erbil's town centre. 'Send three cars,' he says. At 1000, he calls again. Destination is now Salahuddin. I hire a truck for the gear and a Land Cruiser for the crew. Bruno calls again at 1045. The Turks have told the journalists the opposition meeting is cancelled and are not allowing them to cross the border. I tell him the meeting is not cancelled. There are too many delegates here. Bruno sounds somewhat frustrated. So far, a cloak of chaos is keeping our crew and a couple of hundred other journalists out of Northern Iraq. If their luck holds, the Turks will delay them again.

At breakfast on the second floor, I have – someone must be making a mistake – fried eggs! First time this trip. Plus Turkish coffee. Asla worries about the Turks, her people, coming here. When I mention the 'Kurdish-Arab Fraternity' banner outside, she says that was the slogan that went up in 1959 just before a pogrom of Turcomen in Iraq.

I am organising a live interview for *Good Morning America* with Ahmad in Salahuddin. Without a crew or a dish of my own, I am hiring IHA, a Turkish company. Asla speaks in Turkish via telephone to their director, Umit, for me. We arrange to shoot the interview on the roof of the KDP's Public Relations Office in Salahuddin. I wanted to do it on the roof of the KDP guest palace, where Ahmad is staying, but the KDP won't allow it. Ahmad arrives on time with Tamara, Zaab, bodyguards Hussein and Samih and a few other INC people. I try to position Ahmad with the mountains behind, while blocking the TV aerials and power lines that blight the view. It seems to work. The IHA crew are great, and nothing goes wrong. Charles

Gibson, the morning anchor, asks Ahmad questions. Ahmad answers. Nothing interesting. It's over.

Downstairs in the office, I see Hoshyar. He says, 'Their [the Turks'] goal is to destroy what we have achieved, not just to stop us going further.' He says the Turks are massing thousands of troops near the border. He worries that newspaper headlines in Turkey today warn that the Kurds are threatening Turkey. 'The Turkish foreign minister set out plans for our disarmament,' he says. 'We will not disarm until there is a comprehensive political settlement. We who faced genocide, disarm? No way.'

The American plan, he has been told, is to send 80,000 soldiers through Turkey to control the cities of Northern Iraq.

'Here, we are closer [than US forces in Kuwait] to Baghdad and Tikrit,' he says. 'And the Turks know it. If the Americans come here, they will need our support. We are the only force that knows the ground. Mosul city has a half a million Kurds and a very receptive population.'

I ask about the 'Kurdish-Arab Fraternity' banners and the 1959 pogroms. He says the slogan goes back to the 1950s, when Mullah Mustafa returned from the USSR. In the pogrom, he says, those killed were mainly leftists. Nine Turcomen died. 'It is very serious, really,' he admits. But he believes the Turks are using the Turcomen as an excuse to intervene. Turkey did not show much enthusiasm for Turcomen when its relations with Saddam were good and he *hanged* Turcomen. After lunch with Hoshyar, I spend the afternoon at the INC's guest palace gleaning gossip.

Dinner at Chwar Chra Hotel with Allen, George and Kurt of CBS. Hans Blix says Saddam's al-Samoud rockets must be destroyed by Saturday.

Tuesday, 25 February 2003
Tower Hotel, Erbil

This was to be the day of the crew's arrival from Turkey. After many telephone calls and false starts, their buses – with 100 or more other hacks – make it over the border. They end up 100 or so miles north of here, in Dohouk. Allen calls to say one of the journalists noticed an ABC shipping case left on the ground in Silopi. Do I know anything about it? I call Bruno, who is on the Turkish press bus, to tell him. I, meanwhile, buy some carpets to cheer up my dreary room and a mattress and cotton sheets so I can sleep in it. With Jella's help, I also buy a computer. Allen and I have lunch at the Chwar Chra, later joined by Dan Williams, Jon Randal's friend from *The Washington Post*. Then tea at the Tower with Rizgar and Sherwan to talk politics. Elizabeth Rubin arrives from Iran, *sans chador*, and I give her one of our spare rooms. (I am feeling generous with ABC's space. Empty rooms do us no good at all.) She says in 1996 Dick Cheney and Richard Perle published a proposal to make Sherif Ali bin Hussein King of Iraq. What did Bush think of that? I ask. 'The wackier, the more far-out the plan,' she says, 'the more Bush likes it.' Well, if Britain imposed a Hashemite monarch here, why not the US?

In the Tower Hotel's office, the two partners, Rizgar and the younger Sherwan, are having coffee with their manager, the older Sherwan. They are all agitated about Turkey. Nobody seems to care much about Saddam anymore, but mention Johnny Turk and out come the rifles. 'I don't care about Basra and Baghdad,' Rizgar says. 'For the last three days, I've been thinking about Turkey coming here. I decided to join the Special Forces again to fight the Turks.'

The younger Sherwan seconds him. 'I will fight whoever is a threat to us. The Kurds must stand together. This is the opinion of the ordinary Turcomen too – not the Turcoman Front. Only a minority group supports Turkey.'

Rizgar says CNN is on its way with nineteen people. Nineteen? We in the ABC team will be five, if Bruno and the crew make it.

Downstairs in the crowded lobby, Asla is waiting for someone to take her to a meeting with Adham Barzani. And where is her Islamic fundamentalist Hizbullah escort? 'Oh,' she says, 'he's upstairs in the bar, drinking vodka.'

Turkey, which has agreed to accept US money and a piece of Iraqi Kurdistan, will put the agreement to a vote of parliament. The accord did not prevent the Turks from dumping Zalmay Khalilzad at the border, where Hoshyar has had to rescue him with Dave Pierce and a few other stranded US diplomats. Hoshyar then drove them down to Salahuddin. (The Turks could have escorted Khalilzad or flown him down by helicopter. Relations must be tense.) The Afghan-American arrived in time for dinner with Barzani, Talabani, al-Hakim and Chalabi. The conference is scheduled to begin tomorrow afternoon, but you never know.

Asla returns from the press conference Adham Barzani gave to Turkish journalists to say he is backing off his *jihad* threat. The US must have spoken to his cousin. She mentions that today is her birthday, then disappears. What present can I get her in Kurdistan? I seek the counsel of Sherwan the elder, in his office. He takes a key from his pocket, locks the door and takes me outside to his car. We drive through Erbil to an open bakery. The baker pulls a chocolate cake from the refrigerator and ices it in English, 'Happy Birthday Asla.'

Asla and I go to the Hawler for a late dinner. While we are there, Ahmad, who has adopted her as a confidante, calls her. Khalilzad and Pierce, having been snubbed by the Turks, are in Salahuddin with the KDP. They say the US has agreed, in return for Turkey's cooperation on US deployment, to permit Turkey to occupy a fifteen-kilometre zone of Iraqi territory all along the border. Ahmad is furious. We finish our dinner, the last people in the restaurant. Even the waiters are gone. Outside, there are no taxis. The owner, a kindly man named Sawkat, drives us back to the Tower. We go upstairs for a nightcap and the birthday cake. On the radio, Bush warns Saddam to disarm completely or face war. This must be the first war in history in which one side is required to disarm before battle commences.

Wednesday, 26 February 2003
Tower Hotel, Erbil

At breakfast, Jim Muir receives a breathless briefing from his translator, Rasha. She speaks Kurdish, about the only language Jim doesn't know. She says the Turcoman Front just gave a press conference downstairs. The spokesman called for the Turkish army to come to Erbil and

Kirkuk to protect the Turcomen. I ask her for the spokesman's name, but she doesn't know it. Jim glares at her, and she runs downstairs to find out. I wish I hadn't asked. Walking by Sherwan's office, where the hacks check emails on his computer, I hear a feminine scream. Looking in, I see an Iranian photographer named Neshwa, one of the prettiest women here, reading a message on the screen. She claps and says, 'I've won the World Press Photo Award!' I would take her out to celebrate, but her boyfriend, another journalist, is here as well.

I go down to the lobby to watch the television news, when the electricity goes off. I head up to Salahuddin with a truck and two 'Monicas', as the Kurds call the big-ass new Land Cruisers, in honour of Ms Lewinsky. Don and the crew can use the Monicas. (The older models, with oversized fronts, are named after well-endowed actress Layla Alawi.) At about five o'clock, a convoy of buses from Turkey disgorges hundreds of disgruntled and disfigured hacks onto the asphalt in front of the Meedia Palace Hotel in Salahuddin. I board the first coach. Luggage and bodies lie everywhere as if at the end of a battle, rather than at its prelude. For some reason I am wearing a suit. All the other hacks are in jeans, and a French woman thinks I have come from the embassy to help them on arrival. I direct her inquiries to the KDP.

The bus stinks, and some of the journalists are still asleep in their seats. Andy, a good guy, is the first ABC person I see. Nearby are Fabrice, Bruno and Bob. I am meeting Bruno, who is about forty, and Bob, who must be sixty, for the first time. Bruno, though polite and agreeable, is frantic. He worries about camera cases, the lost case in Silopi, his luggage, the cars, the crew, the queue in front of the hotel for opposition conference passes and the hotel itself. Bob has wispy white hair and recently had, I am told, a cancer operation. He does not look well, and I wonder how ABC could send him. When Qassem Dergham arrives from Syria, Bob will be free to go home. He looks like he wants to leave now. Finally, I meet Elif Ural, who works for ABC in Turkey. An attractive young woman, she is the most composed of the bunch. She is also the most welcome, having carried a dozen packs of Lavazza coffee for the espresso pot I bought in Suleimaniya.

They complain that, during their overnight stay in Dohouk, CNN booked the hotel and kept most of the rooms empty – meaning the rest of them had to double up or find other accommodation. Outside I see Don, smiling but exhausted. In its way, Don and Fabrice's journey to get here has been worse, because more mundanely awful, than our trip in 1991. Then, we had to trudge through mud and rain over open fields to get to the front. But there was a front. Today there is a dull conference of once-exiled Iraqi politicians. Don and I desert the other hacks to have drinks and dinner at the new INC guest palace. We are counting on the INC or the Kurds to get us to the front, and possibly to Baghdad, when the war starts.

At dinner, Ahmad says he told Khalilzad that Iraqis must remain sovereign in Iraq. There should be no period of US rule, because the people will not accept it. He implies that Khalilzad was not listening. Apparently, all he said was, 'There are some issues to be worked out.'

Thursday, 27 February 2003
Tower Hotel, Erbil

A morning of journalistic mayhem as hundreds of press folk from Turkey settle into free Iraq. On the Tower's first floor in what was a coffee bar, a dozen journalists sleep in bags on foam mattresses, laid out like a row of tombs. John Simpson of the BBC, always a very nice man, limps in for breakfast, tired from the long trip. He says he's living in Dublin, but keeping his places in Paris and Chelsea, and offers me some tax advice. Dean here of television journalists, John is always reliable and helpful.

Bruno, Fabrice, Bob, Andy, Jella and I hold our first ABC logistics meeting in Suite 901. We agree to make extra room keys and ask the people from CNN Türk, to whom I lent some of our rooms, to move out and make way for our people. Up in Salahuddin, fifty-five of the sixty-five delegates are here. Among those boycotting are Iyad Allawi, five of his followers and Sherif Ali bin Hussein. Sherif Ali may be waiting for the foreign powers who conquer Baghdad to anoint him, as they did his Hashemite ancestor-king. Delegates in Salahuddin say Khalilzad warned fifteen of the fifty-five – including Talabani – that the US does not want a leadership to emerge from the conference. I have coffee at the INC's guest palace, when Ahmad comes in and announces, 'Good news! We have a unanimous vote for a leadership council.' Its members are Ahmad himself, Talabani, Barzani, al-Hakim, Iyad Allawi and the eighty-year-old Adnan Pachachi. Mudhar is thrilled, 'I couldn't have hoped to have it better.' After much celebrating, and much arguing with me, Ahmad says, 'It's a bullshit victory.' Bruno and Don come up to the palace for dinner. There is news tonight: Saddam says he will destroy his al-Samoud missiles.

Friday, 28 February 2003
Tower Hotel, Erbil

Elif Ural, ABC's woman in Turkey, is rushing all over town digging out equipment and information. I hate to see her leave on the bus back to Turkey, because she is helpful here. 'I'm going to the arms market,' she says. 'Want anything?' Bruno wants to hire everyone in Erbil to translate, fix or drive. Don, Bruno, Fabrice and I drive up to Salahuddin to a press conference that was scheduled for 1 PM, postponed to 2 PM, 5 PM, 7 PM, 9 PM, 11 PM and then cancelled. We waste time at the KDP's press centre, in the Meedia Palace Hotel press centre and in the 'Darin Internet-Pizzeria-Dry Cleaner' building. Outside, I do my first stand-up in years for a piece we might not do or, if we do it, might not run. I meet the beautiful Sophie Flamand, Fox's Danish producer, and Fox's absurd security chief, Chris, ex-Rhodesian and ex-British army. He does not allow the Fox team to leave the hotel without armed guards, and in his first few days here would not permit them out of the hotel at all. He appears to be driving the Fox crew mad with restrictions. It turns out he is the one who forced the KDP to put checkpoints in front of the hotel. Everyone accuses him of paranoia.

We wait for hours at the conference for an announcement of some kind. Don and I give up and go to the INC's guest palace for dinner. A bald, buttoned-down American named Chris appears. It is Chris Straub of the Senate Select Committee on Intelligence, who was at the London conference in December. Tall and emaciated, Straub sports the same shaved head and wire spectacles as back then, only his trenchcoat is missing. The Iraqis and I talk politics most of the evening, while Bruno waits at the conference. We give Judy Miller, here for a few days for *The New York Times*, a lift down the mountain to Erbil.

Saturday, 1 March 2003
Tower Hotel, Erbil

Fox Television is colonising the Tower, making it a paranoid outpost of Murdochland. Already responsible for the checkpoints at either end of the road, it is bringing in hundreds of sandbags to barricade the fourth floor. Completely nuts. Next they'll enforce the Patriot Act to detain suspect journalists. Half their team says morale is so bad they'll never work for Fox again. The staircase and restaurant are covered in sand from the leaking bags that workers carry on their backs up the stairs to the Fox Floor, now called the 'Fox Hole'. The whole floor has become a bunker. (If the building blows up, the sandbags won't preserve one floor. If they fear Iraqi artillery, we are out of range.) This is American paranoia at its worst, effected by a Rhodesian-born British private cop.

Sherwan, the mild manager, takes me aside in the stairwell. 'I do not like this,' he confides. 'All this sand. What is this? The owner of the hotel called.' (Rizgar and the younger Sherwan lease the building from its landlord.) 'He does not want this. And he is the one who fixes the hotel.' He complains that Rizgar is letting Fox ruin the place. (There is not much to ruin, but Sherwan does his best – he is a Ritz manager working at a TravelLodge.) A few minutes later, I bump into Rizgar outside the front door.

'Fox made us put up the checkpoints,' he says. 'And now the local people are afraid to come for a drink or dinner.' When we all leave, which we will, he will have to attract local business back. In the meantime, Fox is scaring away the average people we used to talk to in the restaurant and bar. Still, better than CNN, which has turned its hotel into a fortress with bunkers, barricades and security passes. It's like one of Saddam's prisons. No one there meets anyone who doesn't work for CNN.

On the way up to Salahuddin, I read Jonathan Randal's book on Kurdistan. He writes that Kurdish nationalism was, after the First

World War, 'a disease that was considered highly contagious and thus especially suspect to the highly centralised states they were then forging in the West's modernising image.' Nothing has changed.

Fabrice, Bob, Bruno, Jella and I meet at the Conference Centre in Salahuddin, where American guards keep the press back. Rather than stand outside for hours, we drive in two cars to the INC guest palace to record an interview with Ahmad. For the first time, the guards at the front gate do not allow us in. It seems the KDP is banning journalists from the compound – especially those with television cameras. Hussein, Ahmad's chief bodyguard, comes down to help. The security men agree to let us in, but we cannot bring Fabrice's television camera. Fabrice, Bob and I walk up to the house, while Jella and Bruno take the camera to the Darin Internet Café down the road. Hussein goes there to pick it up for us and brings it back in his car.

Inside the guest palace, we watch the Turkish parliament vote on the US military package. Asla is there, along with most of the INC delegation. They cheer when the vote is announced: the parliament ratifies the agreement with the US, 264 to 251, with nineteen abstentions. That should mean the US can enter Iraq through Turkey, and Turkey will receive about $6 billion in grants and aid. A few minutes later, there is dejection in the guest palace when Asla hears from Ankara that the parliament must approve the bill by an absolute majority. The 'yes' vote has only a plurality; the abstentions carry the day. Only Ahmad is sanguine: the US doesn't need a northern front, he says. It is better not to have Turkish forces in the country. (In 1990, the US ceded to Syria full control of Lebanon in exchange for Syrian participation in the war for Kuwait. In 2003, the US was willing to give Turkey a piece of Iraq, but is now losing the chance.)

Hussein returns with the camera, but Ahmad has left for a meeting with Khalilzad. Muafak Barzani, one of Massoud's under-employed cousins, comes to search for the camera. It seems the KDP has made him responsible for security here. Muafak, who reminds me of Inspector Clouseau, is sure we are hiding the camera somewhere – as we are. He wanders with feigned nonchalance from room to room. We get him to sit down and have coffee. This is when I realise Muafak is crazier, in his own fundamentalist way, than his cousin Adham, the *jihad*-declaring zealot. Muafak quotes the Bible, mainly the Old Testament, again and again – something Kurds are not known to do. He mentions that life is hard, and then throws a verse from Exodus at us. Keeping an eye out for our camera, he says he is a convert to Christianity. Bob and Jeanne Dixon of Dallas, Texas, brought him to the Lord. He gives me their telephone numbers and tells me to call them. They are great people, God bless them. He talks about the glories of rebirth in Christ, while fingering amber worry beads. I wonder if his family chief Massoud approves.

Meanwhile, the Iraqi opposition press conference, scheduled for 5 PM is postponed to 7 PM, then 8 PM, then 10.30 PM. When it begins, it is just after 11 PM. Asla leaves for the closing statement, but we are stuck in the guest palace with the camera and the ever-present Muafak. We got the camera in, but we cannot get it out. Fortunately, BBC's Kaveh Golestan is recording the press conference for Jim Muir and for us. We watch it, with Muafak, on Kurdish television. The principals, including Khalilzad, deliver their final pronouncements. Nothing substantive appears to have resulted from this long-awaited event, but Chalabi, Abdel Aziz al-Hakim, Barzani and Talabani look pleased. We wait for Ahmad to return or for Muafak to leave. Neither happens quickly, and it is midnight when Asla comes from the press conference to type up a story for *Saba*. Ahmad arrives and gives her a private briefing. Hussein diverts Muafak with an important discussion in the kitchen, and we set up the camera in a back room to interview Ahmad. With Muafak lurking outside, we go to work.

Fabrice rolls his camera, and Ahmad insists, again, on Iraqi sovereignty over Iraq: 'I believe that the United States' interests, as well as the interests of the people of Iraq, will be much better served if there is an Iraqi authority which is in alliance with the United States, with a clearly defined mission – and there is a clearly defined function for the American forces in Iraq.'

Does the opposition conference that has just ended mean anything?

'I think this conference will be a watershed. The United States has agreed to deal with us as partners in the liberation. And I think the opposition will be treated with much more seriousness by the United States.'

And the Iraqi army?

'The Iraqi army has to be very, very seriously restructured. The army has been turned into a tool of the Party. And in the process of de-Baathification, we must dismantle all the apparatus of the party and its control over the military forces. We hope the Iraqi army will be an army of volunteers, who should be oriented towards the defence of its borders.' Ahmad says he welcomes US assistance in training and equipping a new Iraqi army.

He gives an assurance: 'The Iraqi people will welcome the United States forces as liberators. We will welcome them. Everyone will be grateful to President Bush for having sent the US Army with the support of Congress to help in the liberation of Iraq. But foreign military presence in any country after a few months becomes problematic.'

Previously, he warned of looting in Baghdad, particularly by Shiites from the slums around the city. Is he still concerned?

'I believe that random violence can be contained. But it will not happen because of a wish. We must work hard. We must coordinate. We must do things, positive things, so that people find that their cry for justice will happen through mechanisms of law rather than through acts of random violence.'

Finally, what are his ambitions?

'I seek no office. I am not a candidate for anything. My role, I believe, will end with the establishment of democracy in Iraq.' He may believe it, but I don't.

It's a wrap, but we have to get the camera and the tapes past Muafak. We drink more coffee with him and wait. Elizabeth Rubin arrives to talk to Ahmad, who is busy with Asla. Elizabeth sits on one of the sofas, annoyed that she must wait for an audience. Kanan, Sam, Mudhar and the rest alternate between political discussions, television news and sending emails. They ignore Muafak, who is growing weary of the game. At about two in the morning, Muafak announces he is going home. He lingers outside in his car, perhaps waiting to see whether we rush out with the camera. Finally, he drives out, past his security men and through the gates. Hussein passes the camera out a window, and Fabrice hides it in the back of his Monica. Fabrice, Bob and I drive back to Erbil with the camera and our tape of the 'exclusive' interview. ABC does not broadcast it.

Sunday, 2 March 2003
Tower Hotel, Erbil

At breakfast, Jim points to a discrepancy between the English and Arabic versions of the conference's final statements. 'Well,' he says, 'this may be a bit nuanced for your audience. The English version says that power should be handed to representatives of the Iraqi people as soon as possible. In Arabic, it says power will go to the representatives of the Iraqi people directly.' He asks if I noticed that Barzani spoke in Kurdish, Talabani and al-Hakim in Arabic. Chalabi addressed the crowd in English. 'He knows where power lies,' Jim says.

Bruno, Fabrice and Bob film the streets of Erbil and the Kirkuk front, while Andy and I review ABC and BBC tapes of the opposition conference. Jim asks us to wait before bothering Kaveh for his tapes. 'He worked all night,' Jim says. 'You can look at his tapes later.' Kaveh, who shot most of the conference, comes up in the afternoon and lends us his cassettes. He goes back and forth between the BBC's floor and ours, bringing dubs of most of his work to Andy. He is not required to do this, even under the sharing arrangement between the BBC and ABC; he does it because he is a kind man. We give him a copy of the Chalabi interview, in case the BBC needs it. Jim and Kaveh have a twenty-four hour news service to feed, while ABC has only a few news broadcasts each day.

I transcribe the Chalabi interview for a new spot on the opposition. We offer two pieces to ABC's *World News Tonight* – one on the fears of a Turkish invasion, the other on the apparent race between the Iraqi opposition and the US to reach Baghdad first. They probably won't broadcast either.

Monday, 3 March 2003
Tower Hotel, Erbil

Saddam and the UN destroy six al-Samouds. That brings the total to sixteen. In Erbil this morning, tens of thousands of Kurds march to protest a Turkish invasion. It is peaceful, but they burn a Turkish flag. Don and I go up to Salahuddin to the KDP's Public Relations Office, the PRO (the Kurds seem to be imitating the US armed forces with all these initials), to see Fawzi Hariri. He takes us miles up the mountain to an old Baathist office block where Barzani has his HQ. Massoud's interpreter and his protocol chief greet us at the door and take us upstairs to the leader. Massoud has aged and filled out since 1991, when Don and I spent much of the war with him. Dressed in his red turban and *Peshmerga* uniform, he looks like the young son rather than the old leader that his father was. We all sit down, and he taps his foot on the floor.

He is furious about the Turks, despite the parliamentary vote which he fears could be overturned, and angry with the US for inviting them in. He is going to call on the Turkish troops already here to leave and will withdraw cooperation with the US if the Turks increase the size of their force here. 'The Turks said they would come to Northern Iraq,' he says, 'and their force would not only be larger than the American force, but won't be under American command.' Everyone knows the Turks would deploy in the KDP's heartland around Dohouk, rather than in PUK territory. That is why Talabani is less exercised about the prospect than Barzani is.

'The Turks' basic objective is to disarm the Kurds. They want no Kurdish state. They do not want even the status quo. They don't want Kirkuk or Mosul for the Kurds. Our forces would interfere with that.' A telephone rings, and he answers. When he is done, he says, 'The Turks say, "We would not go there to fight Saddam Hussein". If their intention is not to fight Saddam, if it is to demolish our experience here, Kurds would use all the facilities at their disposal to fight them. And the Iraqis. This does not serve Turkish interests.'

There is a small Turkish force in Kurdish Iraq, at a base near the border, from which the Turks occasionally attack the PKK. 'We will not allow them to come in,' Massoud says, 'and we will ask the remaining ones to leave.'

When?

'We will see.'

How will he do it?

'We will tell the Americans and themselves that if they will not leave, they will be an occupying force. The situation is tense.' So is he. He agrees to do an on-camera interview when he goes public with his demand that the Turks withdraw.

'The problem is that the Americans have not understood how far the Turkish intervention is opposed by our people. If they come under the umbrella of the coalition, it is bad. If they come alone, it is worse. If we do anything, we will be seen as against the coalition. Or with bin Laden.' I try to steer our talk towards the war, but he brings it back to Turkey.

'If they replace Saddam's rule with Turkish rule here, we will tell the whole world the US has betrayed our people.' Again. 'If the Americans want to come here and liberate us and put us under a dictatorship, this would be contrary to the values of the US.'

If Turkey does invade, would that end Kurdish cooperation with the US?

'Certainly. The Kurds would be busy fighting the Turks. How could we cooperate with the US? Let those officials of the US who admire Turkey answer that question.'

Turkey opposes a Kurdish takeover of Kirkuk and Mosul. If the KDP's forces go to either, Turkey could intervene. 'The people of Kirkuk and Mosul should liberate those two cities. Indeed, it's difficult from the time of the uprising. Within one hour, you could gather 5,000 *Peshmergas*.' To fight Turkey, not Saddam.

During dinner the Hawler, Bruno, Elizabeth and her photographer, Lynsey Adario, relive their Afghan days. Another American war in a country the US misunderstands.

Tuesday, 4 March 2003
Tower Hotel, Erbil

As I email a 1,000-word article to *The Nation* in New York from
Sherwan the elder's office, I receive an email from Sophie in London.
I seem to like her more and more, despite the separation. Another
dreary day in Erbil, more a non-day than anything else. The cleaners
say they can clean only five of our eleven rooms. I hand them keys and
money and beg them to do the rest as well. Maybe, they say. They are all
nice peasant women, but an oily young man named Salem orders them
about. He takes the money and wants an extra tip for making the bed.
Rizgar is still worried about the loss of local business since Fox put in
all of its security – the checkpoints, the searches in the lobby and the
sandbags. The Kurds who used to congregate in the restaurant won't
come near the place anymore. Rumour comes to us that the KDP will
order the removal of the sandbags on the fourth-floor Fox Hole.

Don and I spend the early evening in the bazaar among Kurds.
When he sees starlings in a cage to be sold for food, he buys one and
sets it free. It flies higher and higher, circling a minaret, and floats
gently towards us. If it flies back to its cage, Don's merciful act is futile.
At the last second, it turns and disappears into the citadel.

Farewell dinner at the Hawler for Burhan Jaff, who is returning to
Brussels via Damascus to resume work as PUK representative there.
Around the table are the restaurant's owner, me, Burhan's brother,
Jim, Fawzi and six other KDP people. There is much talk of Jalal
Talabani's love of food. They say someone told him he had a fat ass
and a fat gut, and he just laughed. On Saturday, when the opposition
press conference was dragging on towards midnight with one of Jalal's
monologues, a KDP delegate whispered in his ear, 'Mam Jalal, the
food's ready.' Jalal banged the table and declared the conference over.
Everyone at the Hawler laughs at this story.

When he was young, they tell Jim and me, Talabani was thin and
handsome. It seems the ladies loved him. In 1964, he broke with the
KDP. He was supporting his father-in-law, Ibrahim Ahmad, who
demanded a collective Politburo. Old Mullah Mustafa did not see the
need for collective decision-making. He was, after all, the chief. After

that, Talabani moved to Syria and gained weight. He came back to Iraq and to the KDP, but abandoned the party again and formed the PUK.

Return to my dingy room on the ninth floor to call Sophie in London. No answer. I call my son George, who is back in London from Orlando's funeral in Tuscany. Julia went with him and sounds, when I reach her, more shaken than he is. Saddam on the Iraqi news calls Bush one of the world's 'great despots'. They have something in common.

Wednesday, 5 March 2003
Palace Hotel, Suleimaniya

Voice of America broadcasts a chilling editorial on what the US will do here. It is a kind of warning to the Iraqi people that, although not the enemy, they should get out of the way. I remember hearing a similar announcement in Libya in 1985, just before the US bombed Tripoli and killed about twenty civilians in their beds. One of the dead was the teenage daughter of my friends Ghassan and Sania El-Ghossein, and among the wounded was an angry ambassador from Japan. Other radio news: Russia says it will veto a US-British-Spanish war resolution at the UN. Stalin died fifty years ago today.

We set off for Suleimaniya in two Land Cruisers and a Nissan 4x4 this morning with drivers, crew, Don and Jella the translator. Driving into the morning sun, I am glad to be leaving the filthy Tower behind, although I'll miss Rizgar and the two Sherwans. Don and I are with Ismail, the driver with the best sense of humour, in the lead car. My steel thermos is filled with espresso, breakfast for the road. No news yet from Qassem, who has vanished at the Syria-Iraq border near Qamishli. He said he would be in Iraq three days ago. I call the newsdesk and ask them to tell him to go to the Tower in Erbil, where we've left him a room and a letter. We head east over the asphalt roads that Saddam destroyed and the Kurds re-tarmacked, up the hills and down again, over land we had to traverse on foot or tractor in 1991. There have been many Kurdish risings here, and so many defeats, when highland warriors succumbed to superior cutthroats, were cleared from the land and sent into exile. Now it may all come right for them under Bonnie Princes Massoud and Jalal.

At the entrance to Suleimaniya is a huge warehouse with the letters 'WFP' painted twenty feet across its roof to ward off accidental bombing from the air. The only planes in the air over Iraq since 1990 have been the US's and Britain's. The WFP – World Food Programme – sign should spare the warehouse, not that the WFP is doing much to save Kurdish farmers. We drive to the Palace, where we all try to check in. The management there is as bad as Rizgar's is good; it gave away one of our rooms while we were gone and raised the room charges. (I wish Rizgar and Sherwan ran the Palace, and that the Palace managers were stuck in the Erbil Tower.)

The process of settling into the Palace, completing forms and moving a bed into Fabrice's suite for Bob to sleep on, takes hours. Andy and Fabrice repair broken equipment, and Bruno attempts to wrest one of the ABC satellite telephones from McKiernan. Jella and Hazhar Arif are helpful, amid this crowd of insane foreigners with their inexplicable demands. Don and the three Erbil drivers take rooms at the end of town at the disgusting Abu Sanah.

I stop at the Internet room that the Ministry of Cooperation provides on the mezzanine. They charge a few *dinars* per hour to log on and check emails. There are messages from ABC, my son Edward, daughter Julia and Sophie. The young woman who works there gives me a small bouquet of honeysuckle, *nergez*, now in season. The Kurds love flowers, even if most of them seem to keep plastic flowers at home.

Our merry band meets for dinner at the hotel's Indian place on the mezzanine, where we listen to rumours. NBC's Fred Francis does not mention his 4 March start date for the war. His updated prediction is the 7th. Or the 14th. Or … The service is unusually slow and disagreeable, but the food is bearable. Fabrice finds a red wine he can drink, and I stick to beer. Elizabeth and Lynsey sit at our table. Lynsey, a feisty American, makes me laugh. She talks about her young boyfriend, 'Whaddaya mean spend the rest of my life with him? He cheated on me with a secretary. If he'd cheated on me with a really smart woman, it'd be different.' When I ask what he's doing while she's away, she answers, 'Sleeping with my friends.'

After dinner, Don returns to the Abu Sanah with Ismail and the other drivers. Lynsey and Elizabeth, who are also staying there, go with them. I go upstairs late. My friend Ralph Isham calls from New York to say his brother Chris, ABC's investigative unit chief, turns fifty tomorrow. He wants me to send a funny email message to be read with many others at a big dinner in Chris's honour. Today is Ash Wednesday, the first day of Lent when I usually give up drinking. I remember it was Lent during the uprising of '91, and I did not touch a drop until Easter Sunday. That Easter evening, we reached the Turkish border to escape from Saddam's rampaging army and helicopters. We made camp, lit a fire and settled in to await a dawn walk over the mountain. I opened a bottle of Jameson's Irish whiskey which I passed around. This year, I doubt I'll give up drinking. This war is stupid enough without going that far. At about 0230, I fall asleep with a book. At 0300, the telephone rings.

Thursday, 6 March 2003
The Azmer Hotel, above Suleimaniya

The ABC London desk is calling on my Kurdish mobile telephone. I should not answer. A youthful voice tells me of a warning from the CIA. Jack McWethy, ABC's national security correspondent in Washington, received a call from someone at the CIA who said there was 'a credible threat' to American journalists in Suleimaniya. I say I'll look into it in the morning. That is not good enough, so the London desk patches me through to Chuck Lustig, a nice guy, who runs the foreign desk in New York. Lustig repeats the CIA warning and adds the name of the CIA guy who spoke to McWethy. He says a CIA intercept mentioned an attack on the 'Suleimaniya Hotel'. But we're at the Palace Hotel, I say. Lustig does not care and tells me to leave town with Bruno and the crew. There is nothing to be done at three in the morning, so I try to sleep. The next interruption is a panic call from Bruno. Lustig, it seems, just called him. The warning has escalated

Bruno's normal frenzied state to delirium. I worry about his health: blood pressure, ulcers, nightmares. He tells me to pack now. I hang up and try to sleep again. The *muezzin* chants his morning prayer for about ten minutes. I put my head under a pillow. The traffic begins. Trucks and hooting taxis stop and start at the roundabout beside the hotel. I make another formidable attempt to close my eyes, but the telephone rings again. It is Lustig. He checked with the CIA, he says, and they meant the Palace Hotel. He repeats that we should leave. Why? I never believe the CIA. When a senior official of the CIA says something, he says, we should listen. I am too tired to explain what I think of the CIA, and it is too late to recapture sleep. I give up.

Down in the lobby, the hacks are in moderate turmoil. NBC, CBS, the American news agencies and newspapers all had the same call. Farnaz Fahissi from *The Wall Street Journal* says they probably told us at 3 AM to heighten the drama. You don't forget being awakened. Nor do you forgive. Jonathan Landay says Knight Ridder called him at the same time, but its version of the threat, via its Washington bureau chief, was that both Erbil and Suleimaniya were unsafe. Jonathan and I agree it is probably government disinformation to scare the press out of Northern Iraq. I recall that Chairman of the Joint Chiefs Richard Myers has already taken network anchors to dinner and asked them to pull their people out of Baghdad. Jonathan said Myers delivered the same message to the Knight Ridder papers. The Pentagon says Baghdad is not safe, and now the CIA says the north is dangerous. If everyone leaves Baghdad and the north, the only journalists covering the war will be those embedded with the American and British forces.

No one is leaving the hotel. Bruno, however, wants to be the exception. I suspect he is more afraid of ABC than of Iraqi saboteurs. He tells the crew to pack and load the cars for the drive to Erbil. Fabrice does not want to go. He accuses Bruno of returning to the Tower because it's more squalid than the Palace. I propose a compromise between our wish to stay put and Bruno's to go. Elizabeth told me about a hotel called the Azmer on the mountain above Suleimaniya. I ask Hazhar to call the Azmer. If they have rooms, he can book us in for the week. He cannot reach the Azmer by telephone, so he drives up and calls me from there. The place is nice, he says, and has enough rooms for us all. Jella, Bruno, Don and I drive up to see; Hazhar is right. A half-hour straight up the mountain, just past Kurdsat and beyond any other human habitation, the Azmer is a new, mainly glass, two-storey structure, but cosy inside. Fabrice, Bruno and I take the three rooms facing Suleimaniya and the plain beyond. We leave a deposit for our rooms, when the photographer Kate Brooks arrives to take the four remaining rooms for her *Time* magazine group.

Bruno goes to Kurdsat to see the satellite manager, Hiwa Fareeq, and Azad Seddiq about ABC's satellite needs. (I like these Kurdish names. Hiwa means 'Hope'; Azad is 'Free'.) The rest of us return to the Palace to pack, then head to the Azmer, where the excellent and friendly staff rearranges the establishment to suit the bizarre needs of an American television network. They put a long writing table in my room and carry up tons of Fabrice's, Bob's and Andy's equipment. They open the roof for our satellite dish and stand-up location. They cannot be from the same gene pool as the staff at the Palace, who won't do anything for anyone. The only thing they cannot do is find the keys to the balcony doors for our rooms. The doors are sealed, they say, to keep out the 'black dust' that the wind carries up here.

We have a good, if familiar, *kebab* lunch in the Azmer dining room. It is time for coffee when McKiernan comes in. He's in his usual safari suit, but today looks a little sinister in aviator sunglasses. He wants Andy to make dubs of tapes he has shot. Andy is reluctant and complains that none of the cassettes is logged. They could be anything. We leave him in the hotel to go over the tapes with McKiernan while we drive to Chamchamal.

Azad calls. He has a driver at the Palace who needs a job. We stop by there. Fabrice has the final word on cars, and he does not like the man's Jeep. It is too low for him to shoot from. We can use him anyway, although not for the crew. It's about three o'clock when we resume the journey to Chamchamal over wet roads through miles of fields. In Ismail's car, Don falls asleep and Jella looks dreamily at the countryside. Fabrice and Bob are behind us with one of the new drivers, Ihsan.

In Chamchamal, we drive up the dirt track to the old citadel.

Fabrice shoots some GVs (general views) of the town and the Iraqi lines on Bani Makan. I do a few stand-ups, just in case we have a story. Then we drive down to Shoresh, a muddy collective town that Saddam built for IDPs (Internally Displaced Persons) from Kirkuk. There, some of the residents say the Iraqis have established a new position down the hill, closer to Shoresh. Fabrice takes a picture of it. Some of the children gather around him while he works, but they are not in his way. A few older men come too. One of them is Abdullah Amin Ahmed, a truck driver and one of the many Kurds expelled from his home near Kirkuk in the late 1980s. He is as cynical as one would expect. 'I have a question for you,' he says. 'Are the British and Americans going to protect us?' Kirkuk is only twenty-five miles away, and the Iraqi lines are a few hundred yards from where he lives. The only thing between him and the Iraqi gun emplacements on Bani Makan is a clump of trees. If he worries, it is because the British and Americans have never protected him. The US was supposedly backing the Kurds in 1975 and 1991, when Saddam decimated them.

Back at our new digs at the Azmer, Fabrice says an old friend of his called from Baghdad. She told him that Sky television evacuated Baghdad in the middle of the night – it must have been the same time we were warned – and the Australian government is ordering an Australian television crew to leave as well. Australia, now part of the 'coalition', must be learning from its masters in Washington.

The Azmer's dining room is transformed for dinner into an Arabian Nights banqueting hall. Kurdish families sit at long tables, all ages from ancient to newborn, and listen to a Kurdish band on a stage. It is not exactly traditional; the dominant instrument is a synthesizer. There are mountains of grilled meat on the tables with lots of beer and wine. When the Kurds start dancing, Bruno joins in. Men and a couple of adventurous younger women form a line to step in unison and twist their shoulders like Marilyn Monroe. Most of the action is from the shoulder. Bruno is fine with his feet, but the shoulder moves elude him. There is an old saying, 'He who cannot dance is not a Kurd.' Bruno is no Kurd, but he's close – and he's learning to relax.

The hotel's owner introduces the rest of us to his wife and son and offers to help us cover the war. He sends over a couple of *nargilehs* with apple-scented Persian tobacco. I enjoy the families celebrating the weekend, the dancing, Bruno letting go, the coloured lights sailing around the dark dining hall. I worry that, if things go wrong, the Kurds could lose everything they have made here since they came down from the mountains twelve years ago.

Don and I go up to the office suite on the first floor and open a bottle of brandy. He remembers 1991, a much better war for him that he did not have to wait for. He talks about Catherine and their baby, Max, and wonders what he is doing here. Outside, the wind is blowing harder. Enough melancholy. We head to our rooms. The wind has become a storm battering the sealed glass doors that make up one of my walls. Someone built the Azmer on the exact spot that the wind must hit as it sweeps up the valley. It's like cannon fire. Hail joins the wind, pounding and rocking the glass. Lightning cuts the sky, and thunder shakes the whole building. I cannot sleep, again, and call Sophie. She has just come out of a play at the Riverside Studios on a tranquil London night. I read a little and listen to the tempest struggle to get inside.

An hour later, lightning hits Fabrice's room and sets it on fire. Smoke blows along the corridor, and he is up putting out the flames on his ceiling. He saves his equipment, his bed and his life. He curses the weather and ABC for making us leave the Palace. Not only is his room charred now, the lights have all gone out. The electricity is cut. The water pumps don't work. No light, no reading; no water, no washing.

Friday, 7 March 2003
Palace Hotel, Suleimaniya

Having missed a second night's sleep, we are up early for a cold breakfast in the dark. We use bottled water to brush our teeth, but otherwise we are pretty game. The storm is over, and the sky is a film of hazy grey. I put my little radio on the table in the dining room, where we are eating cold bread and cheese. Gore Vidal is telling the BBC World Service, 'It's madness. It's unconstitutional ... Only

Congress can declare war.' That is what the Constitution says, but who reads that anymore? We drive to the PUK's *Peshmerga* HQ to watch their celebratory military parade marking the twelfth anniversary of the 1991 uprising. The troops do amateur acrobatics and drills for the camera. Kurdish officialdom and the foreign press corps watch. Kurdish guerrilla fighters don't make an impression as a regular army. They have the US model now and are trying to imitate it. Don shoots a frame or two; it's not his thing at all. Fabrice dutifully records it on video in case ABC wants a piece.

In the afternoon, the Azmer's electricity and water are not restored. Bruno must go to Erbil anyway, which he seems pleased about. ABC wants to test the satellite dishes all over the region for Day One of the war, and the only dishes we have are in Erbil and belong to CNN and the BBC. ABC has a share in both. Bruno takes a disgruntled Fabrice, along with Bob and Jella, with him to Erbil for the rehearsal. Andy, Don and I move back into the Palace. Hans Blix and Mohamed ElBaradei are on the television delivering their weapons reports to the UN Security Council. Britain's foreign secretary Jack Straw says Blix's report 'shows Iraq in material breach of the resolution [1441]'. Blix says nothing of the kind. He *does* say, 'Disarmament or any verification of it cannot be instant ... It will not take years or weeks, but months.'

Britain and the US give Iraq ten days. When Straw says Britain wants a deadline of 17 March, Don says, 'The 17th? Am I ever going to see my wife and children?' Dominique de Villepin, the French foreign minister, tells journalists, 'France will not support a deadline. We said we were going through Resolution 1441 to choose referees. Blix and ElBaradei are the referees. We should stick to the process.' France is not alone in opposing a deadline: Security Council members Russia, China, Germany and Syria will also vote against. Straw, back in the Council chamber facing de Villepin, says, 'The choice is not ours, Dominique. The choice is Saddam Hussein's.'

Ham'ali Khan takes me for a walk through Suleimaniya's bazaar in the late afternoon. A mad beggar with wild curly hair limps up to him. Ham'ali puts a ten-*dinar* note into the man's hand and squeezes it. The man walks away without a word. 'He's crazy, that guy,' Hama'ali says. 'Saddam killed his brother. He hanged him in Mosul. And he tortured this guy. He put electric shocks in his head. It made him crazy.' Ham'ali seems to have very little money, which is why he wants a job with us. But what money he has, he gives away. Everyone in the streets knows him from his films. The *Peshmergas* greet him as 'Abbas', a character he played in *The Outlaw*, a war movie.

The only other news of the day is an Israeli attack on the Jabaliya refugee camp in Gaza, where helicopters rocketed houses. Three people were killed at once. Five more were burned alive when their houses caught fire in the explosions.

Saturday, 8 March 2003
Palace Hotel, Suleimaniya

At breakfast, Ham'ali explains the plot of his Superman movie. He speaks quickly, with no control over his English grammar. My notes capture only a small part of the monologue:

> Superman dresses all in red. He is a little man and lives under the *agha*. Someone gives him a stone, so he can fly. And he picks up a child and tries to fly. And he falls. But he learns. And he vanquishes the *agha*. But he cannot fly for long. The West takes back the stone, and he has no more power. This is Kurdistan. Here with these Ottomans and Persians and Arabs.

He, like most of the tough Kurdish men in this town, holds a little posy of honeysuckle. Andy, Don and I drive to the PUK security office in Chamchamal. No tea is offered, but everyone seems happy to talk. Bahktiar, the deputy chief, says the Iraqis are digging trenches to fill with oil for burning when war starts. The story does not sound quite right. If they pour oil into open trenches, it will sink into the earth: not much of a weapon. Saddam tried the same tactic in Kuwait in 1991, and it didn't slow the US advance by a minute. Bahktiar says the Iraqi army 'has dug in around Kirkuk city to hide when the attack starts'. The security chief, who calls himself 'Adil', predicts, 'If the attacks start, the Iraqi army will be defeated by the American forces easily. The Iraqi soldiers are very tired and also want to get rid of Saddam Hussein. They are waiting for the war. They want it to start right now.' The Turks fear the PUK and KDP will stage an uprising in Kirkuk as a cover for the *Peshmerga* forces to occupy the city.

What is Adil's prediction?

'It depends on America,' he says. 'If America supports the Iraqi people, they will make an uprising against the regime. The Iraqi army may arrest young people in cities like Kirkuk in order to prevent an uprising. We have an example. They did the same thing in 1991.' He reminds me that Ali Hassan al-Majid arrested 15,000 Kurds and executed thirty young people in Kirkuk in 1991. The people rebelled anyway, and the *Peshmergas* entered the city.

This time, I ask, who will liberate Kirkuk – the Americans or the Kurds? He is silent. There are about a dozen Kurdish fighters in the office as interested as I am in his answer.

He says, 'Both. The Kurds are waiting for American support.'

And what will the Turkish reaction be?

'Now, I am speaking as an Iraqi citizen,' Adil says. 'If Turkey comes to Kirkuk, all the people of Iraq will be worried. If Turkish troops invade Iraq, we will fight them. If they come to support us, it will be different.'

We shake hands with Adil, Bakhtiar and a dozen other men before walking a gauntlet of armed Kurds in the security building's corridor. Our next visit is Shoresh, the IDP settlement about a mile away. It is a grim little town with barely a shop, whose people are waiting to return to Kirkuk. Up at the edge of the concrete buildings, we gaze again at the Iraqi lines. A few soldiers are visible on the hilltops, looking down at us. Children gather as they did the other day. Two men approach. One is Abdullah Amin Ahmed, the friendly Kirkuk truck driver. The other is a very old man, who leans on a stick. Today, it is the old man who talks.

'We do not trust America,' he says. 'We have suffered a lot. Why now are foreign journalists coming? Where were you when we were suffering? You have to tell the truth to your people. Tell them we are not beasts. We are human beings. We are grateful if you tell the American people that we are a people with a parliament. We as Kurds do not like to deceive people who want to support us. America should treat us like human beings. We are not Arabs. We are Kurds. Iraq abused us.'

I ask his name, but he won't say. 'Iraq may come back to this area. They may arrest and torture me.' Iraq did come back in 1991, and people were arrested, tortured and murdered, just after Bush Senior called upon them to rise up.

A mine explodes out of sight, not far away. The people shift their feet, but no one moves away or goes to look. 'Someone who is smuggling must have stepped on a mine,' Abdullah says. It may have been an animal. He points to a spot of grass nearby, where children are playing, and says that was where the Iraqis shot a shepherd two years ago. The casual cruelty of the Iraqi army should no longer surprise me, but it does. Then Abdullah says Shoresh and other complexes like it exist because its people were evacuated during the Anfal to make way for Arab settlers. That was cruel, systematic government policy. But soldiers would not be ordered to shoot a shepherd. That was just fun, I suppose.

Jemal drives fast along the roads back to Suleimaniya to reach the city before dark. He does not stop for checkpoints, where armed guards wave at him, or for pedestrians, who jump. We are back at the Palace in time for the 'storm before the storm' party. NBC sponsors this bash to take everyone's mind off the long wait for war. It is a good idea, and generous. They've taken a banquet room on the ground floor and filled it with all kinds of Kurdish food and imported alcohol. A band plays, and some of the press corps dances. There must be 100 of us in Suleimaniya now, impressive when you remember that everyone had to smuggle or bribe his way in. Landay and I talk about our plan for tomorrow: to tour the front lines with Mam Rostom. We have already spoken to Rostom about it, and he's promised to meet us early and show us his troops nearest the Iraqis. Later, when the waiters clear up, a dozen or so of the younger hacks make their way to Room 108. Landay and a freelance American named Quill are playing blues guitar. People prop themselves up on a bed or squat on the floor, college dorm-style. Just about everyone has paired off, and I suspect I'm about the only hack – apart from a few married people – at the Palace Hotel who isn't getting laid tonight.

Sunday, 9 March 2003
Palace Hotel, Suleimaniya

Voice of America announces this morning that President Bush is demanding a UN resolution setting a 17 March war deadline. VOA says France is threatening a veto, then broadcasts a long report on the hell faced by Arab immigrants in France – anti-Muslim discrimination, violence, police brutality. VOA never fails to live up to its charter.

Landay and I wait in the hotel lobby for Mam Rostom to show up and take us to the front. He's late, so we call his house and are told he has gone to Dokan to see Massoud Barzani. So it's Dokan for us. Jemal loads Landay, Don and me into his Monica. Andy and Azad Seddiq follow with Hazhar in the Mazda. The Mazda breaks down just outside town near Bakrajo Airport. Hazhar stays to have it repaired. Andy and Azad pile into the Monica with us. We ascend the mountain, no clouds over us, towards Lake Dokan, as if to a picnic. Landay's mobile rings. It's Borzou Daragahi: Barzani and Talabani are about to give a press conference in Dokan. He says we should hurry.

We race to the gates of Mam Jalal's house, where a Reuters TV crew are waiting near their Jeep. As the morning grows hotter, more journalists arrive from Suleimaniya. The guards won't let any foreign journalists into the compound. The press conference does not look likely to start any time soon. Azad goes in to see what's happening, comes out and says that Talabani and Barzani are in a meeting. Nothing will happen for hours. He stays there, and we go down to the INC Big House to see Mudhar, just returned from Ankara and Salahuddin. He says he told the Turkish deputy foreign minister that Turkey's intervention in Iraqi Kurdistan would affect Iraqi-Turkish relations in the short and long terms. Negatively.

Today's pow-wow is an internal Kurdish affair, but the big four – Talabani, Barzani, Chalabi and al-Hakim – will meet in Dokan tomorrow. They want to create committees or task forces to work with the US postwar security and humanitarian relief. The INC does not want US soldiers patrolling the streets of Baghdad. Policing should be done, Mudhar insists, by Iraqis.

Andy, who is on the telephone, interrupts to tell me ABC has more than seventy people in Kuwait – plus the embeds. Seventy? We're five in all of Northern Iraq. Better for us.

Mudhar shows me the latest issue of the *Turkish Daily News*. I've met its mercurial editor and publisher, Ilnur Cevik – the Turkish Murdoch – in Suleimaniya. The Kurds say he is there to sell central heating systems. Çevik's editorial, featured on page one, says, 'We also reminded [Kurdish leaders] that thanks to Turkey the Iraqi Kurds had made all these gains in the past twelve years and that Turkey had no intention of hurting them provided they did not declare an independent state.'

Azad calls to tell us to come now. We drive to the Ali Askari Martyrs' Hall for the press conference. Twenty-five journalists are waiting under an increasingly hot sun, but Azad is not one of them. I call and discover he is at the Ashur Hotel, where Barzani and Talabani are having lunch. 'What?' I say. '*Lunch?*' There is an angry press corps here expecting them to make a statement. Too bad, he says. The press conference won't begin for hours. We walk down to the hotel, saying '*Bayani bash*' and '*Chu nee?*' to the *Peshmerga* guards who line the way. Landay, who has been working harder on his Kurdish, says, '*Bayani bash, Korban* [Good day, Struggler].' Talabani, Barzani and their respective politburos are by the swimming pool eating lunch. Massoud wears his turban and baggy trousers, Jalal a dark suit. The security guards wear suits as well and carry light automatic weapons. We have our lunch inside, out of the sun. Later, the KDP politburo goes one way with Barzani, the PUK's the other with Talabani. An hour later, they reconvene in a small dining room. Andy shoots video of the meeting. Finally, they are ready to announce their conclusions to the press.

They drive and we walk up to the Ali Askari Martyrs' Hall. Borzou and several of the other journalists have left, but about a dozen remain. Talabani, Barzani and Hoshyar Zebari take seats on a dais, a portrait of the Kurdish martyr Ali Askari behind them. Preliminaries include statements about the right of displaced people to return to Kirkuk. Barzani announces that the two parties will form a joint military command, primarily to face the Turkish threat. Talabani says the KDP and PUK have agreed to defend each other against Turkey. No one mentions Saddam. Barzani says the agreement is not intended to exclude other parties – 'but this is a bilateral agreement to have a joint [Kurdish] command'. Landay asks whether the KDP is sending forces to the Turkish border. Barzani says, 'I'd like to emphasise we don't want any problems with Turkey or clashes with the Turkish army. Always we have extended the hand of friendship to Turkey. But it is a natural right to take precautionary measures.' I assume that means yes.

Another journalist says the Turkish newspaper *Millyet* reported that Turkish tanks have crossed the Habur Bridge into Iraq. Barzani answers, 'That is not true. There is no Turkish armour crossing. There is a buildup in Silopi.' Silopi is the last village on the Turkish side. Not much more comes out of this day's wait for a press conference, but Talabani looks satisfied after a hearty lunch. 'Thank you very much,' he tells the journalists. 'See you in Baghdad.'

Jonathan and I head back to the INC Big House, and everyone else goes down to Suleimaniya for a rest. Young volunteers and equipment arrive all afternoon. Tents are piled next to the house, and military cars are parked outside. 'We have tents now for 300 people,' someone says. A delivery of new uniforms is dropped off. It begins to look like an army camp. They invite us for dinner with Yarub al-Hashemi, an INC volunteer who says that, while still in the Iraqi army in 1991, he was involved in a plan Saddam devised to kidnap General Schwarzkopf. It was a mad scheme that needed, among other things, decoy airplanes, helicopters and vehicles camouflaged in US colours. It fell apart when the pilots, who would have been immediately shot down, grounded their planes and disappeared. The Iraqi high command discovered later that al-Hashemi had dropped his bombs on empty fields rather than on the rebels in 1991. He was arrested, then released and placed under house arrest in Baghdad. He fled in 1993, with his wife, to Canada.

Mudhar adds that Saddam executed fifty-six Sunni pilots who refused to bomb the Shiite uprising in 1991. Amr Shabandar, a well-spoken young INC man with a shaved head, introduces himself. There are many defectors here, he says, and points to a thin, middle-aged Iraqi on one of the sofas. 'He was in prison for twenty years,' he tells me. 'He was accused of being in a group that would assassinate Saddam Hussein. Imagine, spending your life from seventeen to thirty-seven in prison.'

Francis Brooks, INC man in Washington, arrives. A Virginian and Christian fundamentalist, he is a fountain of glowing quotes. When we meet, I tell him the Kurds just said they were combining their two forces to face Turkey. 'Great,' he says. 'They can run away together.' A few minutes later, he says, 'As far as I'm concerned, Syria's next. When they say Perle and guys like Wolfowitz want to get Syria, they're right. These guys are my friends, and I know.' Fair-haired, tall, nearing forty, he wants only a cold beer.

The television is on all the time at the INC house. Colin Powell is saying that the Security Council may yet pass the US-British-Spanish resolution for a 17 March deadline. The Turkish governing party's real leader, Tayyip Erdogan, wins a by-election to parliament and will assume the prime ministership. He is expected to force a second parliamentary vote to permit US forces to enter Iraq through Turkey. Brooks dismisses Turkey, 'The US military never needed the northern front. They want political support of a moderate, democratic, Muslim country and NATO help.'

Jonathan and I reach the Palace in Suleimaniya after midnight. McCullin and Patrick Cockburn are drinking beer in the bar. We have a drink with them and realise we never did see Mam Rostom.

Monday, 10 March 2003
Palace Hotel, Suleimaniya

The tension may be high in Washington, but all is calm in Iraqi Kurdistan. The BBC says Saddam has destroyed the forty-six al-Samoud missiles, which had a range exceeding the UN limit. Mam Rostom shows up, on time, at 10 AM in the hotel lobby. This time, we're not ready. Fabrice is back from Erbil, where he left Bruno wallowing contentedly in one of the Tower's grisly rooms, but now he's vanished. We give Mam Rostom some tea and let him tell stories of the Kurdish wars. He is not only a military commander, he says, he is a Member of Parliament for Kirkuk. We'll see, he says, how the people of Kirkuk welcome him. Azad Seddiq drinks coffee, smokes cigarettes, looks glum and waits with us. Forty-five minutes later, Fabrice comes into the hotel with a bag of clean clothing. Like the rest of us, he distrusts the hotel's laundry and has it done outside. We've all lost clothes to the Palace. I have someone else's socks, and I wonder who's wearing my shirts.

Jemal drives the lead car with Mam Rostom in front. Landay and his interpreter, Karim Omer, are in the back seats with me. An open truckload of *Peshmerga* bodyguards follows with Fabrice and Bob. Mam Rostom gives us a quick autobiography. He was born in 1953 in Kirkuk. In 1967, after five years of school, he became a *Peshmerga*. Until then, he says, students took their lessons in Kurdish. In 1977, two years after the collapse of Mullah Mustafa's US- and Israeli-backed revolution, the Baath Party destroyed his family's Kirkuk house.

'Why do people start revolutions?' Rostom asks. 'Because they are persecuted. I was a patriotic young guy, and I joined the *Peshmergas*. I was seriously wounded six times. The KDP revolution collapsed ... I was in Iran and joined the PUK there.' His wife, three daughters and one son live in Germany, he says, for their safety.

What is his real name? Rostom Hamid Rahim, 'Uncle' Rostom to his troops. He thinks the *Peshmergas* are better-disciplined and better-trained than they were in 1991. 'In 1991, we were more like a militia,' he says. 'Most of the Jash joined the KDP.' He implies that Saddam's old Kurdish collaborators are unwelcome in the PUK.

The road outside flashes past, one village after another, untilled land all around, on the way to Chamchamal. Rostom does not think the Iranian Mujahideen-e-Khalq (fanatics who lost out in the Islamic Revolution and came under Saddam's control) will fight the Kurds as they did in 1991, 'because this time the Americans are serious'.

I suspect that the US, when it occupies Iraq, will do a deal with the Mujahideen-e-Khalq to use them against Washington's next intended target for regime change – Iran. I tell Landay to expect Mujahideen car bombs in Tehran within a year. He accuses me of cynicism. I think it was Woody Allen who said, "No matter how cynical you are, you can't keep up."

The war is producing strange alliances. The Kurds and US are unlikely friends. But a US air umbrella has given them twelve years of near-independence. What about the other parties? The Mujahideen-e-Khalq is on the US terrorist list, but I am sure Rumsfeld and the CIA can find a *modus vivendi* with them. What about al-Dawa? The US is talking to them, despite the fact that they blew up the Kuwaiti US embassy in 1983. Now, they're friends of Wolfowitz and company and will probably join a US-backed government. And SCIRI, headed by the al-Hakim brothers? They've been in Iran for twenty years, fought for Iran and imbibed Iran's Shiite political fundamentalism. They're on the Iraqi leadership council that the US is about to impose on Iraq. Their Badr Brigade has more men under arms than any Iraqi party except the Kurds. About 3,000 of them are now in Iraqi Kurdistan, more troops than the US has up here.

Mam Rostom does not trust SCIRI and its Badr Brigade: 'They have come only to make trouble for us. Maybe there is an agreement between Turkey and Iran. Their real business is in the south. America will not accept them as fighters in the war. If America is liberating Iraq, it is not for the Majlis. It is for all Iraqis.' Or for itself. 'You know,' he says, 'that Iran and Turkey do not want anything good for us.' To the right of the road is a city of tents, more refugees from his Kirkuk constituency. He looks at them. 'If we listen to the Turks,' he says, 'these people cannot go back.' I ask if he was in Kirkuk during the 1991 uprising. He was. Was he also in Karahanjir, the town between Chamchamal and Kirkuk where some *Peshmergas* tried to kill McCullin, Fabrice, Qassem, Gwynne Roberts and me? He smiles and says, 'Yes.'

The *Peshmergas* fled from Kirkuk in 1991. Why?

'That's because America betrayed us.'

Will America betray you again?

He thinks. We leave the tents behind and are in open country again. 'It doesn't suit their purpose this time.'

We park at the last PUK checkpoint outside Chamchamal. The soldiers salute Mam Rostom and stand to attention. He bounds out of the car and surveys the scene. He points to Bani Makan, the High Plateau, and says the Iraqis have Katyushas, 130-mm artillery, 120-mm mortar rounds, Russian 'Dushka' anti-aircraft guns and some long-range Austrian artillery pieces. What will happen here when war begins?

'The Americans have told us, because of the Turks, not to go to Kirkuk as *Peshmergas*. But the people of Kirkuk will return. We cannot stop them. If the Americans do it seriously, people will rise up. In 1991, around 1,300 people were arrested in Kirkuk. Many were executed. It is best to get rid of the Baath. If there is an uprising, it is not only the Kurds who hate the Baath, but the Assyrians, the Chaldeans, the Turcoman. In the south, there will be an uprising.'

Will there be reprisals by Kurds against Arabs in Kirkuk?

'It's possible,' he says. 'In 1991, we had fewer than in the south.' (In 1991, the Shiites of the south killed hundreds of Baath Party officials.)

Our tour of the front does not, as it happens, take us anywhere we have not been before. It's Chamchamal and the view of the first Iraqi checkpoint again. We had been hoping for a more extended foray along the lines from here down to Kalar in the south. We pack up and go with Mam Rostom to see the *kaimakam* of Chamchamal. He's a former political prisoner from Kirkuk named Tariq Rashid Ali. He looks like a town mayor, all three buttons on his blue suit jacket done up, his red-striped tie tight at the neck. He welcomes Mam Rostom and offers us chairs facing his desk. We ask about civil defence for Kurdistan's front-line town. There isn't much, he admits: a few first-aid teams, a small fire brigade, ambulances to take wounded to Suleimaniya. Mam Rostom corrects him, 'We have all the preparations.'

Tariq Rashid Ali doesn't think so, 'We don't have [gas] masks.' Everyone in Kurdistan complains that, while the US gave gas masks to the Israelis hundreds of miles away, none came to the people Saddam has already gassed. 'We have no shelters,' the *kaimakam* adds. 'If the bombs fall, people will leave.

Back in Suleimaniya, we have Turkish coffee on the terrace of Mam Rostom's house. Landay makes him promise to take us into Kirkuk when he goes. It is obvious that, no matter what the Kurdish leaders say in public, the *Peshmergas* will take Kirkuk and probably Mosul. Landay pulls out some military maps and asks Mam Rostom the best route into Kirkuk. Rostom goes over it, pointing to an Iraqi position in one place, a mined road in another. The Kurdish way is not to find some clever tactic to sneak into Kirkuk. They just get a bunch of guys with guns and drive down the main road. If no one stops them, they carry on. It's warfare from the time before Alexander came here. Rostom says Suleimaniya's Bakrajo airport is now ready to receive US forces.

Back at the hotel for lunch, Don is tired. The wait is taking its toll on him. After lunch I do something I have not done here before: take a nap. While I slowly drift off, Jacques Chirac is on the radio explaining why France will veto the deadline resolution: 'There is no case for waging war for the goal we have set ourselves – disarming Iraq …'. Igor Ivanov, Russia's foreign minister, says the deadline contradicts Resolution 1441 and must be vetoed. Kofi Annan warns that any action undertaken without UN authority will be seriously impaired. Iraq, meanwhile, continues to destroy its al-Samoud missiles.

Elif, ABC's Turkish producer, was detained by Turkish police at the border after her return from Iraq. She was trying to smuggle some ABC personnel and equipment into Iraq. I call her on her mobile, and she is remarkably relaxed. Yes, she is under arrest. Yes, the ABC staff are with her. No, she is not being mistreated. In fact, she is drinking tea with her jailers. She thinks she'll be out tomorrow when she sees the judge. What a woman. Sophie calls from London. She has fired her composer, whose score for the film didn't seem to work. Her new composer wrote ten pieces of music over the weekend that are much better. The backers don't like her film's title and asked her to come up with another. I have not seen her since 15 January. She says she'll be my hot date in Tuscany when the war ends.

Tuesday, 11 March 2003
Palace Hotel, Suleimaniya

We have a jolly morning in the ABC office, Suite 110, drinking tea and joking. We're all here – Fabrice, moaning Bob, Andy, Don, Hazhar, Jella and me, plus a few BBC guys – but Bruno is still in Erbil. He calls from time to time to tell us how bad things are there. CNN will let him use our 'shared' satellite dish on their roof, but they won't let him have any space inside if it rains. The roof is slanted, leaving him nowhere to stand. The CNN guys, who don't give a damn that we gave rooms to their homeless colleagues from CNN-Türk, have the whole hotel to relax in. Poor Bruno. At the Tower, the BBC is more helpful with its roof dish. But then again, Jim Muir and Kaveh Golestan are gentlemen, unlike the savages at CNN. Bruno is consoled, however, with the Tower's terrible food, the filthy room and the dungeon-like hallways.

Meanwhile, here in 'Sully', we plan our day at a story conference in Suite 110. Fabrice says he'll buy electrical supplies and do some filming in the bazaar. We are doing a feature on the Kurds, who they are and why they matter, to run when the war begins. Fabrice is gathering all the footage he can, and Andy is checking with the library in New York to see what archival material – particularly from Halabja and the 1991 uprising – is available. Azad calls from the lobby. We go down and have coffee with him. He tells us about the interview he did for Kurdsat last night with Khosrat Rasul. Khosrat is going to Turkey as head of a joint KDP-PUK delegation. Jemal and I drive up to Dokan.

When we arrive, Ahmad and Tamara are having an *al fresco* lunch at the Round House above Lake Dokan. They have brought caviar from Iran and put a dollop on my plate. Francis Brooks prefers beer. Bottle in hand, he pontificates. 'I think Talabani could play a role. Maybe Foreign Minister. But Barzani is going to be alone up here. The US is going to disarm his militia.' Someone should tell Massoud. The leadership council has everyone but a Sunni, and no Sunni leaders are coming forward. Ahmad says the State Department has no candidates. The only ones available and acceptable to the US are Adnan Pachachi, the former foreign minister and UN ambassador, and ex-General Hassan Naqib. Both are respected men, but they are in their eighties.

Tamara, two bodyguards and I walk by the lake. I suspect the bodyguards are there to protect her from me. She is attractive, and she's just finished her PhD in history at Harvard. She doesn't really like being the only woman in this INC throng of men, but she's determined to stay with her father at least until he reaches Baghdad. If her father becomes Prime Minister or President, her post-Harvard career may be decided for her. We drive with Ahmad and more guards to the summit for a view of the larger of Dokan's two lakes. Ahmad gets out of the car, takes off his jacket and power-walks eight miles down to the house. It seems he does this every evening. I cannot keep up. His healthy, young bodyguards are struggling. Ahmad takes off his shirt, but the bodyguards are sweating more than he is. It is dark when we reach the Round House.

Elif calls to say the Turkish police have released her and deported her two American colleagues.

Back in Suleimaniya to watch the news on television. Rumsfeld has dropped Tony Blair into a bucket of camel dung. He says the US doesn't need British troops, who may not take part in the first phase of the war. What is the second phase? Romania's prime minister, Adrian Nastase, goes to London and announces his support for the invasion. It's Rumsfeld's 'new Europe' at work – Soviet satellites of yore, US stooges today. Bulgaria and Poland are lining up as well, as once they did to support the Warsaw Pact's invasion of Czechoslovakia.

Barzani has been visiting Talabani again, but the Kurds say he always returns to KDP-land before dark. He doesn't trust the PUK enough to sleep this side of the line, and Mam Jalal always accompanies him to the demarcation line. At day's end, more beer and *tikka* at the hotel Indian.

Wednesday, 12 March 2003
Palace Hotel, Suleimaniya

If I'd stayed married this would have been my twenty-sixth anniversary. I didn't, so it isn't. Early morning *VOA* news: there are now 250,000 US troops in the region. Britain's UN ambassador, Jeremy Greenstock, says Iraq's deadline will not exceed the end of March. The US says it may use a new 9,000-pound bomb to achieve a 'psychological effect'. The physical effect will be something as well. The 2,000-pound bombs the Israelis used to drop on Palestinian refugee camps in South Lebanon left craters the size of city blocks. Nine thousand pounds? That should scare, 'shock and awe' the natives. *VOA* reports that the US has suspended surveillance flights over Iraq because some Iraqi jets went into the air. In Turkey, the president has asked Erdogan to form a new government.

The usual quiet, dull breakfast downstairs. Then, while I'm having coffee in the lobby, a Kurdish man comes up to me. We know each other, but it takes a minute to recognise Nizar Said. We met here at the end of 1991, when he returned from San Francisco for the first time in twelve years. His family home was next to the internal security headquarters. We walked through it together and talked about what happened there, how the people in the neighbourhood lived knowing their friends and relations were being tortured there. We filmed a piece that ran on ABC's *Nightline*. (I tried to get a copy of the tape before I left London, because I wanted to do a follow-up on Nizar. But the tape library told me someone had checked it out and did not return it. I wonder how many other bits of history are lost that way.) Nizar, who has just returned from the States, heard I was asking for him at Barham Saleh's office – he works for Barham. His family lives in the same house near the old security buildings. We arrange to meet for dinner.

Don, the crew, Landay and I drive south. Spring is bringing the anemones into bloom, thousands of them scarlet and violet in the meadows. The riverbanks are overflowing with melted snow, and nomads are coming north towards the hills. Driving on the right of the River Sirwan, I am struck by the thought: why not take a boat to Baghdad? Everyone says the US armed forces will establish checkpoints to stop us using the main roads south. They won't think of the rivers. The southern tip of the Kurdish area at Kalar is eighty miles from Baghdad, and the rivers here join the Tigris a little further south. I know from nineteenth-century travel books that most of Iraq's rivers are navigable. It's crazy, but possible.

We pass Lake Darbandikan and descend onto a plain that looks anything but Kurdish. Date palms and mud houses, sand and heat – this is Arab Iraq. This stretch of the 'Land Between the Two Rivers',

Ard ar-Rafidain in Arabic, looks Arab, but most of its people are Kurds. I think of the Kurds as mountain folk, but these are plainsmen. They dress like Arabs in cool, cotton *jellabas*, as the climate demands. This finger of Kurdish-held territory along the Iranian border is 200 miles south of Suleimaniya, on a line about 180 miles below Iraqi-held Kirkuk. It is low and exposed to Iraqi fire.

We come into Kalar town, where Landay hooks up with three Kurdish scouts he has already hired to do reconnaissance for him. Jonathan is thorough enough to be a good artillery officer. His scouts tell him the last Kurdish checkpoint is about six miles south of here. Iraq has been reinforcing its positions, they say, and is preventing smugglers from getting through. We drive further south to the last PUK checkpoint at a place called Ban Asiou, where a few PUK security guards live in a concrete shell of a building beside the road. We park and get out to take pictures of the Iraqi positions. They are even closer here than at Shoresh. Without binoculars, we see the soldiers watching us from a ridge. Their tanks are dug in, and they have some small artillery pieces on a hill behind them. A PUK policeman says this road has been closed for a year. A week ago, he continues, a tank carrier delivered something big – not tanks. We hear some shooting. What is it? He says this is the first time it's happened, probably because our cars are here. The last fighting here was in 1992. The Iraqis had taken Kifri, but the PUK retook it. We continue talking; suddenly, a mortar round falls on the grass about 200 yards away. No one seems bothered.

The policeman says he is about to be replaced by *Peshmergas*. The police will go back to Kalar. Why? I don't know, he says. When the war begins, the *Peshmergas* will have to protect this area. They will want to move south to take Khanaqin, the Kurdish town a few miles south that the Iraqis still hold. A few more mortars hit the ground nearby, and we leave.

We drive west to Kifri, which is on a parallel with Kalar. It's a larger town, with ramshackle houses and a strange mosque in the shape of a pagoda. The PUK security people give us a tour of their front lines and take us to a checkpoint where cars still come from the Iraqi side. There, one driver says, 'The Iraqi army is nothing. From

Jalaula to Kalar, all they have are a couple of worn-out Dushkas and some ragged soldiers.' A passenger in a taxi complains that the Iraqi soldiers stole their oil, petrol and rice. 'We paid them,' he says, 'but it's useless.'

We are only about eighty miles from Baghdad. It would not be a long cruise downriver. Don and I go to Darbandikan to find a boat. We ask some of the fishermen, who are willing to rent us a boat but say we have to obtain PUK permission first.

At the hotel Indian, we have a kind of stag dinner – Anthony Loyd of *The Times*, Landay, Don, Fabrice and me. Anthony says he came to journalism from the British army. He was in the 1991 war in Kuwait, and he served in the Balkans. It was never going to be his career, he says, and he's seen far more military action as a journalist than as a soldier. He's about thirty and married to a beautiful woman I know in London. It makes me ask again why people do this. Why do they (we) leave families and lovers for months with no date of return? Why do they let people they care about worry that they might be killed or maimed? Don mentions Jon Swain, a mutual friend at *The Sunday Times*, who has been doing this almost as long as Don has. Swain was a kid when he covered the fall of Phnom Penh in 1975, and he wrote a beautiful book about Cambodia. Swain is apparently in Amman waiting to get into Baghdad. Don says Swain should have gone onto something else. So should we.

Thursday, 13 March 2003
Palace Hotel, Suleimaniya

Most mornings, Ham'ali Khan collars me in the hotel and tells me stories. They are like a child's, unconstrained by reality. Today, it's his films. 'I make a film about Qazi Muhammad in Iran. They hang him.' Qazi Muhammad was the Kurdish nationalist leader, who with Soviet help established the independent Mahabad Republic in 1945. When Stalin dumped the Kurds, much as the US later would, the Iranian army returned. The Shah hanged Qazi Muhammad alongside his brother and cousin in Mahabad in 1947. There are posters of Qazi

Muhammad in Suleimaniya's shops. Ham'ali says nobody came to that movie. Then he made another serious film, *Anfal*. He was in Erbil when it came out, just about the time Barzani invited Saddam's army to help rid the city of the PUK.

'I ran from Erbil to the mountains,' he says. 'I was not afraid of the KDP. Most of them are my friends. But the Iraqi soldiers know me from the film. My face is on the film. They will take me to Mosul and hang me if they find me. After the Iraqis left, I went back.'

Ham'ali says Kurds prefer comedies, because they are 'stupid'. There are other stupidities, too, 'Islam come to this area,' he says. 'They don't like daughters. They like men.' He flexes his muscles in mock bodybuilder pose, 'They like the big moustaches.'

I tell Ham'ali about my plan to sail a boat into Baghdad. He is at least as crazy as I am, and he loves the idea. 'That is beautiful,' he says, kissing me on both cheeks. 'We'll do it.' His assignment is to find the right vessel and get it onto the river as far to the south as we can go. And off he goes.

In the Palace lobby, Abdel Razzaq Mirza says the UN expatriate staff have left Suleimaniya. 'They just gave us a list of the new local responsibles,' he says. The international agencies never consult the Kurds, they inform them – like the US.

Hiwa Fareek, the satellite engineer at Kurdsat, lost his mother yesterday. He is receiving condolences at his father's house, where Azad takes me. We are all in dark suits, and men fill the small front room. Hiwa is a gentle, tall, kind man in his early thirties. He is in shock, but he makes a point of translating what his father and the other men are saying. The women are next door in the kitchen preparing dinner. Condolences here are a male prerogative. They tell me McKiernan was there earlier. 'He is very good man,' Azad says. 'He is just like a Kurd.' (I don't have much time for McKiernan, but I respect him for his kindness to Hiwa and the way he has befriended many Kurds.) Hiwa tells me how his mother died. She was fifty-seven and had cancer. She was in the hospital when the electricity went out. The power failure cut her oxygen supply. But he is not angry with the hospital for not having a generator to take over during the frequent cuts in electricity.

I am late for dinner with McCullin, Landay and his photographer, Tom, at Mam Rostom's house. They are already on the floor around a big cloth and lots of plates. This is eating-with-fingers time. The main course is wild rabbit. Rostom gives me a glass of whiskey. He loves whiskey. Landay asks him if he trusts the US. He answers that trust is not important; the Americans and Kurds have common interests – for now. Then Rostom receives an urgent call from his office. A suicide bomber has just blown himself up near Khosrat Rasul's house. Tom is anxious to get a picture, so dinner breaks up and we head to the scene. There isn't much more than spattered blood and some human guts on the street. Some of the neighbours are outside talking about what happened. A man named Abdel Qadir Muhammad, who lives nearby, says he was watching television when he heard a blast. 'The children were weeping,' he says. 'I saw a man whose body was broken in two. A pistol was next to him.' It seems the blast decapitated him. 'We don't know him. He's a stranger. When I came out, he was lying in the street. He was wearing a scarf, and only his eyes were visible.' Tom takes photographs of the mess and says he is going to the morgue to shoot the dismembered corpse. McCullin says he's disgusted. The suicide bomber turns out to be a deranged PUK member with a faulty grenade. He was a long way from Khosrat's house. This was more likely an accident than a bungled assassination.

Back at the Palace, we all need drinks. The lobby television is running BBC news. Jeremy Greenstock at the UN says the 17 March deadline could be extended to get a UN resolution on war. Other Security Council members want to wait for Blix's report next week before deciding anything. In Turkey, Erdogan wants to recall parliament tomorrow to consider another vote on the agreement with the US. Turkish public opinion is 95 percent opposed to war, but he must see some advantage in the US aid package and the right to occupy part of Iraqi Kurdistan. Meanwhile, the charity World Vision is sending relief supplies to Jordan. I wonder why. More Iraqis are likely to try to get to Iran than to Jordan to escape war, as they did in 1991.

Friday, 14 March 2003
Palace Hotel, Suleimaniya

The hacks here with Pentagon sources have stopped saying today is D-Day. The US is going through the diplomatic motions, however determined it is on war, and is contriving language with Britain and Spain to sell a UN resolution. At breakfast, Ham'ali Khan swears the war will begin in four days. He says he knows. Everyone knows, except me.

ABC wants us to be ready whenever the flag goes up, so we push the Kurdish feature forward. We take off early this morning in an old, big-busted Layla Alawi and Jemal's new Monica to film in New Halabja. Clouds are gathered over the mountain, leaving the sky clear over the plain. In the bare fields, children rummage in furrows looking for something. Here, it could be rodents, coloured stones or land mines. Cattle graze the short grass. Old men leaning on staffs watch their sheep at the roadside, where the longest shoots are. The two-lane asphalt leads through mud and stone hamlets alongside giant power pylons. Jemal and Hunear, the new driver with the Layla Alawi, love overtaking tractors and farm trucks. We come to a bridge where a sign points to Kara Gol (Black Rose, from the Turkish *kara gul*). Not many roses, but wildflowers grow everywhere, along the dusty roads to the collective village called New Halabja. Saddam built it to contain survivors of the Anfal and the chemical attacks. He called it Saddam City. Jemal tells Fabrice to keep the windows up, because he is afraid of Islamic fundamentalists. I doubt a window would deter a suicide bomber.

To ease some of Jemal's worries, we stop at the PUK security office and pick up two guards. We drive towards the bazaar. Jemal parks his car beside the offices of Komol Islamiya. They are about as fundamentalist as you get in New Halabja. When Jemal sees their sign, he jumps back into the car and moves it 100 yards further on.

We interview people in the streets, and Fabrice shoots much of the town. It's a jolly, colourful place that has shaken off its birth as a Baathist collective town. As soon as we begin doing my stand-up, the *muezzin* launches into his prayer call. Other *muezzins* join in from other minarets. Duelling *muezzins*. It's that kind of town. We wait. And wait. And wait. For some reason, they take about an hour. It must be a holiday. We give up and go to the cemetery outside town to interview the one Kurd who really knows how to talk. Why hadn't I thought of putting him on camera before?

Ham'ali leans forward and rests an arm on a rock wall. I face him on the other side. The mountains and bare sky loom behind him. Fabrice sets the shot, and it is beautiful. We could be interviewing a pioneer in Montana's Big Sky country. Ham'ali, for the most part, ignores my questions. He's one hell of an actor.

'I am like an artist,' he says, in his growl of a voice. 'I need my freedom. This is my land. If I have my flag in the United Nations, it is my right. But until now, most of the leaders are afraid to say we want freedom ... I don't know what will happen when the United States hit Baghdad. I don't know. Even our leaders, they didn't know what will happen ... So, the destiny of Kurds, nobody knows where we go. Nobody know what will happen. But I don't know in the end that Talabani and Barzani go to Baghdad. There must be an Iraqi democratic country ... This area suffer for so many years. I want to be quiet. No war. No killing. I need my freedom. Tomorrow, after tomorrow, my child will some day shout for his freedom. But now the situation is complicated situation. We will go to Kirkuk. We must go to Kirkuk, because Kirkuk is ... Eighty percent of people in Kirkuk are Kurd ... Yes, I need Kirkuk.'

'Even if the United States and Turkey won't let you?'

'So, we will fight again. That's our destiny.'

'Will the Kurds ever stop fighting?'

'They say Turkish military will come to this area, and I will fight with them. I'll be one of the first *Peshmerga* to fight. Because this is my land. This is my country.'

'Why do the Kurds in Iraq feel so strongly about not having Turkey here?'

'They come to destroy everything. We have our hopes and our dreams. They think when they come with their military, they destroy everything ... In this last twelve years, we made something beautiful to Kurdistan. Although there was a war between armies, between

Talabani and Barzani, but we do beautiful things to our country. Now we are living in freedom. We have own government. If they come, they say they will take all of the weapons from Kurd. So, it means we fight again.'

When Fabrice finishes shooting, we split up. Don, Ham'ali and I head to Lake Darbandikan to find a ship. I have decided to call her the *Queen of the Tigris*. From the edge of the lake, we walk down to a fishing village. It is miles along a mud path. We find some fishermen, who lead us another mile on to an inlet. There are ten rowboats, all too tiny for our crew, satellite dish and other equipment. Even if we had a fleet of these dinghies, it couldn't work. There would be nowhere to sleep, and they wouldn't stabilise for satellite transmission. It is a long, long hike for nothing. On the way back, though, Don lights on a small mud village and takes pictures. Its Kurdish family doesn't mind, and the women make bread and wash clothes as if he weren't there. It's the happiest I've seen Don in days. The family know Ham'ali from his films and offer us tea. It's a good end to a good day.

Ham'ali won't give up. He'll find a barge tomorrow in Lake Dokan. If there is one, we can lift it out with a crane, put it on a truck and drive it south. Could be a great adventure.

Saturday, 15 March 2003
Palace Hotel, Suleimaniya

Fabrice, Bob and Jella leave at 0700 to film the al-Hakims' Badr Brigade near old Halabja. Andy and I review tapes for our Kurdish feature. Rick Kaplan, an exuberant executive who has just returned to ABC after running CNN's news for a few years, wants to include it in his three-hour, eve-of-war special. The Kurds look striking, as always, in their battle dress on Andy's monitor. The baggy trousers, the bandoliers and the curling moustaches make them among the world's most romantic-looking fighters. How were these brave warriors beaten by the British, the Iranians, the Arabs and the Turks? They love to tell war stories and feats of valour, always ending with their flight to the mountains. It is impossible to dislike them. Fabrice's panoramas of the mountains are beautiful, as are his Kurdish faces. In the early afternoon, Ham'ali is back from Dokan, 'Good news! I have the boat. It's a big one – for twenty people.' He's going back with a mechanic to check its river-worthiness.

I go to see Kurdish military commanders, who will not answer my questions about expanding the Kurdish region south to Khanaqin. The INC says it is on its way to Ankara, then Washington, and plans to be back here in time for war. Kurds are now leaving Kirkuk at a rate of about 500 a day. Some of them tell us the army is mining the roads. The US used a B-1 bomber for the first time on Iraqi radar today. Don asks, 'How much radar can they have? America has bombed them every day for ten years.'

Sunday, 16 March 2003
Palace Hotel, Suleimaniya

BBC radio reports at 0600 GMT that Bush, Blair and José María Aznar will meet in the Azores to make a statement on their proposed UN war resolution. Landay's interpreter, Karim, is down with typhoid. Don seems very tired and has a bad gut; and I'm worried about him. He was sick during the night. Bob Harle, who has been waiting for Qassem Dergham to come from Syria and relieve him, also has a bad stomach. He cannot hold out much longer. Disney announces it needs to save money, so ABC is recalling correspondents Hilary Brown from Adana and Mike Lee from Bahrain. Seventy-odd are told to leave Kuwait. And the war has not begun.

We hear that, because of French opposition to the war, Americans are now boycotting French wine and eating 'freedom fries'. Don says, 'Then they should send back the Statue of Liberty.' Jim Muir adds, 'What they need is a statue of puberty. To grow up.' Tired of hotel breakfasts, I eat sweet buffalo cheese with honey that I bought last night in the bazaar. Don is wearing a red-checkered lumberjack shirt he bought here. We are becoming local. Jim says he and Kaveh are a two-man band here, while there are eleven people in Erbil with John Simpson. At 0930, Kurdistan observes a two-minute silence in memory of the dead of Halabja. When it ends, Jim says, 'You still have people dying in Tehran from Saddam's gas attacks. The mustard gas stays in your lungs. There are still birth defects from it. We saw children in Halabja with no backs to their heads, eye problems and other defects. Cancers. We saw an old man last year whose eyes were being progressively eaten away.'

Eliza Griswold, an American freelance journalist, comes from Erbil with boxes of equipment that Bruno gave her to deliver to our work suite. An ABC satellite dish has arrived from Turkey, and Bruno is trying to make it work in Erbil. We hope he brings it here. I call him, and he confirms he will come tomorrow. I tell Fabrice Bruno is on his way here, and he shudders. Kurdsat broadcasts footage of the 1988 Halabja massacre all day for the anniversary. Rumours, as always in situations like these, abound: war will commence on Tuesday. On Thursday. At the end of the month. Some say Bush will declare war tonight in the Azores, the launch point for Portugal's original imperial conquests. Did he, Blair and Aznar choose to meet there for its symbolism?

Three brothers of Salar Bapir, a Kurdish friend in London, come to tea at the Palace Hotel. One of them owns a fleet of cars and says we can rent them if need be. Landay comes into the lobby and shouts, 'That bastard [Mam Rostom] has promised to take *everybody* to Kirkuk!' Poor Jonathan. He believed Rostom would take only ABC and himself. The Bapir brothers have no idea what he is talking about.

Panic seizes networkland in our afternoon, New York's morning. Powell and Cheney make their war calls. Bush speaks. ABC sets up a conference call: London, New York, Bruno in Erbil and me. What should we do? Play it by ear, I say. Bruno makes the case to base all of us in Erbil. I push for Suleimaniya: better sources, closer to Kirkuk, clean sheets. Bruno says his new satellite dish is not working. The Kurdsat engineers here offer to repair it, if he brings it over.

Azad says Republican Guards are being withdrawn from Mosul south to Tikrit and from Khanaqin, a Saddam-held Kurdish town south of Kalar, to Baghdad. He has brought his wife and two young daughters to dinner at the hotel; they are all dressed for a night out, perhaps their last for awhile. Eliza and I have dinner at the Indian restaurant. An Episcopalian bishop's daughter, she says she is writing a piece for *Harper's*. So am I. Hers is on American Protestant evangelicals, who are trying to convert Muslims to Christianity. She thinks they are mad. They are in the right place.

Monday, 17 March 2003
Palace Hotel, Suleimaniya

The 0600 GMT news on BBC Radio tells of today's Bush-Blair-Aznar meeting in the Azores, the failure of their UN resolution and the probable announcement of war. The million anti-war demonstrators in Washington, Toronto and elsewhere count for nothing. News from Israel: American peace activist Rachel Corrie, twenty-three, is crushed to death by an Israeli bulldozer. Every day, the Arabs see Israel's crimes in the territories and hear no criticism, let alone condemnation, from Washington. Tayyip Erdogan, who is about to become Turkey's prime minister, says there will be no discussion in parliament of the US aid and military cooperation agreement until 23 March. Although it will be a vote of confidence in his government, it will come too late for the US to use Turkey as a base for a northern front. Washington is furious with Turkey. After freedom fries, I suppose, Americans may celebrate Thanksgiving with 'freedom birds'.

There is no war fever in the Palace lobby this morning. The drivers and translators sit around waiting, as usual, while the hacks decipher the smoke signals over breakfast. Fabrice comes down and asks, 'Do you want the bad news now or later?' Later, I say. He gives it to me now, 'Bruno called.' Poor Fabrice. Bruno told him he doesn't like the location Fabrice chose to cover the front from in Chamchamal. First of all, Bruno says, there is no electricity in Chamchamal. Fabrice tells him we have a generator. It is too far from Kirkuk, Bruno says. Fabrice answers that it is closer to Kirkuk than Erbil is. By the time Bruno calls me, I am braced. I ask him not to worry. Fabrice, who has been in the business twenty years longer than him, knows what he is doing. I tell Bruno, as a new friend, to be calm and follow events rather than devise elaborate plans that will have to change. Slowly, he tries to overcome his natural inclination to panic. He calms down and agrees to bring the dish to Suleimaniya today. He is basically a good guy, who must learn not to fret. When war begins, there will be worry enough.

Rumours of a start date for war abound: Tuesday, Thursday, etc, will be D-Day. Who knows? Landay is still complaining that Mam Rostom promised to take every hack here into Kirkuk. Fabrice, Bob and I return to Chamchamal to interview Kurds fleeing Kirkuk. They seem to want to avoid the fate of those who were arrested during the uprising of 1991. Iraqi soldiers stop them at the last checkpoint before Chamchamal and make them walk. Some say the troops are moving from place to place because Iraq's military intelligence officers do not trust the regular army brigades. They fear, probably with reason, that they are making private agreements with the Kurds to surrender.

One man says a new Republican Guard artillery unit has just moved into a base near Kirkuk. A Kurdish military source says the Iraqis are preparing to burn the Kirkuk oilfields. But, he believes, the US can prevent it if it gives air support to the Kurds. 'People will rise up easily,' he says. 'Except for the Khalid Military Camp [the Republican Guards' main barracks], there is less than a brigade in and around Kirkuk and one artillery unit at Laylan. I think Saddam will not have time to strike us. When America starts, Saddam Hussein will not be able to strike. The *Peshmergas* will defend the area. If they attack us, we can push them back. You will see how people are looking forward to seeing us and to be reunited with their families.'

Back at the Palace, Jim says Khosrat told him there will not be any northern front. There will be no uprising in Kirkuk and Mosul. That is what the US told him. Khosrat believes Saddam will collapse within a week to ten days. He also believes that the US has people inside Saddam's army.

We all have dinner, again, at the hotel Indian. Eliza tells me of three journalistic romances, born in Afghanistan and dead in Kurdistan. One is Kate Brooks and a heavy Australian named Mick Ware, also from *Time*. Eliza points to two other couples in the restaurant who, however loving they were in Kandahar, are not speaking to each other now. Tonight, Bush declares that tomorrow will be the 'moment of truth for the world', and leaves the Azores. The State Department recalls 'non-essential' staff from its Mideast embassies.

Tuesday, 18 March 2003
Palace Hotel, Suleimaniya

I am up at two-thirty this morning: first when a friend calls from London, then to broadcast live after Bush's declaration of war. ABC wants us to go live from the hotel, but a fierce wind has sent our satellite dish crashing down from the roof. We – Fabrice, Bruno, Bob, Azad and Hiwa – drive to Kurdsat and stand outside with the camera in freezing weather to use their satellite. We watch Bush deliver his speech on a television monitor. Apparently transfixed by his teleprompter, Bush gives Saddam and his sons forty-eight hours to leave Iraq, Wyatt Earp in Dodge. 'All foreigners,' he says, 'including journalists and inspectors, should leave Iraq immediately.' He ends, 'God bless America.' To the people of Iraq, he says, 'The day of your liberation is near.' ABC runs, amidst its worldwide coverage, our Kurdish feature including the interview with Ham'ali. We do one short piece to camera on the reaction in Kurdistan, so far as there is any, to the imminent war. At 0600, we break down the equipment, pack it into the cars and return to the Palace to sleep again.

The morning resumes with bad news. Ham'ali says the *Queen of the Tigris* can't be realised after all. With many Shiites on the riverbanks, no Kurdish river pilot will take the chance. The Kurdish captain of the ship won't let us take it without him, and he won't go. Damn. Ham'ali has another idea: an ambulance! We can go south in an ambulance, he says. No one will stop us. Well ...

The dollar is going down and the price of gasoline is up 100 percent. The people of Suleimaniya are not panicking, but they seem anxious.

From the White House, spokesman Ari Fleischer announces that US forces will enter Iraq even if Saddam Hussein departs. Not much incentive, then, for him to leave. Hans Blix's United Nations Monitoring, Verification and Inspection Commission leaves Baghdad. Kofi Annan instructs the rest of the UN's staff to pull out. Zalmay Khalilzad, in Ankara, tells the BBC that the Kurds have agreed not to send forces into Kirkuk and Mosul. This is more or less what Khosrat told Jim, but it is just not believable. Nothing will keep the Kurdish displaced people out of Kirkuk, and among them are thousands of armed men. Most of Kirkuk fell to the Kurds in 1991, when Saddam's forces were much stronger than they are now. The US is peddling the idea that the Kurds will avoid Kirkuk either to satisfy the Turks or because they know nothing about Iraq. Khalilzad says US troops will secure the northern oilfields. Blair wins a parliamentary vote for war, despite a rebellion by 122 Labour rebels, thanks to Conservative support. Robin Cook resigns. Clare Short doesn't.

Wednesday, 19 March 2003
Palace Hotel, Suleimaniya

The war may begin tomorrow at 1800 local time, if my sources are correct. I'm exhausted already. At breakfast, Jonathan Landay says the PUK and KDP have agreed to put their forces under US military command. Is he sure? Well, he says, Khalilzad announced it last night. It seems the Turkish parliament, that spanner in American works, votes today on whether the US may fly over Turkey to bomb Iraq. Don comes down looking healthy. He says he had a good sleep and has not had a drink in three days. I suspect he's better because his wait for the war is nearly over. Anthony Loyd finishes breakfast and says he is going to Chamchamal, where he's rented a house. He'll wait there for war to start. For some reason, Bruno fires Azad, the Kurdsat news director he hired to fix things for ABC. Within the hour another network hires him, and he's off with their crew.

A day of astounding tedium with a satellite dish broken in the overnight storm, car and driver troubles, interpreter problems, pointless calls from ABC in New York and London. Jemal drives me up to Dokan. On the road, we pass a family on a tractor. The women and children are on a trailer behind, covered in a plastic tarp. There is another family, also heading out of town, in a Toyota pickup. Jamal says some people, maybe 30 percent, are leaving Suleimaniya to stay with relations in the villages. They are afraid of chemicals. There is not much traffic, and the small exodus is not a panic escape. At a petrol station outside town, the queue of cars is about a mile long. They say

Saddam has cut the petrol supply from Kirkuk, and what the Kurds have now is smuggled in.

Up at the INC Big House, two former officers of the Iraqi army, General Mahdi al-Duleimi and General Ahmad al-Samarrai, have taken up residence. They say they have just arrived from Turkey. Mudhar says they are part of the INC's 'outreach' to the Iraqi army – as though they were Alcoholics Anonymous. While Fox Television blares behind us, Mudhar says, 'We may go direct to Baghdad. If it takes ten days, we may establish ourselves in Mosul. Then Tikrit. The cities on the line to Baghdad. We are waiting for several hundred US Special Forces to come from Turkey to escort us.' What happens, I ask, if the Americans don't want the INC in Baghdad? He says the US will just have to let the INC go on its own.

General al-Duleimi, a quiet man from the old officer corps and a Mosul native, was on the general staff. He left the army in 1994 and worked with the INC in Erbil in 1995 and 1996. He says the army now has five corps outside Baghdad, one each around Kirkuk, Baquba, Basra, Kut and Mosul. The Republican Guards, he says, are deployed around Baghdad. 'The regular army,' he says, relying on reports from colleagues who remain in the army, 'has shortages in everything – men, officers, tanks, vehicles. It varies from unit to unit.' He does not believe Saddam's army will fight, except in Baghdad.

'He doesn't care about other places. The Republican Guards will go to Baghdad to force street fighting in the city. But I think you should not do this in Baghdad. There should be something inside, a revolution.'

Is that possible?

'If you have a plan before, with the officers. Most of the officers are against Saddam. At the same time, they are afraid of Saddam. The regular army, it would be very good to gather them. It is better if they come with the US into Baghdad. The Republican Guards, when they see the regular army coming towards Baghdad, and we ask them to come with us, they will. I am sure. I cannot say they will never fight. I think there will be some little fighting.' He says some former Republican Guards are now in Ankara, and he has asked them to come to Dokan.

Amar Shawkat, Mudhar's younger cousin, who deserted the army after the 1991 uprising, remembers, 'As soon as the uprising began, there were pickup trucks with automatic weapons everywhere. It will happen again. In 1991, they looted in the south, in Basra, in Kufa. It was anarchy. There was no opposition at that time. There is a mixed opposition now.' He believes the opposition groups, if allowed, can control the violence. An exile for more than ten years, Amar says, 'Normal Iraqis in Europe have mixed feelings about the whole thing. They have been disappointed. That could change in five minutes.' Later, Mudhar tells me that Amar's father, first cousin of his own father, was murdered by Saddam in 1968.

Back at the Palace, Nizar Said (about whom I did a *Nightline* report in 1991 and who now works for Barham Saleh) takes me aside. He says the US-Turkey agreement has three parts: to allow US overflights of Turkey, to open a land corridor for US troops and to permit a Turkish military presence in Kurdish Iraq. Talabani is in Ankara, where he is trying to maintain relations with Turkey while opposing a Turkish invasion. We sit down and watch al-Jazeera on the coffee shop television. Turkish crowds, nationalists who in general hate Kurds, push Talabani as he enters a conference in Ankara. Everyone in the coffee shop laughs when the al-Jazeera correspondent calls Saleh 'the KDP [instead of the PUK] prime minister'. Azad returns from his day in Chamchamal with his new employers. He says Kirkuk is under curfew; the military is arresting people, and only army cars are allowed to drive. Although he is no longer working for ABC, he says he rented a house for us in Chamchamal.

ABC London calls, once again, to ask whether Tariq Aziz has defected to the Kurds. Marcus Wilford, the bureau chief, explains that the story began with a Bulgarian radio stringer in Kuwait. We still have to check. I call Hoshyar Zebari, who laughs at the suggestion.

I go to Khosrat's house. Iraqi Kurdistan is one of the few places you can just drop in on political and military leaders. They usually don't bother with spokesmen. Saleh, Khosrat and the Talabanis have told us we can come by anytime, so we do. A guard takes me upstairs through a large sitting room to Khosrat's study, where a vase of artificial flowers stands on a table. The wall behind it holds two carbines. I ask Khosrat about his understanding with the US on Kirkuk and Mosul.

'Up to this moment,' he says, 'the USA told us not to enter Kirkuk and Mosul. Our forces are ready, though, for the unexpected ... We are ready to cooperate with US troops, to establish a front for the US forces to go by land. We don't like to act to annoy the US.'

Has he, as I was told, put his forces under American command?

'It's not certain. Talabani has not contacted us from Ankara. If they want it, we are ready. Yes. We would like such cooperation. Jalal will be back tomorrow or the next day.'

Have any Turks entered Iraq?

'It's not clear yet.'

Will there be uprisings in Kirkuk and Mosul?

'The level to which the Iraqi army deteriorates will determine this.'

If there is an uprising, will his forces go in?

'There is no decision. I don't want to disturb the Americans. Our intention is to work for the longer term with the Americans.'

Will the Kurdish forces go to Baghdad?

'Politically, we should have a headquarters in Baghdad. It is the centre. Because we are Iraqis, we should have an existence in Baghdad. There are one and a half million Kurds in Baghdad. But we won't be there militarily, unless they need us to be there.' He says his troops will attack the fundamentalists of Ansar al-Islam with US air cover. (I ask whether the Kurds will fight the Mujahideen-e-Khalq; he answers, 'Probably.')

What about WMD?

'I hope that Saddam will never use biological or chemical weapons against civilians.'

He would like the war to have a northern front. It would give territorial gains to the Kurds and give them a voice in postwar Iraq. 'Saddam is finished,' he says. He denies that Tariq Aziz has defected. Others may, he says, when the air strikes begin. 'High Iraqi officials will start surrendering. They will come.'

Does he trust his American allies?

'Let's be realistic. The world today is a world of interests. Churchill said there are no friendships in politics, but there are interests. At this stage especially, the interests of Iraqi Kurds are in conjunction with America's. That is why America needs an alliance, and the Kurds need an alliance. September 11th brought us closer, because Arabs threatened America. On Kurdsat, I said this is the first time the Kurds will be on the winning side. Americans are winners, and the Kurds are with the Americans. So, we will be winners ... We cannot compare now with 1975, '88 and '91. The world has changed. It is unipolar. Until 1990, Kurdish leaders were not received by any ambassador. Two days ago, Barham [Saleh] met with Tony Blair. Today, my son and two other students met Blair and thanked him. So, the world has changed ... There were mistakes by the leadership. It was not able to choose the best ally at the time. [Respected Kurdish nationalist] Sami Abdel Rahman said Americans betrayed us three times. We owe a lot to America. For twelve years, we are ruling ourselves, protected by the Americans. That is not gratitude to talk about the USA in this way. If American troops arrive here now, they will be received with flowers.'

When it is all over, he says, he looks forward to a federal Iraq with a single Kurdish province including Kirkuk. Then, 'the Kurds will be significant allies to the USA'.

Before I go, he writes up a pass that I can use to get through PUK checkpoints when the war starts. It could be useful.

Dinner at the Indian with Nizar and Don. Sleep at 3 AM.

Thursday, 20 March 2003
Palace Hotel, Suleimaniya

At 0545 local time, Zoe Magee of ABC's London desk calls. The US air bombardment of Baghdad is beginning. 'Ari Fleischer is about to go to the podium,' she says. I play with the idea of returning to sleep. My source said war would begin at 1800. This is too soon. But I don't go back to sleep. It's time to work, for real: the waiting is, at last, done. While dressing, I watch the BBC television: static shot of a quiet Baghdad morning. At the White House, Fleischer announces the opening stages have begun. Most of the television channels – MBC, LBC, RTL, DW – show tranquil Baghdad scenes; al-Jazeera shows the roofs of Baghdad's skyline on fire. Their reporter, Tariq Ayoub, is wearing a helmet and flak jacket. Above his voice are the air raid sirens. The skies here in the north, perhaps in sympathy, are rumbling with thunder. Marcus Wilford calls from London and tells us to be ready to go live. He adds, 'We fell for the oldest trick in the book. The Pentagon told McWethy it would start on Friday night.' My source said it would begin today, but not until 1800. He was a little closer.

Bush, in a red tie, white shirt and blue suit, delivers his address to the universe, 'We have no ambition in Iraq.' No ambition? He ends, 'We will defend freedom. We will bring freedom to others. We will prevail.'

When we try to go live from the balcony of Suite 110, our satellite dish and videophones do not work. I have to go alone through the empty streets about five miles to the Sarchnar Hotel on the western outskirts of town. There I find two Lebanese journalists, Joseph and Abdel Hakim of Sawatel, in a car park beside their truck, with an old satellite dish. As rain falls, they hook me up to New York. Under an umbrella in an empty car park, I'm live in no time. *Nightline* is on, but they don't want anything from Suleimaniya. I wait in the rain for the next broadcast, due in an hour. Listening to the reports from Washington, I learn that the bombing began ahead of schedule because the US found 'a target of opportunity'. The Pentagon says the targets were 'very senior Iraqi leaders'. That is, they were trying to murder Saddam at some Baghdad restaurant and killed civilians instead.

Thus begins a long day of live shots to camera that does not end until 0530 the next morning. Between appearances, I go inside the hotel to watch television reports in the manager's office. At 0830, Saddam Hussein, wearing a field marshal's uniform and reading glasses, condemns the 'shameful crimes against Iraq and against humanity ... the honest family that is being unjustly treated.' He tells Iraqis, 'These days will add to your record. This is your share of dignity and victory. You will be victorious, O Iraqis! Draw your sword. I am not afraid.' He may not be afraid, but I am. The Iraqis must be tired of his idiotic speeches, the same kind he made when he dragged them to war in Iran and Kuwait. I go back outside, where the rain turns to hail. It is freezing. Joseph points the camera at me, and I hear a woman in New York ask how many UN troops there are in the north. UN troops? There aren't any here. There never have been. I say the northern front is quiet, and she goes to ABC News consultant Anthony Cordesman in Washington. A minute later, Jack McWethy of ABC says F-117 stealth bombers were the first planes to hit Baghdad today. They were also the first to bomb the city in 1991. That should give its manufacturers something to celebrate and a slogan for ads in *Jane's Defence Weekly*.

Afshin Abtahi, ABC's Tehran office manager, and a satellite engineer named Najafee arrive from Iran to do repairs. Bruno takes them to Chamchamal, and the US escalates its invasion. At 1500 local time Geoff Hoon, the UK's defence secretary, cautions Parliament against the notion that the campaign will be short. He announces that British forces are already engaged in operations, but does not disclose casualty figures. Russia, France and China demand an end to the war. At 1930 local, BBC World Service reports that the US bombed Southern Iraq this evening. The Turkish parliament approves a US air corridor for the bombing of Iraq from the north. At 2030, we are scheduled to go live again, this time from Suite 110 of the Palace. Our dish is not ready, but Sawatel has moved to the car park below. Sawatel, unfortunately, has its own technical problems. Andy rushes to their van and does some repairs. Forty-five minutes later, we are on the air. Nothing in the north competes with footage from embeds with the US Marines in the south or the bombing of Baghdad. My only contribution is commentary on the politics of Northern Iraq and Turkey. I add that Kurdish military sources tell me air raid sirens are going off in Mosul, but there are no signs yet of any bombing. Through my earpiece, I hear Donald Rumsfeld warning Iraqis not to go to work and to stay away from military targets. Good advice, but I doubt many of them are trying to get to work tonight.

At midnight, Bruno, Fabrice and Bob return from Chamchamal. They saw no US bombing of Kirkuk from there, no northern front yet. They could not get the second ABC satellite dish to work there. Afshin and Najafee remain in Chamchamal to repair it. At 0230, I am still standing on the balcony, trying to stay dry and to keep from freezing. New York comes to us occasionally, but not often. It looks like they are going to let us stand down, when someone reports that bombers just left Britain on their way here. They may bomb Mosul or Kirkuk, so we cannot sleep yet. An hour later, it seems the bombers are not coming this way. ABC has no more questions for its northern contingent, and I go next door to bed – but not to sleep. I read to calm myself and drift off an hour later. Then, at 0430, someone calls from the London desk. He says the air raid sirens are going off in Mosul, and I say I reported that a few hours ago. He checks with someone else on the newsdesk. 'Al-Jazeera reports there is bombing around Mosul,' he says. That is different, if true. I get up to make some calls and return to the balcony, tying on a microphone and ear piece. At 0500, an anchorman in New York asks me about the bombing in Mosul. I say we cannot confirm anything. With that, I am released to go back to sleep.

The television networks, taking their lead from the Pentagon propaganda apparatus, officially christen this Day One of 'Operation Iraqi Freedom'. How many days lie ahead? And how much freedom?

Friday, 21 March 2003
Palace Hotel, Suleimaniya

At 0843 this morning, the London desk calls to ask all the questions about conditions here and our plans that Bob Roy, a senior producer in New York, asked last night. BBC radio news at 1000 local time: US armour moves ninety-three miles north from Kuwait into Iraq and up the Fao Peninsula. John Simpson reports from near Erbil that US Special Forces have secured the Kirkuk airfields. But no one in Kirkuk, where the PUK and INC have agents with satellite phones, has seen them. They do say the US bombed Kirkuk during the night. All morning, we are in frantic mode, trying to repair equipment. Neither the new dish nor our electricity generator works. We cannot find parts or a mechanic, because everything is closed for Nowruz, Kurdish and Persian New Year.

Najafee is worried that US troops will arrest him at a checkpoint because he is Iranian. My solution is to issue all our local staff with identification cards, but we don't have any. We need a photocopier and passport photographs. Ham'ali to the rescue! He persuades the owner of a photo shop to open. I make some cards, and Ham'ali has them photocopied and laminated. They look as good as the ones ABC gave us in London. Meanwhile, there are no mechanics to fix the generator on account of the holiday. Undeterred, Ham'ali goes to the bazaar and stops everyone he sees to ask if one is a mechanic. Finally, one turns up. Ham'ali brings him to the hotel, and he gets to work. The problem was that someone put diesel into a petrol-driven generator. The mechanic cleans it, puts in petrol and restarts it. We pay him, and Ham'ali gives him a drink to celebrate.

Over whiskeys, Ham'ali says he learned three new English words today, '"Infamous", like Saddam Hussein. And "forger". And "including".'

'Including?'

'Yes, "including the war". "Including the Kurds." Like that.' For some reason, he recalls going to Baghdad in 1976 against his father's wishes to study at the Institute of Fine Arts. He was so broke that he worked nights in a bakery. His father relented and came to Baghdad to give him five *dinars*. He was there for five years, until Saddam drafted him to fight in the Iran-Iraq war. He returned home to join the *Peshmergas*. 'Not killer *Peshmerga*,' he says, 'but media *Peshmerga*.'

News reports say a US helicopter crashed in the south, killing eight British and four American soldiers. They are the first coalition deaths of the invasion. Some of Saddam's palaces are on fire in Baghdad. Azad says his man in Chamchamal called: Iraqi execution squads in black uniforms are taking people away in Kirkuk.

At 1515, Ahmad comes to the hotel, buoyant from his visit to Turkey, to do an interview with ABC's *Good Morning America* that makes NBC upstairs furious – they wanted him exclusively for their morning news. Ahmad's bodyguards, Hussein and Samih, are not wearing their usual jeans and T-shirts. They are in what looks like US Army combat gear with INC logos on the pockets. At 2215, Turkey announces its skies are open to US aircraft, and that it has no territorial ambitions in Iraq. I go live much of the day and all night. Zaab Sethna arrives from London, bringing a welcome delivery of chutney, the newspapers, *Private Eye* and mail that my son George gave him. After a late cognac with Fabrice, I head to bed at 0415.

Saturday, 22 March 2003
Palace Hotel, Suleimaniya

Zaab says the US bombed the Republican Guards' Khalid Garrison in Kirkuk, the only place in the city that did not fall to the Kurds in 1991. Nizar says the US hit Ansar al-Islam near Halabja with about 100 bombs overnight, causing 200 Ansar casualties, but eyewitnesses say most of the dead were from the popular, moderate Islamist group Komala Islami. The PUK followed up the bombardment by taking positions in the village of Khormal. I go to Barham Saleh's house. He insists the US will land thousands of troops here by air tonight. Bruno and the crew are in Chamchamal with a dish, but I have to wait here in case the troops arrive. All day, we have technical failures with our equipment. During my first 'live' of the day, the screen goes blank. Jeanmarie Condon in ABC's New York 'war room' calls to say an ITN crew are lost in the south (maybe dead), and an Australian journalist has been killed here. It turns out the Australian was a young cameraman named Paul Moran, a close friend of Zaab's. He was filming at a PUK checkpoint near Halabja when a suicide bomber detonated his car. (The correspondent was injured.)

For most of the day, we try to go live and our equipment breaks down. The frustrations of television ...

Sunday, 23 March 2003
Palace Hotel, Suleimaniya

For the first time since coming to Iraq, I suspect there will be no northern front. The US never needed it for military purposes, any more than it needs the British army. It wanted to involve Turkey, and thus NATO, for political reasons. NATO would not cover Turkey, and Turkey won't let the US come overland into northern Iraq. So

US forces will not conquer Kirkuk and Mosul and drive south to smite Tikrit on their way to connect in Baghdad with the southern offensive. When Baghdad falls, they will let the Iraqis in the north surrender. What else can the Iraqis do when their president is gone? Despite Kurdish assurances, no planeloads of US Special Forces or infantry arrived last night. The Kirkuk front is quiet.

Bruno calls to say that *This Week*, ABC's Sunday morning interview show, wants to interview Ahmad live from Dokan. Poor Bruno is frenzied – he always is, but more so today because Azad told him the PUK would attack Ansar al-Islam tonight. Don comes to Room 106 for a coffee, which I make with the espresso pot and hotplate I bought in town. He had a good night, albeit on the floor of a primitive house in Chamchamal. Landay also comes in for an espresso. He tells Don and me that he was in Khormal and Halabja, soon the front line between the PUK and Ansar al-Islam. He had his photo taken with *Peshmerga* fighters in a spot that took seven mortar rounds a half hour after he left. In Chamchamal, he went with smugglers to get closer to Iraqi positions. He did not say why. The PUK says 280 Special Forces landed in four planes during the night. At 1830, al-Jazeera broadcasts images of four captured and stunned American prisoners of war. It shows, as well, the battered corpses of four other American soldiers. Later, we attend a memorial at the Palace for Paul Moran. Among the speakers is his correspondent, whose head is bandaged. I did not know Moran, but everyone says he was a good guy.

Najafee and Afshin are mounting a satellite dish on one of the Monicas. If it works, we can go live anywhere. If it doesn't, we're screwed.

Monday, 24 March 2003
Palace Hotel, Suleimaniya

Two calls at dawn, one from Nizar and the other from Landay. Nizar says the US is bombing Ansar al-Islam near Halabja and the Iraqis in Kirkuk. His mother is in Halabja, and she says one US bomb hit the home of Sheikh Ali Bapir, who heads Komala Islami. Nizar believes there may be 200 dead among the Komala and Ansar. Landay in Shoresh can see American planes bombing the hills towards Kirkuk. I tell him Fabrice stayed all night on a hill above the Bakrajo airbase to film the US forces. By the time he left, no planes had landed. We should head to Chamchamal to see the bombing of Iraqi positions between it and Kirkuk. I ask Bruno to let us take our newly mobile satellite dish there. He agrees. Then he reneges and insists on keeping the dish in Suleimaniya. An argument follows. The point of a mobile dish is that it is mobile, and we should go live from Chamchamal to report the bombing of Kirkuk. Bruno disagrees. Fabrice and I overrule him.

By 1115, Bruno is still not ready to leave. I pass the time watching Saddam live on Iraqi television via the BBC. The leader praises his people's courage and promises, 'We are going to be victorious.' If the US is not winning, it is losing. For him, it is the opposite: if he is not losing, he is winning. Given the disparity of forces, every day he holds out is a victory until, that is, the fighting stops.

Fabrice, Bob, Ham'ali and I head to Chamchamal, praying that Bruno, Andy and Najafee will follow with the dish. We stop at the PUK headquarters in the village of Takiya to ask for an update before proceeding onto Chamchamal a few miles further on. From the PUK's roof, we see the hills between Chamchamal and Kirkuk. The bombing has stopped, but the PUK recorded the earlier air raid on video. I call Bruno and ask him to come here with Andy and make a dub of the PUK footage. Luckily, Bruno, Andy and Najafee are already on the way, about twenty minutes behind us, with the dish. We go on to find our grubby house in Chamchamal, film a little late aerial action and wait for them. They arrive with the PUK dub. From then on, we make television. We send a story that Andy cuts, do live shots from 'the front' and receive praise from our masters in New York. It is strangely satisfying, although nothing of importance is actually happening. Chamchamal is mostly deserted, but a few hearty souls have stayed behind to guard their houses and keep a few shops open. I am getting to like the place, but not enough to want to sleep on the concrete floor of a house without furniture or running water.

Don arrives by taxi from Halabja, where he says nothing much is happening yet between the PUK and Ansar al-Islam. Just before dark, he takes another taxi up to Dokan to see the INC people about their proposed trip to Baghdad. If they go into battle, Don wants to be with them. I suppose I do too, but not as enthusiastically as he does. I'd prefer to cruise on our own aboard the *Queen of the Tigris*.

Tuesday, 25 March 2003
Palace Hotel, Suleimaniya

Allen Pizzey comes by the Palace in the morning. Since he and his CBS crew left Erbil, he has been stuck near Chamchamal, tied to his satellite dish in an abandoned prison. He is as fed up with new-style network television as I am: lives, dishes, lives, question-and-answer, no reporting, no stories, no analysis. We have some espresso in Room 106 and hear, on the BBC at 0950 local, Paul Wolfowitz explaining the Iraqis' lack of enthusiasm for the American invaders, 'I think this is a people terrorised into silence.' Is it? Maybe, like most other people, they don't like foreign armies in their country. Bush is asking Congress for $75 billion for the war. At lunch at the hotel Indian, Allen tells stories about John Borrell and other friends from Africa days. Pizzey used to share a house with John in Lusaka and remembers just about everyone from the Rhodesian and Zambian press corps of the 1970s. Borrell, a New Zealander with *Time*, used to offer me dinner in Lusaka. Later, we were neighbours in Beirut. Then he hit the jackpot: married a beautiful Pole, bought some land in the forest south of Gdansk, built a lodge and became a wine importer. When I stayed with them a few years ago, I asked if he missed journalism. He took me for a walk with his two sons around his pristine lake, where ducks paddled, without another house in sight. What did I think?

Adnan Mufti, the PUK deputy prime minister, is in the Palace coffee shop. He says the US is being forced to review its strategy with the Kurds and Turks in the north, and with the Arabs in the south. 'Without Iraqi popular support, there will be a lot of difficulty for the Americans and British,' he warns. He expects more US coordination with the Iraqi opposition groups, because of the hostility of people in the south and disagreements with Turkey in the north. Even from here, I see that the invasion is a mess. That's no light at the end of the tunnel. It's fire. The British are falling back on saying there are 'unconfirmed' reports of a rising in Basra. CNN reports it later, leaving out the word 'unconfirmed'. If Basra rises against Saddam, we will know it, as we did in 1991.

Wednesday, 26 March 2003
Palace Hotel, Suleimaniya

At 0900, BBC radio reports that Iraqi forces stopped the US advance at the southern Shiite city of Nasiriya. To date, Americans and British killed: 40. Iraqis: 500. The Iraqi figure is a US estimate. The British are attacking Basra, where the 'uprising' remains unconfirmed. That is, no one claims any longer that there is an uprising. British artillery shells are, according to BBC reports, falling day and night on the city. Our ABC team here has a morning meeting in Suite 110. Fabrice and Andy say they want to leave Iraq by 8 April. Fabrice promised his daughter a holiday over Easter, and Andy wants to see his girlfriend. I pass this onto ABC London to give them time to send replacements. They tell me Qassem is not coming. He went twice from Beirut to Qamishli to cross the Euphrates from Syria; the Syrians stopped him both times. This is bad for us. Not only do we need him as a sound engineer – he's the best fixer alive and would be invaluable if we reach the Arabs south of here.

Worse still, Bob Harle is too ill to continue and asks to leave. The only way out is through Turkey, which has closed its border to the journalists who did not return on the bus that brought them to the Iraqi opposition conference in Salahuddin. ABC News in London, New York and Washington work hard for Turkish permission. A local doctor writes a letter confirming that Bob needs treatment in London. By early afternoon, he is on his way by taxi to the border. Andy, already working flat-out editing tapes, offers to do sound as well.

US Special Forces flew into Bakrajo last night, the first night we were not watching. An ABC News correspondent, Jim Sciutto, is embedded with them and is covering the proposed onslaught on the Kurdish Islamists near Halabja. We decide to do a story on American reassessment of policy towards the opposition in light of the lack of popular support for the invasion. Fabrice goes out to shoot some 'vox pops' in the bazaar and at the university. One man who criticises the Americans on camera is shouted down by the crowd. The PUK declares it is giving Ali Bapir and his Komala Islami party three days to evacuate the Halabja area or suffer American wrath alongside Ansar al-Islam. Mudhar, Zaab and General al-Duleimi come for lunch with us at the Indian. We tape an interview with Mudhar in Suite 110. The 'desert storm' in the south is blowing up here, and rain is dropping mud on the north. I write and track a script that Andy edits. We work late on it, but *World News Tonight* decides not to broadcast it. Zalmay Khalilzad arrives here in the dark to see Jalal Talabani, and 1,000 paratroopers of the 173rd Infantry Brigade are expected to drop somewhere near Erbil tonight. A British military spokesman refers to the war for 'hearts and minds' in the south. We refer to the 'credibility gap' between what Washington says and what is happening. It's *déjà*-Nam all over again.

Thursday, 27 March 2003
Palace Hotel, Suleimaniya

An anti-war consumer boycott of US products has begun in Europe and the Middle East. In Suleimaniya, all is mud on the ground and rain in the air. On the summits, new snow is falling. The 173rd Infantry Brigade did drop last night into Harir at the airstrip that Ahmad told me in January had already become a US base. Why they parachuted instead of landing in their planes is a mystery to everyone here. The base is far from Iraqi lines, and it is secure for landing. I would have said it was a publicity stunt, but they tried to keep the press away.

Fabrice goes to the PUK military headquarters with Ham'ali to film the US Special Forces who arrived here on Wednesday. When he finishes, one Green Beret demands that Fabrice hand over his tape.

Fabrice gives him a blank cassette. At 1730, Fabrice, Andy, Ham'ali and I drive to the western edge of town to do a stand-up. While waiting for Fabrice to set up his camera, I call Landay to see what he knows. He's in a car on his way to Chamchamal. 'You'd better get over there, Charlie,' he says. 'Those Iraqi positions on Bani Makan are gone.' The Iraqi army has abandoned its front and withdrawn to Kirkuk. We race towards Chamchamal. I call Bruno and ask him to meet us there with the mobile satellite dish. After some argument, he agrees.

By 1820 we reach what had been the first Iraqi checkpoint on the Kirkuk road. Mam Rostom is crowing as though he conquered the Iraqi army himself. The truth is that the Iraqis fled without a fight three hours earlier. The looting has already begun. *Peshmergas* are returning from the hills with gas masks, rifles, mortar shells, binoculars – equipment the Iraqis left in their empty bunkers. Fabrice films everything, and we interview Rostom in Kurdish. Ham'ali, himself swept along in the enthusiasm, translates. There is a lot of 'see you in Kirkuk' among the Kurds, and reporters surround Rostom in his triumphal hour. All the fighters know Ham'ali as 'Abbas', from *The Outlaw*; it's like going to the front with John Wayne.

Long after dark, the looters are still returning with war junk, but the journalists have left to file from Suleimaniya. Bruno arrives with our mobile dish, Afshin, Najafee and Mohsen, another satellite engineer just in from Iran. The engineers point the dish at the right satellite, and we are feeding material to London. We set up camp on the lonely road. The crew breaks out some food, and Afshin lights a little fire to brew tea. We do a spot then and there on the first evacuation of Iraqi positions in the north. The producers in New York thank us for the exclusive. Later, we are told that the piece was not broadcast: no American troops are involved.

We decide to return to Suleimaniya, but Don wants to stay the night in Chamchamal. We stop by Landay's house in Shoresh to see whether Don can stay there. After Landay's bodyguard scrutinises us, we go to the door. Landay is in stocking feet. We ask if Don can have a spot for his sleeping bag, because the rest of us are leaving. Landay says it's fine with him, but he has to check with the 'other guys' – his photographer Tom, known as 'Deputy Dawg' to his colleagues; Mick

Ware and Kate Brooks. After disappearing for a few minutes, Landay returns to say the guys don't want Don to stay. This is outrageous. It is unknown for journalists to refuse shelter to a colleague. Landay is ashamed, but he shares the house and abides by majority decision. Don is sixty-seven years old. He is probably the finest war photographer of the post-World War II era and an exceptionally kind man. Landay's three colleagues fall into another category. We go back to Suleimaniya, have lots of cold beer with our Indian *tikka* and sleep on clean sheets.

Friday, 28 March 2003
Palace Hotel, Suleimaniya

The war, such as it is, goes on elsewhere, and there is not much for us to do. We send a short spot to *Good Morning America* on Iraq's Chamchamal evacuation and have lunch at the hotel. Don, Fabrice and Andy are bored. Bruno leaves for Karahanjir, about halfway between Chamchamal and Kirkuk, then aborts the trip. Don and I drive up to the INC house in Dokan and have dinner at the Ashur Hotel bar with an American colonel from the US embassy in Cairo, Ted Seel, and some INC people, including Francis Brooks. Ted knows Jim Ritchie, another army colonel who was Defense Attaché in Beirut in 1987 and whom I liked. When Ritchie was a major he told young Lieutenant Seel to move to the Middle East for an interesting life. (Ritchie told me many years later that the Middle East was a graveyard for military and diplomatic careers. Ted agrees.) We drink a lot before and during dinner. When the food is cleared away, Ted and Francis open up.

Don and Ted talk about Vietnam, where Don took some of his most memorable photographs and where Ted did two one-year tours. Ted served in what the army called 'helicopter observation'. He flew as close to the ground as *this*, he says, his hand gliding a foot above a bowl of pistachios on the table. I do not write while he speaks, but make notes later in my room. This paraphrases his words:

'And I could see them, just like I see you,' he says, looking at the INC's Nabil Musawi opposite. 'Observation? It was assassination. You get used to it. We just shot them at close range. I didn't care anymore. Then I asked myself, was there anyone I would not kill?' He stops speaking, and we wait for the answer. I think he will swallow more whiskey – he is already through half a bottle of Teacher's – but he doesn't. He says, 'No.'

Then he says he never took R&R. Why not? When he arrived in country, his platoon lieutenant took R&R with his wife in Hawaii. When he came back, he shot himself. Then two other guys in his unit went on R&R. They came back, took more drugs and had nervous breakdowns. So, Ted stayed in Vietnam for the full year, both times. He was a Private First Class for a long time – too long, he says. Then he worked up the ranks. He says that, in his unit of assassins, one was an opium addict, two were homicidal maniacs and one was an alcoholic. (I guess Ted could have been the alcoholic, but I might be wrong. He drinks a lot, but holds his liquor.) At the end of his first tour, he boarded a military transport for the States. He had a window seat and looked out at Vietnam. Then he thought about all the people he shot. Suddenly, he says, the tears came. He hid his face, pressing it into the window. He looked at the guy next to him, hoping he had not noticed his tears; the guy didn't see anything – he was crying, too. Ted looked around the plane, he says, and everyone was crying. He was nineteen.

That was in the late 1960s, when John Wayne made the movie *The Green Berets*. At sixteen, I worked on that film part-time as Wayne's driver. One of the technical advisors, whom I more or less hero-worshipped, was a Special Forces major named Jerry Dodds. One night after filming at Warner Brothers, I asked Dodds about Vietnam. He was drunk, and grabbed me by the shirt. I remember him saying, 'You don't know what we're doing there. I kill people. I would kill anyone. I would kill your father if they told me to. I would kill you.' He was shaking. Because I was a young patriot who still believed the war was right, I tried to ignore what he said. That was before I read about the murderous Phoenix Program and Operation Speedy Express.

Francis and Ted talk about the American Civil War. Ted's grandfather fought for the Confederacy and killed himself after the war. Francis's people also fought for the rebels, although one ancestor was an abolitionist. My great-grandfather was in the Union Army. We argue about that war, 150 years later, in the midst of a war in Iraq, still getting angry about it; we three Americans are colonising the table, all at one end, while the Iraqis listen from the other.

Ted and his wife have six children. Their two sons were in the army, but left. One son is doing well as a civilian. The older boy, thirty-one, attempted suicide. Ted is not sympathetic and told his son so. If you kill yourself, he says he warned the boy, I won't feel guilty. Perhaps that was Ted's way of preventing another attempt. I want to tell Ted my mother killed herself, that you cannot stop it. It's like an incurable disease, a cancer, that eats you up. But the conversation takes another turn. We drink more. Then Francis talks about Saddam.

He says he would support the elimination of Saddam, even if every single Iraqi were killed in the process. I ask him to repeat what he said, and he does. He means it. 'I'm coming from a place different from you,' he says in that soft Southern drawl that you hear from preachers and conmen. 'I believe in good and evil. That man is absolute evil and must be destroyed.' That Virginian voice honed itself for twelve years in Decatur, an Atlanta suburb, and mellowed in the corridors of Washington. But I don't know where the ideas come from. He says he believes in Jesus, resurrection and eternity. If all the Iraqis die, he says, they will live in eternity. But the 'human Satan' must go, no matter what. Ted tells Francis he knows where he comes from, but he cannot go as far.

Ted knows more about killing than Francis does.

Saturday, 29 March 2003
Ashur Hotel, Lake Dokan

We are about to leave Suleimaniya when Patrick Cockburn, Allen Pizzey and ITN Channel Four correspondent Gaby Rado arrive in the Palace lobby from Erbil. Pizzey says he left Chámchamal after ten days in the filth of an old Baathist fortress on the morning the Iraqis withdrew from the front. He went, he said, to chase the American paras at Harir. He moans that he missed the story he waited ten days for. I reassure him: although we were there, we didn't get on the air. After lunch Don, Fabrice, Andy and I drive to Dokan and take rooms facing the lake for a weekend off, more or less. We go up to Ali Hassan al-Majid's Round House to see Nabil, Mudhar and Ahmad. Fabrice and Andy shoot B-roll of Ahmad.

Don and I go to the Big House to see Francis, Zaab, Amar Shawkat and the rest of the INC group. They and the US say the PUK and Special Forces beat the hell out of Ansar al-Islam, killing about 200 and expelling the rest to Iran. Marie Colvin of *The Sunday Times* is staying in Dokan, having just entered the country from Syria. She tells funny stories about all the journalists waiting in Qamishli for Syrian permission to cross the river. Two of them attempted to sneak across the water on inner tubes. The Syrians, however, caught them and stuck them back in their hotel. I remember that hotel from years past; worse than prison. Cockburn has also come here. We meet for dinner in the bar. Later, I stand on the balcony of my room and stare at the dark lake and the barren hills. Someone calls to tell me Molly Bingham, whose cousins I know in New York, has disappeared with three *Newsday* journalists in Baghdad. I try and fail to sleep on nylon sheets. This is Day Ten of Operation Iraqi Freedom.

Sunday, 30 March 2003
Ashur Hotel, Lake Dokan

While Fabrice, Andy, Don and I are outside listening to BBC World Service reports on the war in the south, Bruno comes out to the pool. 'Gaby Rado died,' he says. It seems he fell from the roof of the Abu Sanah Hotel in Suleimaniya. Hungarian-born Rado was a very nice guy and an excellent journalist. We hear that he fell in the dark while making a call on his satphone. Later versions of this story reach us during the day. He was shot; he was pushed; he jumped. It seems the last might be true. The body fell too far from the building, apparently, for him to have fallen, which means he must have run and jumped. Why?

Yesterday, a suicide bomber killed himself and four US Marines in the south near Nasiriya. Francis, up at the Big House, says the INC sent Hamid Shraeder, INC member and former Iraqi Republican Guard, to Qatar via Saudi Arabia aboard a US C-117 transport to act as INC-CENTCOM liaison. Putting a man in CENTCOM HQ is a coup for the INC, meaning further Pentagon recognition of them. Francis is exultant.

The US and PUK declare victory over Ansar al-Islam. Francis says the operation – involving B-52 strikes, Special Forces observation posts and *Peshmerga* light infantry – will be a 'template' for US cooperation with the Iraqi opposition in the south. Zaab says Iraq is press-ganging young boys into service and killing those who refuse to fight the US. Maybe. Nabil, Mudhar and Zaab join us for dinner in the Ashur bar. Even after drinking much whiskey, I cannot sleep on the nylon sheets.

Monday, 31 March 2003
Palace Hotel, Suleimaniya

Driving down from the lake, Don and I see a convoy of Humvees carrying American soldiers west through Dokan town. They stop, and we talk awhile. They are heading towards Shaklawa, but they do not say why. We drive down to Suleimaniya for lunch with Bruno, who left Dokan yesterday. We are waiting for tomorrow's trip to Kalar with Zaab to see the INC's 'army'. Zaab calls to say the opposition groups met US military brass in Dokan just after we left. Ahmad, he said, was the only leader there. Abdel Aziz al-Hakim and Massoud Barzani sent representatives. When Jalal Talabani saw that Barzani had not come in person, he left rather than sit with any KDP person lower than Barzani. Zaab says the US is furious that all the leaders did not attend.

Tomorrow's trip to the 'front'? Zaab says the PUK apparently arrested some of the INC troops near Kalar, so our trip to see them is cancelled. I call Barham Saleh to ask him why his people would arrest their allies in the INC, and he promises to investigate. At 2120, he calls back. He is suppressing anger. He calls the INC soldiers 'thugs', many of whom came from Iran without identification papers. He says a few other things about the INC's irregulars, but I don't write them down.

After dinner at the Indian, Pizzey offers me a cigar, my first since I got here. We have brandies and light up, as if in the smoking room at White's. He says that CBS embeds with the Fourth Infantry Division are hearing that the delay in the southern offensive could last months. There are equipment shortages on the road from the port at Umm Qasr to Baghdad, and the troops have to wait for supplies. The docks are clogged and unable to process the backlog. That, at least, is what the military says. *Months?* Meanwhile, US warplanes bomb the Iraqi Ministry of Information and buildings near the Palestine Hotel in Baghdad.

Tuesday, 1 April 2003
Palace Hotel, Suleimaniya

BBC World Service reports this morning that US troops at a checkpoint in the south shot a car carrying thirteen Iraqi women and children. Six are dead, seven wounded. Colin Powell goes to Turkey today. Landay believes Powell's trip means that, at last, the northern front will open and provide a story. Combat footage from the embeds in the south is making ABC forget us lonely wanderers of the north. That leaves me this morning to write a piece for *The London Review of Books* in Room 106, where I am surviving on espresso and visits from colleagues. The Special Forces and PUK give a joint press conference in Halabja to advertise their victory over a few hundred Islamic irregulars, whom they expelled to Iran. They insist the Ansar operation is a model for joint US-PUK attacks on Kirkuk and Mosul. Zaab and Nabil venture down from Dokan for chicken *tikka* and rice at the hotel with Don and me. They say the US is getting ready to fly nearly 700 INC volunteers to the south. That means the INC – and, more importantly, Don and I – may finally see the war. They will tell us within twenty-four hours whether we can accompany them. For the first time in weeks, Don seems happy. I suspect an April Fool's connection. I suspect it even more when Nabil says Saddam is either dead or wounded. He does not say why he believes this. The INC, meanwhile, are not the only volunteers in Iraq. Several hundred young men are coming through Jordan from Palestine, Yemen, Sudan and Jordan itself to fight *for* Saddam.

Wednesday, 2 April 2003
Palace Hotel, Suleimaniya

We waste the day in the hills and on the roads between Chamchamal and Karahanjir, in and out of abandoned Iraqi positions. Bad as our

day was, it was worse for the journalists who went to Kifri. Kaveh
Golestan is dead. He, Jim and their young producer, Stuart Hughes,
went to Kifri to report on Iraqi shelling of the Kurds' southern front.
They stopped at the PUK office there, where security chiefs warned
them about Iraqi mortar fire. A *Peshmerga* guide took them to a grassy
field to film. Stuart opened the car door and stepped on a land mine.
When the others heard the explosion, they thought it was a mortar
round. Kaveh jumped out of the car to take cover. His foot detonated
another mine, and he fell forward onto still another. Stuart, meanwhile,
was in agony from the pain of losing most of his foot. Jim rushed to help
him. While tending Stuart, who was bleeding badly, he realised that the
body on the field in front of him was that of his close friend Kaveh. Jim
did not know he himself had taken a piece of shrapnel until later, when
he noticed blood coming through a hole in his trousers.

I see Jim this evening, when he comes back to the hotel. He has
just left Stuart at a US field hospital; Jim is in shock. We have some
whiskey, but his voice seems disembodied. Three journalists have died
on our non-front in the north: Paul, Gaby and now Kaveh. This is
Day Fourteen of Operation Iraqi Freedom.

Thursday, 3 April 2003
Palace Hotel, Suleimaniya

BBC radio this morning reports CENTCOM's claim that US
forces are thirty kilometres from the southern outskirts of Baghdad.
Convoys of US troops cross the Tigris at Kut, where the British lost
their biggest battle to Turkey in the First World War. BBC World
broadcasts a report on Kaveh. It features a sympathetic tribute from
John Simpson and much of Kaveh's work, both as a Pulitzer-winning
photographer and as a cameraman. Two things are missing: Kaveh's
voice and mention of Stuart, who may lose his entire foot.

I declare a day off. The crew are tired. Bruno needs rest. We all
mourn Kaveh, who had worked many extra hours dubbing his tapes
for us and was generous with advice. Andy and Fabrice welcome
the holiday, but they do not trust Bruno to leave them in peace. I

ask Bruno to read a book or walk in the bazaar or lie around doing nothing. He hates the thought of it.

Landay shows me a story he wrote, with two other reporters, on the Knight Ridder newswire, putting the case that the northern front is about to open: US soldiers arriving here, supplies on the ground, *Peshmerga* available as cannon fodder, Powell's trip to Turkey, Iraqi pullbacks from the outskirts of Kirkuk and Mosul, meetings between American and Iraqi opposition officials, the expanding southern leg of Kurdistan near Kalar and Kifri. Mix it all up and what do you get? The northern front, I guess.

We have some of my Lavazza in Room 106 and examine a map of the north. Landay says he promised his son he would be home for his ninth birthday on 28 April. If he breaks his promise, he says he'll take the boy camping in West Virginia. I tell him not to risk his life, but he says the Knight Ridder papers love it when he does. All his reports on the battle against Ansar al-Islam near Halabja, where he did risk his life for what was not an important story, ran on the front page. It helped that he was with the US Special Forces, who gave him gung-ho quotes and did a lot of shooting. This is what the papers want, he says, and what helps the career.

Don and I walk to new parts of the Suleimaniya bazaar, where I buy shirts, pens and cakes. We see the roastery, a corner of the marketplace with huge, rotating, gas-fired metal drums. Nuts burning inside are poured into barrels to cool. The shopkeepers all offer us tea. One says two of his brothers live in England, but he is not sure where. Don goes back to the hotel, and I stop by Mariwan the barber for a shave. Sophie calls my Kurdish mobile from London. She is finishing the music on her film.

When I return to the Palace, the hacks and drivers and hangers-on fill the lobby. Someone tells me the US advance is now twenty kilometres from Baghdad. The tanks, they say, are within sight of Saddam International Airport. Some of the Kurds insist the US is also moving on Mosul, but there is no evidence to support this. What seems to be happening is that some Special Forces are directing air strikes on the city. Mosul would probably fall to the Boy Scouts by now. The 173rd Airborne Brigade is receiving supplies by land from

Turkey, despite Turkey's insistence that the US would not use its territory for the war. The Turks are permitting food, medicine, fuel and trucks. Weapons are ostensibly excluded.

At 1900, Barham Saleh gives a press conference in the hotel mezzanine. Hacks, who have nothing else to do, jam into the small reception room. In a blue suit and red tie, the bald Saleh says, 'The environment is one of flux ... We had a meeting yesterday with Chalabi and the US ... We are working from the same sheet of music.' Same sheet of music? Saleh lived in Washington a long time.

'The PUK will not move against Kirkuk – as Kurdish fighters ... but as the Iraqi opposition and in tandem with the US. We and the KDP have decided not to wage any unilateral military action. It must be in the context of the drive to Baghdad. It requires consultation between the Iraqi opposition and the US ... We don't have representatives in Doha, but we have American officers here. We need to operate as the Iraqi opposition. Baghdad's fate cannot be settled by the Kurds alone. We have a deliberate policy decision to act as Iraqis, to move to overthrow the dictatorship ... We have one single objective: Baghdad. We might as well claim our part of this country, and to do that we need to be in Baghdad.'

Most Kurds, I know, want an independent Kurdistan. Because Turkey, Iran and the Arabs will not allow them to have it, they'll take an autonomous Kurdish state within a federal Iraqi republic. So they say. But what will they do to Baghdad? Will the Arabs of the capital welcome the baggy-trousered warriors who have fought against Iraq since its birth?

'We were in Kirkuk in 1991,' Saleh says. 'And we are very proud of those two weeks. But they were only two weeks. But we were not in Baghdad.' He praises the *Peshmergas* for their role in eliminating Ansar al-Islam. 'The success of it was a testament to what can be achieved between the indigenous forces and the Americans. This shows that the participation of the Iraqi opposition can make the liberation of Iraq easier.'

While making notes of Saleh's talk, I see Bruno come into the room. He leaves when I remind him this is his day off. That means no work, not even a press conference.

American tanks are, by nightfall, said to be at the airport in Baghdad. Rageh Omar of the BBC, who is in Baghdad, reports that forty-odd journalists taken by bus to the airport saw 'no signs of military presence. We didn't see anything'. The electricity has gone off in Baghdad. The BBC runs a report from an embedded ABC correspondent, who says, 'We had to keep firing and keep pushing north.' *We?* The embedding seems to be working – for the Pentagon. The quote of the day comes, once again, from the Iraqi Minister of Information, the unflappable Muhammad Saeed Sahaf, 'They are trapped everywhere in the country.' He is, strangely, referring to US rather than Iraqi forces.

At dinner at the Indian, Pizzey tells war stories. We have cigars and brandy again, and he recalls a run-in with Robert Mugabe's ZANU guerrillas during the Rhodesian war. The guerrillas in Mozambique, near Rhodesia's eastern highlands, said they were going to execute him. Something distracted them, and they forgot to shoot him. That was twenty-five years ago, when we were young.

Do we need more war stories to tell?

Friday, 4 April 2003
Palace Hotel, Suleimaniya

Baghdad is falling, and we are stuck here north of the war. American forces are all over Saddam International Airport, as the television pictures are showing. Just when I fear we have missed the war, Zaab calls, 'Come to Dokan. We're leaving. Don goes tonight. You can go tomorrow.' Finally. If Saleh is right about cooperation between the Iraqi opposition and the US, the deployment of Ahmad's volunteers could replicate the Kurdish-American cooperation against Ansar. Such is our hope.

Bruno leaves for Erbil, whose squalor calls to him, and is on the road when I ring to ask him to stop in Dokan to lend Don the digital camera. Don can shoot for ABC until Fabrice, Andy and I follow him to the south. We meet Bruno at the Ashur Hotel on Lake Dokan. Bruno shows Don how to use the camera and continues on his way to

Erbil. Don and I drive up to the INC Big House, where enthusiasm for battle is uncontained. A new checkpoint of armed men and oil drums guards the driveway. Men in uniforms, carrying AK-47s, parade about the concrete yard in front of the house. A few American officers are among them. Inside, the usual INC tea drinkers slouch in stuffed chairs watching al-Jazeera. Ahmad, Ted, Francis and Nabil are outside on the terrace near the satellite dishes. Behind are a lake and hills, far more beautiful than the desert they seek. Zaab says the place we are flying to is near Nasiriya and is now called 'George W. Bush, Jr Airport'.

We go into the room Francis and Zaab share, where two Kalashnikovs lean against a wall and paperback thrillers and Iraqi histories are piled on a table. I borrow *The Saddam Reader*, a collection of articles and interviews. Francis infects Don with his excitement over the coming campaign. The INC is taking 700 men south to join the Americans – shades of Davy Crockett heading to the Alamo with his Tennessee volunteers. What Francis wants, he says, is for Don to take a picture of Ahmad's historic arrival in the south. Ahmad will fly there tomorrow, and Don will be waiting. To Francis's disappointment, Don is shooting black-and-white film. Francis offers to lend him a digital camera so he can email colour pictures to newspapers everywhere. I know Don: he won't do it. Francis and Don are drinking beer when I leave.

On the road down, I see Kurdish families having Friday picnics on the riverbanks. A child rides a donkey. Men and women lie on rugs or tend wood fires for grilling meat. Youngsters drag bare feet in the freezing stream. I am reading Michel Aflaq in *The Saddam Reader*. Aflaq, the Christian founder of the Baath Arab Socialist Party, was a theoretician who lived to see his ideas embodied in his pupil, Saddam Hussein. His was both a mad and a reasonable dream: mad with its Nazi-like emphasis on race and power, reasonable in urging Arab independence and unity. The madness prevailed.

There is a seductive beauty to some of Aflaq's thoughts. His 1935 *Age of Heroism* tells the Arabs, 'We want independence and liberty because they are right and just and because they are the means to the release of our great gifts and creative capacities, so that we can realise

on this earth, which is our land, our aim and the aim of every man
– complete humanity.' Forty years later, when his party held absolute
power in Iraq and Syria, Aflaq's vision was more brutal. He told the
'advanced cadres of the Baath Arab Socialist Party' in 1974:

> A few minutes ago I said to our dear comrade Saddam that
> the idea of the Party was from the start a rigorous idea that
> required a rigorous revolutionary standard as you know
> from the writings in the early life of the party. I told him
> that the conditions of Syria where the Party emerged were
> not of the same degree of difficulty and cruelty. It was natural
> that Arabic Iraq, with its tragic and cruel conditions, be the
> starting point for a serious realisation of this idea.

What hell this idea of Aflaq's inflicted on the Kurds. Now, he is
forgotten here. Lounging beside their river, they need no longer fear
his and Saddam's Baathism. It is burning in the American conflagration
to the south of us. The genocide that Arab Baathism forced upon
them, like the chemical attacks and the burial in the southern deserts
of thousands of Kurdish men, is over. Aflaq's insane dream, far from
ending imperial rule in Iraq, has brought it back. I wonder, putting
the book on my lap, whether the US Army will provide a foundation
for the liberty the Kurds are enjoying today beside the river, or take it
away.

In Suleimaniya, Fabrice and I go to Mariwan the barber for our
desert haircuts. At the hotel, I shampoo my newly cut hair for what
may be the last time. I wrap presents to send to my children. I pack up
my winter clothes to be sent to London. In the south, in that grimy
desert, I won't need heavy sweaters and ski jackets. Let's hope we
reach Baghdad before Saddam goes down. Suddenly, he appears on
television. He or one of his doubles strides amid a Baghdad crowd,
kissing babies like a candidate for mayor of Boston. The people cheer
him, burying today's 'Saddam is dead' rumour.

In the evening, I have a long talk with Wendy Steavenson. She
confesses an unbearable loneliness and angst that afflicts most in this
peripatetic profession. It is so sad to hear her at the start of something
that has become a part of me. She is twenty years younger. If I were

her, I'd quit, but I don't say that. Instead, I offer her a cognac.

By the time I am ready to sleep, Don must be on his way to the southern front.

Saturday, 5 April 2003
Suleimaniya to Tallil Air Base, Southern Iraq

The INC asks me not to tell anyone it is going south. When I see Pizzey, I want to say goodbye. He is an old friend, but he will understand when he finds out. In the hotel lobby, he says he is fed up. No war. No story. He has been trying to reach Chamchamal, but the PUK is blocking the road. Saleh gave him a permit to enter the town, but the *Peshmerga* checkpoint took no notice. 'I want a no-"stans" clause in my next contract,' he says. I have heard him say this before – no Kurdistan, Afghanistan, Baluchistan, nowhere ending in -stan. That leaves some dreadful spots: Chechnya, North Korea, Texas. He is going back to Erbil, there to try his luck getting nearer the front with the KDP. I leave presents for my children with Ali Wharf of BBC's *Newsnight* programme, who is leaving for London. She promises to mail them when she arrives.

Fabrice, Andy, Bruno and I drive up to the Big House. Zaab issues us some jungle camouflage uniforms and numbered badges that he says we must wear to get on the plane. Wouldn't desert camouflage be more useful? He says the INC's 'troops' are at a 'muster point' just outside town, assembling to board buses to take them to the airport at Harir. We drive there to film them and find them fighting among themselves. They wear identical fatigues but they are not, to borrow Saleh's phrase, singing from the same sheet of music. Northerners and southerners, Kurds and Arabs, exiles and those who stayed, veterans of Saddam's army and veterans of no army, they have their differences. They are 'mustering' on a big field, while buses stand empty waiting for a few of them to stop beating each other up. Just before we arrived, an officer says, one of them took a shot at another.

US Army Colonel Grosso warns Nabil, who is trying to establish order, that there must not be any more problems. He cannot allow men onto expensive American transport planes with weapons: one more incident and he will recommend that his 'chain of command' cancel the flights. Nabil orders the Iraqis into queues, where US soldiers frisk them and guide them onto the buses. Some of those on the buses call out to Bruno to give them water. Bruno hands up several bottles from our store, and Fabrice tells him to stop. We are going into the desert, he says, and we will need that water – we have only three boxes of the stuff. Bruno is staying in Suleimaniya, so he is not as concerned as we are.

We drive up to the Round House, where our last Kurdish sunlight struggles through mist to the lake. A guard in a sharp new uniform opens a gate, smiles and salutes us. The first person I see in front of the house is Mudhar, wearing khakis and carrying a weapon. 'I left Baghdad on June 24th, 1986,' he says. 'I'm going to Baghdad. We'll go straight there.' Will the INC do checkpoint duty to spare the US the chore?

'No. We're here to do politics. There isn't much politicking at checkpoints.' About fifty men, thirty or so in desert or jungle fatigues, kill time in the steep car park. I ask whether the US issued the uniforms. 'No way,' Zaab says. 'We bought these in the *souk*.' Cars and vans are waiting to take them to the airport. Ahmad and Tamara are inside the house. They show us a flag that Nibros Kazimi designed. Is this the new flag of Iraq, or their unit's battle colours? No one seems to know. A blue diagonal stripe divides a green triangle at the top from a sandy one at the bottom: the green hills of Kurdistan, sand of the southern deserts, blue for the rivers. On the stripe are two five-pointed orange stars, ten points in all, for the tributaries of the Tigris and Euphrates. Is there a subliminal influence of other stars and stripes?

When Ahmad comes outside, the 'troops' erupt in a war dance around their new flag and their leader. Fabrice films it for ABC and for posterity. Ahmad bids farewell to the tribal chiefs, including 'Kaka' Hama Haji Mahmoud of the Social Democratic Party, who have come to see him off. At dusk, it is time to leave. We go to our cars, and Bruno returns to Suleimaniya. With Ahmad's Land Cruiser in the lead, we head towards Dokan village. There, we stop to buy fruit and nuts for the journey. Afterwards, the villages we pass are in darkness, without electricity, as in 1991. Unlike 1991, they are standing; then, most of them had yet to be rebuilt following their destruction by Saddam.

Candlelight blinks from a few windows. We see a roadside fire, where a man and two children are warming themselves. In one village, a large family standing in front of their stone house shout in English: 'Hello! Welcome!'

The road moves up and down the hills, and headlights bring lone trees and bare villages into focus. After an hour, we reach the border. It is the point where the last PUK checkpoint faces the first KDP checkpoint. We stop in the town of Shaklawa, where breezy *kebab* smoke flavours the air, and we have dinner. The restaurant is a large concrete shack with floor-to-ceiling windows, plastic tables and chairs. We take seats and order our last Kurdish *kebabs*, my staple diet since January. The grilled chicken and lamb pieces are salty and good, but there is no beer – beer is for city people. Marie Colvin sets up her computer to let us read her *Sunday Times* piece on Ahmad, so favourable to him that she can show it without embarrassment. Ahmad comes in wearing a black T-shirt, holding his Thuraya phone. Someone has just told him about a piece in *The Washington Post* saying that the State Department opposes an interim authority of Iraqis. At meetings, Rumsfeld and Bush apparently supported it. And, the report says, the US would not crown Ahmad head of any authority. 'Good,' Ahmad says. 'I don't want them to. It would be the kiss of death.' So, who will it be? He smiles. 'They're still saying, "ABC": Anyone But Chalabi.'

After dinner someone turns on a television by the wall. BBC news at 2300 Iraq time shows battles in and around Baghdad. Everyone in the room laughs when Sahhaf, the information minister, denies that the US has taken Baghdad Airport. The next report shows American soldiers stepping over broken glass in the airport. CENTCOM in Qatar says American troops have been through central Baghdad and are going in and out of the capital 'at times and places of their choosing'. In Najaf, local people are pointing US forces towards an Iraqi army position. Behind me in the restaurant, Nabil shouts: 'Good for you!' The BBC plays a portion of Bush's weekly radio address: 'These are war criminals, and they will be treated as war criminals.' There is more night bombing of Baghdad. A nightscope shows starbursts of bombs blotting out stars in the sky. An American spokesman says the

Republican Guards around Baghdad have been 'crippled'. I think the Guards have vanished.

When the television shows a British tank in Basra dragging down a giant statue of Saddam, Ahmad laughs as it hits the ground. The next scene is less appealing to the Iraqis here: British troops arresting young men, putting bags over their heads and tying their hands with plastic strips. Basra has yet to fall, and the British are bombing the city. In the north, the BBC says, US Special Forces and Kurdish irregulars are cutting the exits from Kirkuk. An ABC News report on the BBC says the Kurds are 'racing to Kirkuk'. Ahmad says: 'That is a bad report.' We are all in the north and have seen no sign that any Kurds are rushing to take Kirkuk. The BBC newsreader asks John Simpson, who is outside Erbil, about it. 'It doesn't feel like a rush there,' he says. 'Nothing happened all day, really.' It is hard for one journalist to contradict another on air, but the ABC embed was relying on information from the Special Forces; Simpson was on his own.

It is unsatisfying to sit in a lonely restaurant in a country at war and watch the war on television. Marie lights a cigarette. The waiters clear the plates. The BBC's Caroline Hawley in Amman interviews an Iraqi artist, who says: 'Saddam Hussein is bad, but Bush and Blair are worse. They have not come to liberate Iraq, but to rob its wealth.' Nabil pipes up: 'That's right.' Then a report from the *USS Kitty Hawk* says the ship has fired 300 tons of explosives at Iraq, 90 percent of it precision-guided, since the war began. No one mentions the General Accounting Office report on weapons fired in the 1991 war, which said 80 percent of the 'smart' bombs missed their targets. The 'dumb' bombs were even less accurate. Television remains mesmerised by smart bombs and military videos of buildings blowing up. Finally, the BBC shows the only verifiable report of the evening: Monty's Pass wins the Grand National.

It is nearly midnight, and I wonder why we haven't left Shaklawa for the air base. Outside the restaurant, beside the main road, INC guards and officials are agitated. Ahmad and others are speaking on their satphones. What's up? Someone takes me aside: 'Washington does not want AC to go to Nasiriya. The rest of us can go, but he must wait another twenty-four hours.' He does not tell me who in

Washington issued this *diktat*, or why Ahmad shouldn't go. A half hour passes. Ahmad and Washington reach a compromise. The INC, including Ahmad, will fly to Nasiriya as planned, Ahmad is to go on to Qatar to see General Tommy Franks before returning to Nasiriya.

Our convoy resumes its journey. It is a half-hour from Shaklawa to the new US checkpoint at Harir, where we wait for fifteen minutes at the barbed-wire entrance to the base. An American officer with our convoy speaks to the sentries, and we enter through a zigzag of dirt obstacles that have become a feature of US overseas bases since the destruction by a suicide bomber of the Beirut Marine HQ in 1983. We rumble slowly onto the tarmac. What was a bare strip of asphalt when I arrived here in January is now a massive US Air Force base with tents, equipment stores, vehicles, medical facilities and weapons depots. So many cars and Humvees are driving around the base that a soldier must direct traffic. This is at two in the morning.

We get out of our cars and wait in the dark. An Air Force sergeant named Dino Julia shows Tamara his night goggles. He tells her not to drop them, because they cost $8,000. When I put them on I see a twilit horizon, every soldier on the base as clear as daylight. I wonder how the Iraqi army can fight these people, who not only drop 2,000-pound bombs from the sky but can see in the dark. A C-117 transport, big as a flying fortress, lands. We are told to board her. A vast platform door opens at the back of the plane. Our drivers, Jemal and Sardar, help us carry our luggage and equipment a few hundred yards to the plane. We say our farewells to them; they have kept us going for the past two months. I regret that I couldn't find Ham'ali before leaving Suleimaniya. I should have had a last whiskey with him.

There are two planes for the 280 INC troops. They are now officially the Free Iraqi Forces (FIF). The US has issued them shoulder patches and made them part of the 'coalition of the willing'. One plane carries Ahmad, Tamara, Abu Muhammad, Mudhar, Kamran Khoshnan, Marie, Fabrice, Andy and me. The troops are on the floor of the plane, and Ahmad's entourage sits on benches along the sides. It is as dark inside as out. We take off at 0335 Iraqi time.

Ahmad's soldiers stretch out and sleep, as they would in their village houses, on the floor. I cannot sleep at all. Ahmad listens to classical music on his Discman, removing himself as ever from uncomfortable realities. This is the end for us, of the northern front, of Kurdistan and of waiting. We approach the conquered Tallil airbase, 190 miles south of Baghdad. The time is 0630, and the wheels rumble like an earthquake. The cargo door drops. Our eyes adjust to the desert light. The sun is harsher in the south.

Sunday, 6 April 2003
Tallil Air Base to Tallil Air Defence Base, Southern Iraq

At first, no one knows what to do. We unload our equipment and pile it onto a pallet. We stand in the hot sun, waiting. The INC party should be joyous, but is bewildered amid the desolation. Is this what they came home to? They climb onto open trucks without a word. Ahmad, Tamara, Marie and most of the FIF troops leave in convoy. Andy, Fabrice, Zaab, a retired American colonel named John Faley, about twenty of the FIF and I remain. Waiting for their five trucks to return empty, we examine the base under a hot morning sun and in constant wind. Tallil is a long and wide concrete interruption of desert, with lakes of sand between the steel frames of a destroyed warehouse and massive earth-covered hangar-bunkers. Hundreds of military trucks, Humvees and forklifts are painted sandy brown. We stand in the open, without shade, for more than an hour. No one tells us where we are going. Zaab, usually the eloquent spokesman, has nothing to say.

The trucks return, but one has a broken axle. The second C-117 from Harir lands, and with it another 140 FIF troops. They are led straight to the trucks, and their luggage is squeezed on with them. We climb aboard the last truck and watch a sergeant manoeuvre a forklift to drop a pallet onto one truck, then lift another from which an Arabic-speaking American colonel helps the men disgorge our camera equipment and other cases. This takes almost another hour, until the trucks drive out of Tallil Air Base towards what was, until the USAF destroyed it in 1991, Tallil Air Defence Base, about four miles away. On the road, we pass hundreds of US military vehicles. Beside the road are sheep, goats and shepherds, the first liberated Iraqis we see. One, a man in brown *jellaba*, says hello in English. The rest ignore us.

Suddenly the trucks ahead slow down. Ours stops. The big luggage truck behind rams us, hard. When it reverses, we see its headlights and grille are smashed. After a cursory check to make sure no people are hurt – the military does not seem to give a damn about wrecked trucks – we resume the short drive. At the gate, a young Iraqi in a FIF uniform waves us through the gate. He checks nothing – no inspection of ID or vehicles. Then we are on the base, actually in the shit. It is not a base so much as enclosed wasteland. Single-storey brown buildings remain collapsed from the heavy bombs of '91. Wind scatters sand through glass-less windows. Rubble and rubbish lie everywhere. Our trucks stop in the middle, and we unload the luggage: our boxes of water are missing.

Don waves from an abandoned building and walks over. He looks exhausted, and he's sweating. He shows us our billet at the far end of the area. It must have been the motor pool. Workshops are arranged around a central well, where there are two dugouts for working on the undercarriages of military vehicles. Rusted spare parts lie amid the banks of sand. In the five-room compound, a half-dozen FIF troops are already camped. The only decoration is filth. Don has one room to himself, where he spent the night on the cement floor. He marked a clean space for himself with bits of cardboard. Andy, Fabrice and I pile our gear along one battered wall. Ahmad and his group are in a large warehouse a few hundred yards away. They are already sleeping when we walk down to see them; they must be dreaming of palaces in Baghdad. We go back to our barracks, where the FIF troops are grumbling about conditions.

Col. Ted Seel comes over and explains that CENTCOM does not care for this mission. That is why it is providing no logistical support. I realise why our water was taken: there isn't any on the base. Ted says there are shortages of cars, trucks and armoured personnel carriers for the American forces, who are a higher priority than the FIF. The supply of transport for American forces is at least two weeks behind schedule, he says, something Seymour Hersh already reported in *The New Yorker*.

FIF volunteers ask us for water, *ma-ee* if they are Arabs, *ab* if they are Kurds. Some come with empty plastic bottles and hold them out forlornly. The pathos would have been unbearable but for the fact that, having no water ourselves, we are as thirsty as they are. Some of them scavenge a bag of flour, but without water they cannot make bread. The ones who arrived yesterday have repaired some abandoned Iraqi army trucks, but they dare not drive them off the base. If they do, the US Marines on the roads will shoot them. Ted says the Marines have already shot one Special Forces soldier in the neck at a checkpoint, and he was in a US Army Humvee. Imagine how they would react to a bunch of uniformed Iraqis in an Iraqi army truck. He adds that the Marines just killed the relatives of a prominent Shiite cleric who was cooperating with the US and trying to persuade his people to do the same. 'They,' Ted says of the Marines, 'are scared and are killing people.'

Don, Fabrice and Andy try to sleep, and I tour the base on foot. A dozen long buildings, all damaged, look like stable blocks. The youngsters of the FIF are sleeping on floors. Some ask me for water, and I ask them for a car. I have no water, and they have no cars. All I want is to get off this base and into a town or village, but I cannot do it on foot. The nearest village is a thirty-mile walk. Our little Thuraya satphones are working, and ABC calls to ask for two pieces on Ahmad's return to Southern Iraq, one for *Good Morning America*, the other for *This Week*. We have the material, but we have no fuel for our generator. Without the generator, we cannot transmit pictures. We have a story, but no way to tell it on television.

I cannot sleep or stay still. I have to find a way out. I walk to the centre of the camp, where Ahmad, Mudhar, Tamara and Zaab are sitting in the shade of a concrete Baathist monument – one of the few structures the US missed in '91. Ted is giving a shopping list to a big, dark-skinned man in a black shirt that has an unlikely Chinese dragon emblazoned on the pocket. A black *keffiyeh* is wrapped like a turban around his head. He is called Abu Zaman, 'Father of Time'. His English is as rough as my Arabic. Ahmad says he is an Iraqi exile who has just come home. His vast family and tribal network in the south will find us some supplies. Abu Zaman and Ted go over the list, at the top of which is water. Lots of water.

A Special Forces Humvee drives up. In the front passenger seat is Francis in an army uniform. He and Ted confer with some Green Berets, who agree to take Abu Zaman up to the main road to cadge a lift to Nasiriya. I jump on the trailer in back. We go up to the road and stop beside some other army Humvees to talk to the MPs. Ted tells them he is looking for a lift for Abu Zaman to buy necessities in Nasiriya. 'I gave him 500 bucks,' he adds. Not much, to supply 500 men.

Just then a huge civilian truck pulls up on the highway. Abu Zaman and Francis walk over to the driver. A half-dozen men in *jellabas* and *keffiyehs* materialise from the cab. Abu Zaman talks to the driver while Francis, who does not speak Arabic, makes some comments in English. Ted, who knows some Arabic, leaves the MPs to move the negotiations forward. The driver agrees to take Abu Zaman to Nasiriya and bring him back. Abu Zaman climbs into the cab. The driver tells four of his passengers, all young men, to stay behind. They are hostages against Abu Zaman's safe return. They climb into the Humvee trailer. One offers me a cigarette. We drive back to the base, where Ted and Francis argue about what to do with the hostages. Ted wants to leave them at the gate's guardhouse, and Francis wants them to come onto the base and meet the FIF people. Perhaps he sees recruiting potential. Ted deposits them at the gate.

The afternoon bears down hard. Abu Zaman does not return, and there is no water for 500 volunteers, for Ahmad and his group, for the four of us. Mass thirst is frightening. More and more boys wander the base, holding empty plastic bottles and begging for water. Without water, food, electricity, toilets or beds, Fabrice cannot work. He says he won't stay any longer. Andy feels the same. If they want to go, I say, I'll go with them. Fabrice begins making calls. He wants a car to take him to Nasiriya and then to Kuwait. Marcus Wilford in London promises to see whether the Air Force will fly Fabrice from Tallil to Kuwait. Calls are made to ABC's operation in Kuwait, and someone emails General Franks at CENTCOM in Doha, Qatar. No one can say ABC does not help its troops in trouble.

I take a short nap, at last, and feel better. I tell Fabrice we should stay. He and Andy cannot stand it any longer and are angry with me for changing my mind. I understand they were leaving in a few days anyway, but I always planned to stay until the end of the war. Meanwhile, we try to work. Fabrice gamely shoots the base, and we interview some American and FIF troops. We are shooting a stand-up at dusk when an Air Force Humvee suddenly drives up. Major John Anderson, Air Force Public Affairs Officer, tells Fabrice and Andy to get in. They have to leave right now if they want to fly to Kuwait. In a rush, they grab their luggage and equipment. Our farewells are too quick for guys who have worked day and night together for two months. They leave me the small digital camera and some tapes. Then they are gone.

Don and I are on our own now. We move from our billet to the warehouse where the INC people make room for us against one wall. This is a dark, windowless barracks for forty men, with Tamara and Marie the only women in a somewhat private corner cubicle. I walk outside into the darkness, bereft without my crew. There is not much I can do. I wish I had gone with them. Mudhar and some other INC people are as angry about conditions as Fabrice was. Ted tries to calm them. He tells Ahmad and Mudhar CENTCOM has a plan for them, but it needs two days. 'I talked to Bill Luti today, to Wolfowitz today,' he says. 'The CIA was convinced that we'd never get here, but we got here. Before we can be integrated into the war plan, those guys over there' – he means a Special Forces A-Team stationed nearby – 'have to tell the Combined Land Forces commander ...' Mudhar, the most vocal of the Chalabi crew, interrupts. Ted, sounding more New Age psychologist than army colonel, tells him: 'I'm trying to help you get your frustration into focus ... I have to tell HQ that there are contributions you can make. During seven years in Saudi Arabia, I learned: never ask permission.'

It is dark, and someone has found fuel to get a generator going. They have hooked up an arc light, and it shines from the front door of our warehouse. Mudhar takes me outside the perimeter of light to confide that he wants to go with fifty armed men and 'take' Nasiriya. Take it from whom? I cannot tell from this desert who controls the town. He says he wants to drive out the Baathists and Fedayeen

Saddam. It's none of my business, but I ask him whether it might be better to offer to organise and help people in Nasiriya.

I do phoners for newsbriefs and *World News Tonight Sunday*, walking on sand in the dark and speaking into a satellite telephone. The trip here should have been a coup. Instead, it's a disaster. On the radio, I hear a BBC report from John Simpson in the north near Kalak. American warplanes have just bombed US Special Forces and Barzani Kurds, killing eighteen, putting Barzani's brother Wajih into a coma and wounding many others, including Simpson. Simpson's translator is dead, and John's rage is unmistakable. Here, in the south, young Marines at checkpoints are so terrified that they shoot at any perceived threat. Most things look threatening to them.

I listen over the telephone to ABC's *This Week*. General Peter Pace of the Joint Chiefs says the FIF is to be the 'nucleus' of a new Iraqi army. From here they look like a bunch of untrained, thirsty and hungry young men abandoned in the desert. As I wander from place to place in the nucleus's first home, I am surprised that Francis has not put a Gideon Bible beside each sleeping bag.

Don goes to sleep in the warehouse, and I sit outside in the unending wind and write in my diary. It is all I can do. This has been a long, trying day, begun without sleep and reaching a low moment with the abrupt departure of my colleagues. We worked well together, and I am sad to see them go. Moreover, it is hard to do television without a crew. No camera here. No dish.

You sit out in the desert alone and think. You want to go home, and you think every day about going home. I always did that, in Beirut and Sarajevo and Baghdad and lots of other places. But you are away so long that home isn't there any longer. The children grow a little more and share jokes and stories that you missed. As for your wife, her life is different too. While you are absent, she has new friendships, thoughts, worries and discoveries in which you play no part. Home has moved, so have you. There are things that you see in wars or famines that you don't talk about. You don't want to worry them or seem pompous. Or you think they just don't want to hear. You make friends who will not meet your wife or children or know what you are like at home. After a while you just stop talking and spend more time in some quiet place waiting for the next reunion, the next hunt, the next story factory. This is a place where home is not home, and you are not you. The desert feeds regret.

It is after midnight when the generator goes off, taking the light with it. One by one, those who are not already asleep find a place to lie down. Some are out in the sand, others in the abandoned buildings. Far, far off, explosions break the silence. Incoming? Outgoing? I really don't care.

Monday, 7 April 2003
Tallil Air Defence Base

At 0300, I go out to piss in the desert. Lying outdoors, at peace with the world, Ahmad is sleeping on an army cot. I wander away from the warehouse in the dark and realise this is the first moment since my arrival that I have not been hot. I go back to sleep.

At first light, I find Andy's sound mixer and microphone in the warehouse, left behind in the rush to pack. I do not find my coffee. All I have left is one bag of the many Lavazza packs Elif Ural brought last February, and one can of Pringle's potato crisps. Andy left his equipment and took our food box; I am not sure why – he won't need it in London. ABC wants some spots from here with pictures that Fabrice can send from Kuwait. The only problem is that Fabrice and Andy, who call early this morning, are stuck at the airbase. There are no flights, so the Air Force is making them wait on the tarmac. Things are not much better for them than for us. Ahmad takes a morning power walk with his Thuraya and bodyguards. During the night, Abu Zaman brought boxes of water in plastic bottles. There is enough stored in the warehouse for everyone, for a day or two. Abu Muhammad makes some tea, and we sit and ponder what to do next.

We are sitting on planks and damaged chairs outside. 'They've got enough supplies for 10,000 people on the base,' Ahmad says, referring to the US forces, 'and this is all we have.' He points to the generator. 'They said we wouldn't come.' In his black Hugo Boss T-shirt, he tells me Abdel-Majid Khoi, son of Grand Ayatollah Khoi (who was killed by Saddam) has returned to Iraq. '[Abdel-]Majid Khoi called from Najaf and asked us to show up, even for a few hours.' Will he go?

'It depends on the transport situation.'

I ask about Condoleezza Rice's announcement that the Iraqi Interim Authority will exclude him.

'Condi Rice said it? The interim authority is irrelevant. Only the constituent assembly matters. It's not a big deal. There will be elections in two years. The Interim Authority cannot influence elections. The important thing is to make the constitution go right.' He thinks again about Rice. 'She thinks I'm waiting to be crowned? I don't want to be crowned by her.'

The sun is hiding behind a relentless sheet of wind-blown sand. The horizon is a permanent beige, and it makes people nervous. On this, our second day, visitors begin coming to the court of Chalabi. First an Iraqi soldier, who has deserted. Then a tribal chief in a light robe. While Ahmad meets potential supporters, US troops arrive in full battle dress with flak jackets, helmets and rifles. Five of them march up to us and announce they intend to do DNA tests on all FIF volunteers. Good luck.

Ahmad wants to get into the war, albeit not as much as Mudhar. The INC needs to claim some credit for overthrowing Saddam, but the US is determined to do it alone. Ahmad, as ever, beams optimism. 'They've agreed to take our guys to Amara by helicopter,' he says, after speaking to his friends in the Pentagon. They will break up his force, now about 700, into three groups: a battalion, several fifty-man special-operations units and a political group. 'The battalion will hold places and fight the Baathists. The smaller groups will work with local forces. The political groups are to mobilise the local population, the nucleus of a political party.' Someone delivers boxes of FIF flag decals. These would go on vehicles, if the FIF had any.

More FIF volunteers arrive from the north via Tallil's George W. Bush, Jr Airport. They bring a locked trunk Bruno sent. Taped to it is an envelope with a note and a key. Don and I open what turns out to be a treasure chest of supplies: tea, coffee, sugar, biscuits, whiskey, pot noodles and baked beans. It may not seem like much, but to us it means survival. Good old Bruno. He was thoughtful enough to include napkins, cutlery and cups.

Abu Zaman comes from Nasiriya with news: Ali Hassan al-Majid is dead. 'The people of Basra shot him,' he says. The people of Basra and just about everywhere else would like to shoot the man who dropped chemicals on the Kurds and tormented the Shiites, but they probably didn't. A report on BBC World Service says British forces claim al-Majid was killed when an American bomb hit his house. I wonder if the house was round, like the one Ahmad borrowed at Lake Dokan. Abu Muhammad returns from a shopping trip in an old pickup, bringing fresh tomatoes, onions and eggs, as well as pots and pans to cook them in. Slowly, the supplies come. Soon Abu Zaman will have cars. We look forward to leaving the base for a cooked lunch.

Abu Zaman's convoy arrives – two passenger vans and a pickup. An FIF soldier sticks a flag decal on a windshield, seals it and salutes it. If the uniform makes the soldier, the flag makes the nation. Ahmad readies himself for the excursion to visit Sheikh Ali al-Ghizzawi, whose ancestors were friends of his ancestors. He comes out wearing a pressed suit and a new red-checkered turban. As we get into the vans, an American colonel telephones, worried about the convoy's security – not from Saddam loyalists, but from Marines guarding the road. Ted puts a white T-shirt on the aerial of the lead van for the checkpoint Marines to see. It might discourage them from shooting. The wind stops for the first time, and the air becomes hotter. The convoy does not budge. We cannot sit forever, waiting. Ted goes to the Special Forces communications room to try and reach the Marines.

John Faley, who now works at the Pentagon, explains the US battle plan for the FIF. 'What I'm telling you isn't in any book. We plan to leap from Amara and Nasiriya, north.' He does not mention obstacles on the way, like the Shiite holy cities of Najaf and Qarbala. His goal is Baghdad. I ask what the political programme is.

'That's nothing to do with me. I'm just interested in the operation.'

They are going to do operations?

'Yes. Maybe take a house where *fedayeen* are. But we have to make sure [the forces] are trained, so that none of our guys get hurt.'

We are still waiting, when Ahmad receives more bad news. For the first time, his anger shows. With INC operations chief Aras Karim, he marches into the Special Forces building looking for Ted. He mentions someone called Abu Hatem, whose full name is Karim Mahmoud al-Muhammadawi. Taking Ted aside in the Special Forces communications room, Ahmad says: 'He's cursing us.' Soldiers at the radio ignore him. They are trying to communicate with the Marines manning the checkpoints on the road to Ahmad's lunch with Sheikh Ali. They have no direct means of contacting the Marines and must go through channels – to the army in Qatar, which contacts CENTCOM, which contacts the Marines in Qatar, which tells the Marines on the road to Nasiriya not to shoot Ahmad.

We walk back through the compound corridor. Ahmad always walks so fast that it is hard to keep up. I ask him, on the trot, who is cursing him. 'Karim Mahmoud al-Muhammadawi ... He went into the governorate at dawn and cleaned out the Baath in Amara. At 0930, this Kuwaiti interpreter comes in and tells him he has to leave. Or he'll be killed.' The interpreter works for the US forces outside Amara. I ask whether CENTCOM knew in advance that Abu Hatem was doing this.

'Yes,' he says, as if the answer were obvious. 'Abu Hatem has been fighting Saddam for twenty-two years.' Abu Hatem was made to withdraw from the town he conquered, condemning the US and its chosen Iraqi, Ahmad Chalabi.

Ahmad gets back into the van and orders the drivers to go ahead. Ted jumps into the lead car, apprehensive that there is no okay from the Marines. We were scheduled to leave at noon, and it is just past two. Don and I ride in the pickup at the back of the convoy. Ted waves his white flag in front. As we turn off the base and onto the main road, the back wheel of our pickup flies off. We stop. Don and I crowd into the second van with the bodyguards. I miss the mountains of Kurdistan. All we see here are mud villages and sand.

The drive takes a half-hour on the main highway to Nasiriya. What we all notice is that there is not a single Marine – or any other checkpoint – on the entire route. Someone in CENTCOM did not want Ahmad to go, and phantom Marine checkpoints were the excuse. Why do they want him confined to a base in the desert? Part of the answer is waiting for us just a few yards away from Ahmad's bedouin welcoming party at a black goatskin tent. Five guys in jeans, bush jackets and baseball caps are sitting in a Humvee taking pictures. If they are meant to be in disguise, the CIA doesn't know much about blending in. When I take their picture, one shouts: 'Hey, reporter. Don't take our picture. And tell all your colleagues not to take our picture.' I answer that if they tell me who they are, I will warn my colleagues. They look like they might seize my videotape, but they don't. Instead, they drive away.

Sheikh Ali welcomes Ahmad with hugs and kisses and introduces him to his Ghizzi tribesmen. A mass of men part to let Ahmad and Tamara, the only woman, enter the tent. Rice and boiled mutton appear, and about 100 tribal retainers sit on the ground and grab at the giant platters. Lunch takes fifteen minutes. We retire to a hut near some eucalyptus trees, and the politicking begins. Ahmad and Sheikh Ali discuss the past, their fathers, the old monarchist prime minister Nuri al-Said and the old Iraqi army. Sweet tea is served, then the meeting is over. Nothing is said, but something happened. If Ahmad becomes president, people will remember that the first tribe to give him hot food and tea was the Ghizzi. If he doesn't, they will forget.

Back at base, Abu Muhammad is about to go on another shopping run. Don and I join him for the ride into Nasiriya. The road is free of checkpoints. Bombed-out buildings mark the town's entrance, but people are on the streets – not many, but some. A barber, a butcher and a tea shop are open. Most other businesses, however, are not. The town is not 'secure' yet, as far as the US is concerned. When we reach the Euphrates, I see why. A line of cars is stopped 100 yards before the bridge. We hear shots. Ahead, at a checkpoint, a young Marine points a shotgun at people. I get out of the car – it is usually safer to approach a checkpoint on foot – and ask what is happening. Behind me, Iraqis are anxious to get home. The boy is very nervous, shaking. 'We have one man wounded,' he says. 'We're awaiting a MEDEVAC.' His orders are to keep the bridge free of traffic for a helicopter to come in. He cannot explain this in Arabic, and these people do not speak English. He is afraid of them, and they fear him. We try another bridge half a mile upriver, but the Marines have blocked it as well.

The shops Abu Muhammad wants are on the other side of the river, and we cannot get to them. We explore Nasiriya. Locals call the air defence base where we are barracked 'French Radar'. I don't need to ask who supplied the radar to Saddam.

Back at the base, the INC men are sitting outside in the dark. The arc light we had the night before is off, because the generator is off. It is gasoline-powered, and the army only has diesel. No light, no power to charge our telephones. INC liaison Hamid Shraeder sits next to me with a glass of tea. 'Now,' he says, 'I've fought twenty-three years to hand this country over to the Iranians. Badr and the Dawa are fighting in Qarbala, and the Free Iraqi Forces are not allowed to go there. We were promised $60 million in weapons and uniforms and other support by Tommy Franks. And nothing.' Shraeder was on Franks's staff in Qatar for a few days, but then came here to French Radar: 'An Agency guy came, and next thing I was told to leave.'

Ted joins us in the dark and says the Marine wounded in Nasiriya today died. A short while later, Ahmad says Marines in a place called Souk al-Shuyukh (Sheikhs' Market) killed seven Iraqi civilians and wounded thirty. It seems that while we were in Nasiriya Sheikh Sayid Hamza al-Musawi, the leader of Souk al-Shuyukh, was visiting Ahmad at the base. Sheikh Hamza had, like Abu Hatem in Amara, cleared the Baath Party out of his village. More than that, he organised one of the rare welcomes for American forces in Southern Iraq. When the Marines arrived, Sheikh Hamza said, people were in the streets to greet them. The Marines saw armed men, who had just expelled Saddam's people, among the crowd and opened fire. Later in the evening, the number of wounded in Souk al-Shuyukh rises from thirty to fifty. Sheikh Hamza returns to Souk al-Shuyukh. Aras says the sheikh was behind the 1996 plot to assassinate Saddam's son Uday. Uday was wounded, and three of the conspirators were captured. 'They executed all of their families,' Aras says. 'One had seven brothers.' The sheikh escaped to Ahvaz in Iran and returned to Iraq three months ago.

ABC calls to say two Polish journalists were just kidnapped in Nasiriya and I should not go there. Next call is from Fabrice. He and Andy are still at Tallil Air Base, closed for much of the day for a visit by General Franks. When it reopened, there was no room on their flight because it was full of wounded Americans. They hope to leave tomorrow. I wish they could get back here, but the Air Force won't let them leave the base.

So, Tommy Franks was here today, and the Pentagon did not tell Ahmad. Shouldn't the coalition commander visit the 'nucleus' of the new Iraqi army and the only Arab member of the coalition? If Ahmad has any reaction when I tell him, he does not show it.

At 2330, as we sit in the dark desert, flares shoot into the sky and light the horizon. More and more flares go up in twos and threes, then float down. We hear some thuds. Ted gets up and walks away from us to listen. He says: 'Maybe there are some infiltrators. There's some machine-gun fire.'

Tonight, for the first time since we left Suleimaniya, I shave. With some bottled water and canned shaving cream, I scratch my face clean by flashlight. It makes me feel a little better. I take my sleeping bag outside and set up to read e. e. cummings with a miner's lamp on my forehead. The wind rattles the loose corrugated tin roof of an open storage shed. Wild dogs bark and howl. Sleep is impossible.

Tuesday, 8 April 2003
Tallil Air Defence Base

Ted says he could not sleep in the warehouse, where twenty men were snoring. He grumbles and marches into the desert with a water bottle to brush his teeth. When he sees Faley, he says: 'I got about an hour's sleep last night, because these motherfuckers were moving around all night shouting at each other. So, if you want to move over there' – with his fellow Americans in the Special Forces – 'you should.'

Francis, who has replaced yesterday's army uniform with a T-shirt and baseball cap, shouts: 'Where are the cars? Can you get us some vehicles? We've got to go to this crisis meeting.' The meeting with the Marines is intended to avoid more conflicts, like those in Amara and Souk al-Shuyukh, between Iraqi civilians and the American forces.

The FIF begin training this morning. Two platoons of thirty-six men, aged nineteen to fifty, stand at ease on a dirt road between the Special Forces house and the INC workhouse. Ten US soldiers are talking with Hamid. Sheikh Hamza, who was forced out of Souk al-Shuyukh by the Marines, is back. He sits on an army cot smoking a cigarette. His car, sporting several Marine bulletholes, is parked nearby. Wind blows sand and scraps of paper. Ahmad comes to speak with him. More sheikhs, all in desert robes and *keffiyehs*, gather to see Ahmad. They seem glum; perhaps liberation is not what they had hoped. Ahmad tries to reassure them, but no one on the American side reassures him of anything.

Hamid leaves the Americans and sits down.

'What are you going to do?' I ask him.

'I don't know.' He tells me how he got here. He was born in Baghdad, but his parents were Basra Shiites. He went into the army when he was fourteen, then commanded a unit of teenagers against Iranian teenagers in the Iran-Iraq war. When he came of age, the army put him into the Republican Guards. He deserted after the revolt in 1991 and joined the INC. Because of his military experience and reliability, Ahmad sent him to CENTCOM in Qatar. 'Before that, I distrusted the politicians. They're like politicians everywhere. But I trusted the military.' He had seen the US Army in Qatar but did not trust it now, especially after the CIA overruled the Pentagon and expelled him from CENTCOM. The INC, however, is still relying on American politicians and soldiers. 'What choice do we have?'

In a convoy including a Special Forces Humvee to protect it from the Marines, the INC takes Sheikh Hamza to the power station outside Nasiriya. The plant is said to be the second-largest in the Middle East. The Marines are in control, but the generators are not working. Aras, Ted, Faley and Francis want help for the fifty wounded in Souk al-Shuyukh. They have been unable to reach any hospital because of Marine checkpoints. I see a group of officers inside the compound with an Iraqi man in a suit. Ted tells a Civil Affairs officer about Souk al-Shuyukh. 'Fifty people were wounded,' he says. 'We'd like to get some help for them, and we'd like more than that to have an understanding. Because he's [Sheikh Hamza] one of the good guys.' She tells him to go to the Marine headquarters in an old Iraqi army base a few miles away.

Driving to the next base, Aras says: 'The Iraqis with the Marines are Baathists. They are bringing in their friends to run the plant. Only Baathists wear this type of suit. It's silvery. And only Baathists can afford a Rolex.' Francis adds: 'They've formed something called the City Council and say everyone has to answer to them.' What happened to de-Baathification? Francis complains that the Marine translator is CIA. 'Most of their units have Kuwaiti translators working for the CIA.' The CIA-INC hatred runs deep. The INC has not forgotten that the CIA left INC people to die in Erbil in 1996.

Don and I sit on plastic chairs on the formerly Iraqi, now American, base. Ted, Aras, Francis and Sheikh Hamza negotiate with a Marine colonel. An hour later, Francis says the colonel responsible for the area has agreed to allow medical supplies into Souk al-Shuyukh for the wounded, to clear the INC's path through checkpoints and to pull the Marines back to an observation post there. 'The facts on the ground are that in the village there are good guys, but a village about a kilometre away is filled with bad guys,' Francis says. 'The plan is for US forces to enter the friendly town. Our guys will go into the other village and get the bad guys and hand them over to the Americans.' If this happens, it will be the first FIF operation.

We take Sheikh Hamza to Nasiriya, and Ted clears him through a checkpoint so he can drive home. Ted says they have saved lives by establishing a procedure for resolving such conflicts. I am not sure how you can stop Marines from shooting at armed Iraqis, even if they are 'good guys'. How can they tell?

The wind turns everything sepia, leaving no horizon, no bearing. A dry, sandy mist makes our unwashed skin filthier. Back at French Radar, the generator is working. Ahmad and I sit down to talk. He admits at last that his forces will not be allowed to assist in the conquest or liberation of Baghdad. At Dokan, they said marching first into Baghdad, like de Gaulle into Paris, was why they came. The whole idea was to enter Baghdad and organise support for Iraqi sovereignty before the Americans rolled in. Ahmad's objective, at least since we began talking last November, was not to allow an interruption of Iraqi sovereignty. Now, he says, his troops will remain here, helping the US occupation forces get along with the people. God help the people. Most of the US soldiers I have met so far are nice, all-American guys and girls – Marines, Army and Air Force. But in hostile terrain, they will kill people, including unarmed, innocent people, rather than risk their lives.

I meet a few of them at the entrance to the airbase where we arrived. Fabrice and Andy have boarded a flight to Kuwait, but I need to get inside to the press centre to transmit my material to ABC. While awaiting authorisation to admit me, the sentries tell me last night's flares were tripped by armed men trying to infiltrate the base perimeter. The Air Force then sent up many more flares to see the attackers. Each side shot at the other. I ask one of them, who seems about twenty, whether anyone was hit. He said: 'No. Thank God.' He apologises when the base commander orders him not to allow me inside.

A Special Forces sergeant at French Radar tells me a Delta Force team here has killed about 1,000 Iraqis to the loss of only three of their own. 'That's what I call a good kill ratio,' he says. It sounds unlikely, when the total number of Iraqi dead the US admits to date is a few hundred, most of those from aerial bombardment. Delta also 'rescued' Private Jessica Lynch from the hospital in Nasiriya, he says. He doesn't like this war. In Afghanistan, he says he 'popped twenty-six guys'. He has yet to shoot anyone in Iraq. His assignment is to keep an eye on the FIF.

More sheikhs visit Ahmad. Meanwhile, the Special Forces train his troops. Weapons arrive, crates of captured Iraqi AK-47s. I watch the FIF train: some are not ready; others will never be ready. There was a knife fight in the camp today. They are now dividing the men into sections based on region to avoid trouble. Some of them are ill. Tamara says Ahmad was so ill that he threw up during the night, although by morning he showed only his perpetual health and self-confidence. No one here feels well. There is no washing, no detergent for clothes, dishes and plates. Filth is everywhere. No one has assigned details to keep the camp clean, dig latrines or dispose of rubbish. Garbage is dropped everywhere. Worst of all, I suppose, I cannot get my stories out. Although I filmed all day and prepared a story for ABC, no one will ever see it thanks to the US Air Force .

The Arab Revolt of 1917–18 must have had moments like these. In a way, Ted is Lawrence, working with local forces, and Ahmad is his Feisal, potential leader of the new nation. But that revolt had real battles and advances to compensate for times like these. This Arab and Kurd force will not fight. It will not protect the American flank as it moves north. The US, unlike Britain in 1917, does not need or want the locals involved. The FIF is ready to do something, but the US will not let it earn a place at the table.

This empire has what it wants: many servants and no allies. It also seems to want enemies, and it has those too. Many of the young American soldiers here have spent months in theatres of conflict – Afghanistan, Yugoslavia, Iraq. After the fall of Saigon, that wasn't supposed to happen.

ABC calls. The two Polish journalists kidnapped in Nasiriya have escaped. That is good news. Now, the bad: the US bombed the al-Jazeera office in Baghdad and killed correspondent Tariq Ayoub. A half-hour later, it bombed the Abu Dhabi Television bureau. An hour after that, a US tank fired into the Reuters office at the Palestine Hotel and killed another journalist. Most of the press dead have been killed by the US, including Terry Lloyd of ITN, who was shot up by the Marines in the south. While they kill journalists, American forces are still trying to get Saddam Hussein. They dropped four 2,000-pound bombs on a restaurant in Baghdad during the night. They missed him and the restaurant, but they hit the apartment buildings around it. A 2,000-pound bomb's crater looks like a small lake.

Marie Colvin has inherited Asla Aydintasbas's role as Ahmad's confidante. He seems to need a woman to talk to, to try ideas on. (I remember that when I first met her, Marie was playing the same role with Muammar Gadafi in Libya. She worked for UPI then, and Gadafi would call her late at night just to talk.) Ahmad tells her his plans, but I wonder whether he confides his disappointments to anyone.

We now have dried food, HRRs (Humanitarian Relief Rations) – substandard versions of the Army's MREs (Meals Ready to Eat). I eat some kind of Pop Tart and throw the rest away. I return to the spot where I tried to sleep last night, but someone has dumped rubbish

all over it. I walk about a quarter-mile from the warehouse into open
desert, far from the forty or more sleeping, snoring, arguing men,
and set my bag down. I put the miner's light on my head and read.
Here there is no corrugated iron roof to bang in the wind. Here the
wilderness howls. I wake a few times in the night to brush sand from
my face.

Wednesday, 9 April 2003
Tallil Air Defence Base to Umm Qasr, Southern Iraq

Sandflies and voices wake me at dawn. The sandy mist stopped
blowing during the night, and the sun is rising for the first time on
a horizon of blue. The tension the wind brought yesterday is broken.
BBC radio says the US is tightening its hold on parts of Baghdad. The
surviving journalists from al-Jazeera and Abu Dhabi Television plead
with the US troops who bombed them for an evacuation to safety.
Here in the desert, a new Subaru four-wheel-drive is parked next to
the warehouse. Sam Chalabi, who left the north weeks ago, is here. He
drove up from Kuwait with an ex-Navy SEAL, Terry Sullivan, who
works on General Jay Garner's staff. They came in a military convoy
most of the way, then broke off with the help of the car's GPS to look
for us. Sam seems as discouraged as ever. He finds the US command
less and less trustworthy. I tell him what is happening here – Nasiriya,
Amara, Souk al-Shuyukh – and say the US is fucking his uncle over.
He does not contradict me or put a spin on the treatment Ahmad is
receiving.

The morning routine commences: find a water bottle and brush
teeth, make coffee from my last pack of Lavazza, sit outside with Ted,
Ahmad, Marie, Don, Mudhar, Zaab and everyone else on canvas cots
to talk as the sun makes itself felt. The wind resumes, forcing the sky
and sun back into hiding. Another day begins. The next BBC radio
news says the US is accusing Syria of harbouring members of Saddam's
regime. 'Syrian assholes,' Ahmad says. I remember his speech at the
December conference in London, lauding Syria for its stand against
Saddam's occupation of Kuwait.

Ahmad makes his first public appearance today. In all his time up north and down here, he has yet to address a crowd. He says he expects about 1,000 people for a speech he is delivering at the governorate in Nasiriya. We leave at 1020 in a long convoy of passenger vans and Special Forces Humvees. Aras and I share a van. For the past two months, during which I have seen him most days, I have not talked to Aras. He directs the INC's operations, including its intelligence, and doesn't say much. Having run agents in Iraq for the INC for the past ten years, he has fed the press stolen documents and a stream of defectors. I ask where he came from, how he happened into the INC. He tells me most of the story.

He was born on 6 August 1967 in Baghdad's Ibn Sina Hospital. His parents were Kurds who moved back to Iraqi Kurdistan when he was a baby. At the time, his father was a senior official in the KDP of Mullah Mustafa. Aras went to school near Haj Omran, on the Iranian border, for three years, until the KDP's rebellion collapsed in 1975. His father, Habib Karim, moved to Egypt for a year, then returned to Baghdad at Saddam's request. Aras spent the next three years at a school in Baghdad, al-Kirkh Primary, where Saddam's wife Sajida Khairallah al-Talfah was headmistress. He went on to Mansour High School and the Engineering College of Baghdad University. For two years, Saddam's son Uday was his classmate. Uday, however, did not attend class often. The army drafted Aras in September 1990, a month after the invasion of Kuwait.

'I didn't want to go to Kuwait,' he said. They took him to Tikrit. 'They put us aside,' he says, 'and told us we were not Iraqis, because we were Failli Kurds.' The Failli are Shiites, a small minority within the Kurdish minority. During the Iran-Iraq war, Saddam exiled many of them to Iran. The army moved him to Mosul for two months and was about to despatch his unit to Kuwait. 'I left on January 14th, 1991, four days before the [American] attack.' Thus began his clandestine life. His family was arrested in Baghdad, then released. He fled to the Kurdish areas, first in Iraq, then in Iran, then back and forth between the Kurdistans of both countries.

He took a job with the KDP as a public affairs officer. 'I spent most of my time playing chess with Massoud's bodyguards.' Barzani asked him to translate for an American who was teaching Iraqi dissidents to make television programmes. Aras was not interested in translating. 'My father said, "I want you to work with my old friend, Ahmad Chalabi". Ahmad asked him to organise the founding meeting in Iraqi Kurdistan of the INC in September 1992. Aras found rooms and cars for 400 delegates and 300 journalists, an astounding feat in a country recovering from the Anfal of the late 1980s and Saddam's revenge attacks in 1991. Ahmad made him operations director.

For a few years, Aras cooperated with the CIA in Erbil. The civil war between the KDP and PUK led Barzani to call for Saddam's help in 1996. The CIA, aware that the Iraqi army was about to invade Erbil and kill its local allies, evacuated without telling Aras or anyone else in the INC. The INC people who did not find hiding places were killed in house-to-house searches by the Iraqis. Aras survived, but his trust in the CIA did not.

We enter Nasiriya before noon. On the wide boulevards, a few children wave at our convoy. Most of the adults ignore us. The Humvees are American, but people may wonder who the Free Iraqi Forces are. As we approach the centre, the roads narrow and more people crowd the streets. Most of the shops are open now, and people are smiling. Some wave at the convoy, including adults. 'That's right,' Francis says from the front seat. 'Wave. These are my friends.' He does not know them, their language, their beliefs, their worries, their names. People approach our car, all demanding the same thing: electricity.

A crowd masses around the convoy. Men stand ten and twenty deep on the sidewalks. This is the governor's headquarters, still charred from the war. The guards rush Ahmad around some eucalyptus trees through the back of the building, clearing a path through the crowd. A religious sheikh who drove with Ahmad from the base addresses the people in back. A few hundred young men, most of whom seem to know him, are cheering. I go inside the building, where every office has been burned. Windows, tiles, cornices and desks are charred black. Torn documents lie on the floor. Most of the furniture has been ripped apart. This is not bomb damage; the people destroyed this place, local symbol of Saddam's authority, as they did in 1991.

I look for stairs to see where Ahmad has gone. I stop outside an exit at the front and see something I have never seen in Iraq before: a real crowd. Ahmad may have expected 1,000, but there are two or three times that many, shouting and waving. Ahmad addresses them through a bullhorn from the apex of an outside staircase. I hear the words in Arabic: 'Your government. Your country. Your Iraq.' These are the phrases they want to hear. The megaphone carries his voice all the way back, hundreds of yards to the river and the edge of the crowd of men. They chant: 'By our blood, by our souls, we will die for you, O Iraq!' Until now, that traditional Arab mantra ended, in Iraq, with 'O Saddam!'. Ahmad is still speaking when suddenly there are two loud explosions from the other side of the Euphrates. The crowd ignores them. I see, coming from the left, perhaps another 1,000 men. They look much like those already there, but their chant is different. Some beat their chests. I listen and hear the words: *'Ya Hussein! Ya Hussein!'* – the name of their ancient Shiite martyr. Among them are men in turbans, looking as if they have come from the mosque. The two crowds melt into one without conflict.

Concentrating on the people I'm filming with the digital camera, I do not realise that Ahmad has stopped speaking. I reenter the building and see him pressed against a wall by his guards. They are holding his new supporters back and trying to make an exit for him. Mudhar pulls out a pistol, and the guards hold up their AK-47s. No one fires. The crowd is not threatening Ahmad, but the guards rush him down the stairs at a run. Ahmad tries to stop, to greet some of his admirers, but they won't let him. They nearly slip on fallen plaster and shards of glass. At the door, they push through the young men still massed at the back, force Ahmad into his car and tell the driver to leave. Abu Zaman, relaxed and in control of the crowd, stands outside and tells us all to get into one car or another. He is a good man in a crisis. He gets us all in, smiles at the crowd and bangs on the car roofs like horses to get them moving. We drive away from the governorate, away from the crowd, but our convoy is now separated. Our group, including the Chalabis, Mudhar and Ted, stops in a quieter part of Nasiriya to wait for the others. We then try the riverbank, where boys are diving and swimming. We call the other cars, which are already on their way to French Radar.

The bodyguards need not have taken Ahmad away. The religious crowd that came late was not threatening him or his supporters. This was the first time most of them had ever been to a rally that had not been organised by the Baath Party. They were in a receptive mood, and most looked like they were enjoying the gathering. Ahmad should have taken control of his guards and of the crowd. But he and the crowds are finding their way in the new Iraq, and no one is sure yet how to behave. It is hard for him after a lifetime in exile, hard for them after a lifetime during which one man controlled every aspect of their lives.

Yet Ahmad, for all his intellectual gifts, offers them nothing better. His promise of independence and democracy is an illusion, part of the massive fraud that is the US invasion of Iraq. As an actor in the drama, he shares responsibility for its consequences. Already, his accomplices in Washington – Cheney, Rumsfeld *et al.* – are distancing themselves from their local client. I know they will not let him play de Gaulle in Baghdad, will not let the Iraqis maintain Iraqi rule and will not allow Iraqi politicians to award contracts to Iraqi companies. We in the press are part of the fraud, and that makes being here more futile.

In the afternoon, Terry Sullivan offers to take Don and me to Kuwait. Sullivan works as a contractor for Garner and the new Office of Humanitarian Relief Assistance (OHRA) that President Bush has sent to administer post-Saddam Iraq. I have several days of video material that I have not been able to transmit and want to get some of it on the air. Don wants to go home. We accept Sullivan's offer. Kuwait means hot showers, hot food, clean clothes, beds. If we have two days there to restore ourselves, we can return to face all this again. We should have a better chance of making it to Baghdad as well. At the moment, we are imprisoned along with the INC by the US Army. None of the taxi drivers we met in Nasiriya was willing to drive us to Baghdad, and a CNN crew has arrived with its own mobile dish. Whatever exclusive we had with this little story is gone. CNN can file, and I can't, from here.

Sam persuades Tamara to come with us. She needs a rest more than we do. Ahmad sends Mohsen, one of his aides, to protect her. I say this is not a good idea. I like Mohsen, but he is an Iraqi, wears a military uniform, has a beard, carries a pistol and has a US travel document rather than a passport. The Kuwaitis will be suspicious and may not let any of us cross the border. We say our farewells in the late afternoon. Strangely, I am going to miss most of them. Ahmad Chalabi is an interesting man, hard to comprehend and vulnerable to criticism that he is an American puppet and a crooked businessman. He may have positioned himself as America's man in Iraq, but he opposed Saddam's crimes back in the early 1970s. America did not come around to his point of view until Saddam trespassed on its oil in Kuwait. Ahmad hides whatever emotions he has, but this goodbye is difficult for me. Mudhar wishes me well, and I tell Zaab that I am leaving all our supplies here. We won't need them in Kuwait, and they may come in handy if they have to stay here much longer. He can keep my Italian coffeepot.

Sullivan, Sam, Tamara, Mohsen, Don and I drive south for a couple of hours on a six-lane highway. Sullivan tells us a little about his military career as a Navy SEAL. He talks about some of his secret operations, mainly in the Middle East. It turns out he was in the unit Ronald Reagan ordered to rescue American hostages on a plane, TWA 847, in Beirut in 1985. Three of us in the car have connections to that story. I covered it for ABC News. Sam had a cousin in Amal, the moderate Shiite militia which effected the release of the hostages from the more radical Hizbullah, and met some of the hostages at the time. Sullivan almost rescued them. His mission was called off after I reported that the hostages had been taken off the plane at Beirut's airport and moved to safe-houses in the city. If I had not discovered that fact, he and his team would have rescued an empty plane. We all remember the pilot, the late John Testrake, who behaved with dignity. Sullivan retired from the military in 1986. He married an army officer, one of the first women to pass jump school at Fort Benning, Georgia, and now a big deal at the Pentagon. It is a useful connection for a military contractor.

Most of the traffic is heading north, long military convoys of supplies from Kuwait and Umm Qasr's port. These roads are the best in the Middle East, among Saddam's few achievements which will not be remembered with bitterness; he probably did not reckon they would be used by an invasion force that would come to depose him. There is only one checkpoint on the road, and the soldiers let us through without an inspection. The Kuwait border is another story.

The frontier is a fifteen-foot berm, sand piled high along the length of the disputed frontier between Iraq and Kuwait. The crossing point is a gap in the line of sand, where American MPs stand guard. Sullivan hands them his OHRA identity, but they do not recognise it. Nor have they heard of General Garner. They look suspicious of Mohsen, whose travel documents do not withstand scrutiny. A sergeant politely tells Sullivan to try the Kuwaiti border post 500 yards east along the berm. Sullivan turns around and heads along an unpaved track to another gap in the berm. Kuwaiti border police stop the car and ask for passports. Tamara whispers to me that she has a Lebanese passport, but is not going to hand it to them. They don't seem interested in a woman anyway. They look at Mohsen. His travel document means nothing to them. It says he was born in Iraq, and they question him in Arabic about this. Kuwaitis tend to hate Iraqis, particularly since the 1990 invasion when Iraq plundered the country. (Mohsen looks a little like Yasser Arafat, I realise, which cannot help.) Luckily, he has hidden his pistol under the seat. He and the Kuwaitis argue.

One policeman orders Sullivan to move the car to the police post and unload the luggage. That seems a good sign. If they are searching the bags and the car, it could mean they are going to let us in. A more senior officer arrives. He orders the police to take Mohsen away. The officer then demands to see Tamara's passport. He inspects it and orders us back into the car. On his instructions we follow a Kuwaiti jeep to the police building where they are holding Mohsen. They examine all our passports. Only Sam has a Kuwaiti visa. Sullivan has military papers that should work for him. Don and I have no visas, but we do have British passports. The discussions go on and on. The Kuwaitis hold Mohsen for questioning and tell us to go back to Iraq.

We turn onto the track and head towards the American entry point. Sullivan waits for a returning British army convoy and jumps into it. It might work. The MPs let the British vehicles through, but one of them recognises us and orders us to stop. He calls his sergeant, the same one who sent us away a couple of hours ago. The sergeant calls the Kuwaitis and searches the car. He does not find Mohsen's pistol, but there is one belonging to Sullivan in the glove compartment. The MPs are clearly annoyed. Kuwaiti police drive to the American checkpoint, and the sergeant gives them Sullivan's weapon. The Kuwaitis say they will keep it, but release Mohsen.

If Sullivan and Sam lose the rest of us, they can return to Kuwait. We drift around the Iraqi desert, deciding what to do. Tamara calls Aras, who tells Tamara and Mohsen to return to Tallil. Don and I decide to take a taxi to Umm Qasr, where the British have established a naval base. Terry drops us at a taxi stop in Safwan, a dire Iraqi border town. Tamara and Mohsen jump into a taxi to return north to Camp Desolation. Don and I grab our bags and wish everyone well. Waiting at the stop, I call ABC London, which connects me to the ABC office in Kuwait. Kuwait puts me through to some ABC people with the Seabees (US naval construction battalion) at Umm Qasr. The ABC producers are not at all excited by the prospect of our barging in on them. They are in a tent there, and there are not many cots. They have a satellite dish, but they are a *Nightline* team and don't want to go out of their way for a regular news correspondent. I say we are coming anyway. We have nowhere else to go. I have material to send to New York, and there is no dish back at French Radar.

I find a taxi willing to take us to Umm Qasr. The driver is not enthusiastic. The sun is setting, and he does not like passing through American checkpoints in the dark. He has a big van and wants to take three of his relations with us. The fare, he says, will be US$50. I ask whether he knows the way to the port at Umm Qasr. '*Ma'aloum* (Of course),' he says. He speaks a little English, much less than my Arabic, and says his name is Mubarak. We speed through Safwan and its palm trees, and he tells Don and me, 'America very good. Mr Bush, very good.' He pokes his thumb into the air like a Marine and says, 'Haji Bush, very good.'

He asks Don, 'You American?'

Don says, 'British.' Mubarak's tone suddenly changes.

'Americans no good,' he says. 'Bad with people. Hit people.' He shakes his head and says, in an unpleasant voice, 'George Bush. He want oil. Mr Tony Blair, he very good man. He down Saddam.'

'Is Saddam dead now?' I ask. We have not heard any news.

'Yes,' Mubarak says, smiling.

'*Akid* (Sure)?' I ask.

Mubarak hesitates. 'Maybe down,' he says. Returning to a safer theme, he blurts, 'Mr Tony Blair, very good.'

It is a long ride, with no lights anywhere. Worse, Mubarak talks all the way, mostly in Arabic, a bit in English. He doesn't like the war. He has no electricity. There is no money in Safwan. Then he borrows my telephone to call his cousins in Amman. This evening, there are few other cars on the highway.

A half-mile ahead of us, a klieg light shines onto the road. Soldiers' silhouettes roam back and forth in the light. Mubarak says, 'British.' He stops the car 100 yards short of the checkpoint, and Don walks over to talk to the troops. He comes back a minute later. The troops, he says, are American. I go to ask permission to clear the checkpoint and, just as importantly, for Mubarak to return this way to get home. The young soldiers say, 'Sure. No problem.' I wave for Mubarak to bring the van to the checkpoint. He waits behind another van which soldiers are searching. The family, a man with several women, nine small children and two babies, get out. While a woman soldier examines the women, my Thuraya rings. A voice in New York says, 'Hold on for TV-3.' Bob Roy, the producer, comes on the line. 'Hold on a second,' he says. 'We'll get you into the hybrid. Do you hear programme?' I do. Peter Jennings is talking about a statue of Saddam falling down somewhere in Baghdad. I can hear the sounds of a crowd below his voice. I am on a desolate road in the desert between Safwan and Umm Qasr, listening to the war in Baghdad. I ask the soldiers if we can wait while I go live to New York. They are fine about it, but want to know how I am going to send pictures. It is voice only, I say. I ask Mubarak to wait and wonder what he makes of this, an American reporter talking to a television presenter from nowhere in the desert. I wonder about it as well. I walk away from the checkpoint into the dark. Jennings says the statue has fallen, sounding as though this were the end, at least the symbolic end, of the war. Perhaps it is.

Just before I left Suleimaniya, I finished reading Borges's collected nonfiction. Something in an essay entitled '*L'Illusion Comique*' struck me, and I copied it into my notebook: 'From a world of individuals we have passed into an even more passionate world of symbols: the clash was not between parties or opponents of the dictator, but rather among parties and opponents of an effigy or name ...' The effigy has fallen. The regime is dead. It does not matter where the man is.

Jennings does not have much to ask me, and my telephone battery is dying. I tell Roy I am going to turn it off and head to Umm Qasr, where there are other ABC telephones and battery chargers. On the drive into town, Mubarak rhapsodises about his home in Safwan and how he will invite us to stay there if we find nowhere to sleep in Umm Qasr. This worries me. Why wouldn't we find a bed in Umm Qasr? The answer becomes clear when Mubarak gets lost. Neither he nor any of his relations in the van knows the town or where its port is. Mubarak drives around and around, back and forth, through the unlit streets. He asks men on bicycles how to find the port, and their instructions prove too complicated for him. He tries to wave down a US military convoy whose gunners will, I am certain, shoot us all if he drives too close. I tell him to keep back. He drives aimlessly. By now, my mind is on a shower. I know there will be showers at the Umm Qasr base. I order Mubarak to go directly to the port, now. He turns around and asks if I would like a hotel. No, I say, you told us you knew where the port was before we left Safwan. Where is it? Ahead, we see a British military checkpoint. We walk up to the sandbags and ask the squaddies where the port is. This *is* the port, they say.

Don and I unload our bags, and I pay Mubarak the $50 fare. 'It's $70,' he says. No, I remind him, we agreed $50. He argues. I ask why I should pay another $20, especially when he didn't know where he was going. It does not matter. I give him two more tens.

At the gate, the soldiers say we will have to wait for someone inside the base to fetch us. We can enter only in an authorised car. Fair enough. The ABC people know we are here and should come to collect us. I call the ABC *Nightline* producer, and he says to wait an hour at the gate. An hour? Is the base that big? His tone makes it clear we are not welcome. We can bloody well wait. Don and I chat with the soldiers. They are not interested in me, but know Don. They love his photographs, particularly from the wars in Cyprus and Vietnam. A lot of British soldiers seem to know his work. Don does not mind the attention.

A Kuwaiti television truck comes to the gate. We ask whether they would take us inside. The soldiers have no objection, but the Kuwaitis are going only to a little car park just inside the perimeter. They are not authorised to enter the base itself. There are, apparently, other journalists already there. 'You might be among friends there,' one of the soldiers says. The Kuwaitis, living up to traditions of Arab hospitality, are as welcoming as our ABC colleagues are not. They rearrange their equipment in the pickup to make room for us and for our bags. They stop at a car park that has empty buildings along one side. The Kuwaitis make us tea and give us sweets. We stay with them for about forty-five minutes, until some ABC people come to take us onto the base. Officially, it is a civilian port. The British have just turned it into a naval base; but US forces, mainly the Seabees, are using it as well. I am up most of the night, filing my footage from French Radar and Nasiriya.

A few nights ago, I spoke to my father in California. He was at Umm Qasr and Basra in 1943, when the US Navy was delivering supplies to Russia via Iraq and Iran. I never thought, he said, that my son would be there sixty years later. Nor, in 1943, did he suppose the US armed forces would be back.

Thursday, 10 April 2003
Umm Qasr

At seven in the morning, when I finish my broadcast to New York, I have a shower and put on clean clothes. Don and I eat a hot breakfast in the canteen. A fresh ABC crew arrives from Kuwait. The cameraman is Johnny Saunderson; we covered the war in Bosnia together. In 1993, he risked his life to drive me through a battle in Kiseljak to get me home in time for my daughter Julia's First Communion. A Northern Irish Protestant, Johnny has a tenor voice that could make you cry when he sings 'Danny Boy'. Standing on the roof of his Jeep, he hands me down a camera case, which I carry into the ABC tent. Johnny complains he has been waiting for weeks in Kuwait to get into Iraq. 'Story's over,' he says. 'Now they want me to do this guy

who's gonna run Iraq.'
  'Ahmad Chalabi?'
  'No.'
  'General Garner?'
  'That's the one.'

Sunday, 13 April 2003
London

Don and I arrive from Kuwait in the afternoon. He goes back to Catherine and their son in Somerset, where he will develop and print photographs. I check into the St Martin's Lane Hotel between Soho and Covent Garden. There are three things I have been looking forward to for the past three months: a steak, good red wine and Sophie. Most of the places that serve good steak – like Christopher's in Wellington Street – are closed on Sunday night. The concierge says Chez Gerard in Charlotte Street is open and makes a reservation. Sophie comes to the hotel, and we walk there. It makes me very happy, if a little apprehensive, to see her at last. I tell her about Iraq, and she talks about her film. At Chez Gerard, I order Château Margaux and the *côte de boeuf, bleue*. This is the rainbow's end: the girl, the steak, the wine.

Before the food comes, she says she has to tell me something. But she doesn't have to tell me anything, not now. Whenever a woman has to tell you something, it's bad. 'I met someone else,' she says. I cancel my order. We talk for a little while. I do not blame her. This sort of thing happens. She must not feel guilty. I must not be angry.

Meanwhile, Washington is warning Syria and Iran that they could be next. The struggle for Iraq, despite the fanfare of victory in the US, has begun.

Index